INTERCULTURAL ATTITUDES
IN THE MAKING

PARENTS, YOUTH LEADERS, AND TEACHERS AT WORK

Yearbook Committee

WILLIAM HEARD KILPATRICK, *Chairman*
Professor Emeritus
Teachers College, Columbia University

C. O. ARNDT
Professor of Education
New York University

PRUDENCE BOSTWICK
Supervisor, Department of Instruction
Denver Public Schools

BERNICE BRIDGES
Director, Youth Division of the
National Social Welfare Assembly, Inc.

CHARLES E. HENDRY
School of Social Work
University of Toronto

JAMES L. HYMES, JR.
Co-ordinator, Early Childhood Education
State Teachers College
New Paltz, N. Y.

HELEN TRAGER
Director of Age-Level Studies
Bureau for Intercultural Education

WILLIAM VAN TIL
Director of Learning Materials
Bureau for Intercultural Education

Other Contributors to Yearbook

EDWARD HAYDON
Director of Mid-West office
Commission on Community Interrelations
of the American Jewish Congress

RUSSELL HOGREFE
Research Associate
Commission on Community Interrelations
of the American Jewish Congress

MYRTLE F. SUGARMAN
Supervising Teacher in the Department of Instruction
Denver Public Schools

INTERCULTURAL ATTITUDES IN THE MAKING

Parents, Youth Leaders, and Teachers at Work

Edited by

WILLIAM HEARD KILPATRICK

Chairman of the Yearbook Committee
and Professor Emeritus of Teachers College, Columbia University

and

WILLIAM VAN TIL

Director of Learning Materials
Bureau for Intercultural Education

HARPER & BROTHERS PUBLISHERS
NEW YORK AND LONDON

CONTENTS

PREFACE

A most serious evil in our modern world is the active survival of intergroup tensions, with their accompanying prejudices and hurtful discriminations. The evil is age-old and opposed to all honest democracy and every decent ethics. Fortunately, conscious opposition to the evil seems now both strong and widely increasing, but far too much prejudice and active discrimination still survive in our country at the very time when our prominence in world affairs calls emphatic attention to all our shortcomings. Education is crucially concerned in this evil.

With such facts as these in mind the John Dewey Society decided to devote its Ninth Yearbook to the cause of intergroup, or intercultural, education as its part in the effort to overcome this intergroup evil which is still so active in our midst. In the pursuit of this aim the undersigned was appointed chairman to organize the committee to bring out the Yearbook. He in turn sought the help of the Bureau for Intercultural Education; and this organization generously agreed to give hearty support to the enterprise. How generous and how effective the Bureau's aid has proved will appear at the close of this Foreword.

This book, while addressed primarily to teachers and school officials, should concern all good citizens who deal actively with children and youth. The aim of the book is to give better insight into the processes through which the attitudes of children and adolescents are actually shaped: hurtfully toward hostility, or helpfully toward wholesome human relations. The focus of the book is on the social forces immediate in, and vital to, the person-to-person experiences of child and youth: the family, the auton-

omous and the adult-sponsored groups, and especially the school
as the one agency most amenable to conscious influence.

The foundation of the Yearbook then is the fact that the intercultural attitudes of the child are in the making day by day
through all the varied experiences that his life brings. These attitudes, let us be clear, are not given in the germ plasm; they come
to the child and youth through the environment. Education does
it, education broadly understood. The homes give the beginning;
youth groups build on this foundation, both the autonomous and
the adult-sponsored; schools have in the matter great possibilities.

In their turn, family, group, and school are heavily influenced
by the climate of opinion fostered by accepted ways of living
and by the mass media of communication; many excellent studies
have been dedicated to this theme but it is not the function of
this book to duplicate their messages. Instead this book examines
the working of family, group, and school in relation to children
and youth. For teachers and others dealing with the young must
understand these forces at work in child and youth development
and take adequate account of them if proper human relations
are to have the opportunity to prevail.

The first chapter by common consent has been given to a re-
examination of our values and the method of their acceptance,
specifically how one comes by the values that govern his life. This
meant in effect a re-examination of how effective learning takes
place, and so how intercultural education must in fact go on.
It fell to the undersigned to write this first chapter, the *Basic
Principles in Intercultural Education*.

Next comes a study of different type homes, homes differing
widely in their social orientation. Each such home shapes its
children, usually unwittingly, at times wittingly, but in either
case effectively, in the pattern of its attitude toward other
groups, of friendliness or of hostility. This chapter 2 by James
L. Hymes is named *Parents*.

In chapter 3, *The Primary Teacher*, by Helen Trager, we
meet a teacher who becomes conscious of children as persons

and learns ways of understanding them and their beginning attitudes. Next comes (chapter 4) a range of approaches used by adults in working with youth groups, by Bernice Bridges writing on *Adult-Sponsored Youth Groups*. The efforts of two junior high school faculties to change school-community situations, as seen by teachers troubled by the discriminations and hostilities they observe, are reported (chapter 5) by Myrtle Sugarman and Prudence Bostwick in *The Junior High School Teacher*. The impact of *Gangs* upon youth's outlook is starkly described (chapter 6) by collaborators Russell Hogrefe, Charles E. Hendry, and Edward Haydon, who take us into a day and a year in the life of a gang before recommending a new group work approach to remediation. The contemporary high school curriculum as a medium for building attitudes is critically examined (chapter 7) by William Van Til, as his protagonist examines current approaches to attitude-formation in a chapter, *The High School Teacher*. C. O. Arndt continues (chapter 8) the group exploration with reflections on *The School as a Whole*, considering in turn the citizenry, the board of education, the administration and staff, the parents, and the students, as these severally affect the making of intercultural attitudes. In a final chapter, the editors then recapitulate some implications of the whole discussion.

The John Dewey Society and the chairman are deeply grateful to the Bureau for Intercultural Education for its generous support of the Yearbook enterprise. Dr. H. H. Giles gave cordial cooperation in every way. The Bureau furnished not only the specifically helpful services of Dr. Van Til, Dr. Dix, and Mrs. Trager; but also it supplied a place of committee meetings and a very generous amount of typing and other clerical work. Dr. Lester Dix took charge of certain more practical matters, the correspondence and other arrangements for meetings. Dr. William Van Til not only furnished a chapter; but, even more, as co-editor he, with the aid of his staff, did practically all of the actual editing and handled numerous mechanical details—a skilled service excellently done for which the chairman, the other co-editor, is especially grateful.

The following were particularly helpful and generous with their time in the early stages of shaping the project: Adele Franklin, L. D. Haskew, Warren Brown, R. Freeman Butts. Others who helped in the planning of the book were C. Leslie Cushman, Dan Dodson, Samuel Everett, Father George Ford, Lois Murphy, H. H. Giles, Mary Fisher Langmuir.

Children's records for Chapter 3, *The Primary Teacher*, were graciously supplied by Fran Dortort and Hazel Thomas, Philadelphia Early Childhood Project teachers. Among others who aided individual authors in the preparation of chapters are the following: Emanuel Berlatsky, LeRoy Bowman, George Corwin, C. Leslie Cushman, Edna Daly, Mary Ely, Adele Franklin, Benjamin Goldenberg, E. Urner Goodman, C. Frances Loomis, Jean Maxwell, Elise Moller, Frances C. Morse, Dorothy P. Osborn, Beatrix Parks, Elizabeth H. Purnell, and Mary Thompson.

WILLIAM HEARD KILPATRICK

CHAPTER I

BASIC PRINCIPLES IN INTERCULTURAL EDUCATION [1]

Dr. Kilpatrick here discusses the nature and the goals of inter-cultural education. A restatement of the principles of learning is utilized to emphasize that the same principles apply to intercultural education.

Some Basic Questions

Intercultural education is new to our schools and to our people, new both in effort and in name. Certain questions naturally arise: What does the term *intercultural education* mean? Why wish such education? How is this education related to education in general? What values does it seek to foster? What goals does it hope to achieve? How shall we so "teach" intercultural education that children will truly learn? One further question sets the theme of this book: How are children's intercultural attitudes shaped by home, by community forces, and by education? Some considera-tion of the earlier questions will prepare us the better for a discus-sion of this last one.

Consider the following words: Negro, Jew, Catholic, Mexican, West Indian, Japanese, "Dago," "Hunky." Taken separately, all except the last two carry to the right-thinking person no implica-tions; they are, we may say, simply everyday words, "neutral"

[1] This chapter was written by WILLIAM HEARD KILPATRICK, Chairman, Pro-fessor Emeritus, Teachers College, Columbia University.

I

terms, each denoting a more or less identifiable group of people. But put all the words together and consider the prejudice and discrimination the groups which they represent too often meet. Then we see illustrated the regrettable tendency on the part of some of our people to refuse full citizenship to certain groups among us, as if the members of those groups do not fully "belong," are not to be granted full acceptance, are even to be denied certain of the rights that supposedly belong to all legal citizens.

Discrimination Denies Democracy, Ethics, Religion

Fortunately these excluding and denying tendencies do not dominate the American scene. On the contrary, an increasing number among us positively reject such discrimination as being fundamentally opposed to democracy, to ethics, and to any adequately sensitive religion. Our Declaration of Independence, as if to anticipate and forbid all such discriminations, declares that "all men are created equal"—not equal in body or in mind, but equal in their rights before the law, and specifically equal in the right to "life, liberty, and the pursuit of happiness" and in the right to share in governing. And our Constitution guarantees "the equal protection of the laws" for all persons. Going beyond the formal law to the activating spirit of proper human relationships, ethics demands that human personality as such be respected wherever found, that each such personality be granted an equal right with all others to the fullest possible development and happiness that conscious social arrangements can effect. The Hebraic-Christian religious tradition sums up all this in the twin rules: "Thou shalt love thy neighbor as thyself" and "All things whatsoever ye would that men should do to you, do ye even so to them."

It is on those premises of democracy, ethics, and religion that intercultural education has come into existence. The word *intercultural* as here employed is now in accepted usage; it means much the same as inter-group and implies a scope that reaches beyond "race" to include also cultural differences.

Man's Nature Is Social

That the human individual can reach his full stature only in and through full group relationships is now increasingly seen. It was said in early times that "no man liveth to himself," that "we are all members one of another," and later that "no man is an Iland, intire of it selfe." In fact, it is only with others that one does truly live —in the family, in the community, in the nation, in humanity. Also, only in and through a socially built and socially transmitted culture do any of us live civilized lives.

Even more, one's very selfhood is socially constructed. The sense of self always implies and involves a sense of others. Out of one's relations with others and by their help does each one build his selfhood. And this selfhood is in fact compounded of both self and other components. Little John sees sister Mary fall and hurt her head, sees and hears her cry. Yesterday he fell and hurt his head, and he cried. Mother calls his attention to Mary. He understands better now how Mary feels; he felt the same way yesterday. Also, he understands better now, from how Mary looks and sounds, how he looks and sounds when he cries. In this he is building his self, partly through what he first saw in himself, but also partly through what he first saw in others. As the days go by, these learnings accumulate. Then, when others watch and criticize him, he learns to watch and criticize both himself and others. He is thus becoming self-conscious. In that way does each one build his selfhood which marks his superiority to the brute, his capacity for critical thinking and for moral conduct.

From all the foregoing we conclude that, without satisfactory relationships with others, the life of any individual is, as old Hobbes well said, "solitary, poor, nasty, brutish, and short."

Values for Intercultural Education Derived from Man's Social Nature

It is out of this social nature of man and on this basis of the life good to live that intercultural education gets the values it specifi-

cally seeks. One such value is recognition and acceptance by others. Since man is self-conscious and must live in society with his fellows, to feel oneself accepted by others is essential to satisfactory living. No privation so surely denies satisfaction in life as does exclusion by others, the sense of not being accepted by the group. Life in any full and satisfying sense involves and essentially demands one's active participation with others in the group life on terms of mutual acceptance and respect. The premises of democracy, ethics, and sensitive religion necessitate the value of full respect for all other persons irrespective of the accident of group membership.

The Meaning of Intercultural Education

It is a denial of the values of equal participation with, mutual acceptance of, and full respect for persons of all groups which has brought intercultural education into existence. Whole groups, as previously stated, are still in some measure excluded from full participation in the life of the community. Intercultural education aims at the best possible achievement of the values of participation with, acceptance of, and respect for others. It is an effort to bring education to bear as constructively as possible on actual and possible intercultural tensions and on the evils of any and all bias, prejudice, and discrimination against minority groups. In short, the effort of intercultural education is to ensure to all the adequate realization of these social values and to remove and cure the bias and prejudice leading to such discriminations. This is the fundamental meaning of intercultural education, and it explains the presence of intercultural education as an integral part and aspect of modern democratic education.

Goals in Intercultural Education

Because bias and prejudice come only by learning, the combating of these hurtful attitudes must be a matter of preventive and remedial education. We come then to the school as a chief agency in American life to combat and correct the evils of bias, prejudice, and discrimination. The goals of intercultural education as aims to guide schools and teaching may accordingly be stated as follows:

1. That all the pupils shall live well together—each to be conscious of friendliness for all; no one to feel unwelcome, or even questioned, because of the group to which he belongs; all to live in mutual respect and appreciation of one another on the basis of personal merit.

It has been found that the youngest children will live together in this desirable democratic fashion almost naturally. But as they get older the attitudes of certain parents and other elders will begin to interfere. The teachers must then work, in season and out, to make the democratic ideal prevail as far as possible and become increasingly effective on the conscious basis that "this is how I would like to be treated." The children of the dominant or discriminating groups must be increasingly brought to understand the feelings of those who suffer discrimination. Since most children do acquire at least some prejudices from the surrounding life of the community, each one as he grows older must be helped to become conscious of whatever prejudices he has thus acquired, so that he may correct them. Teachers specifically must be careful to examine themselves in the same way, lest they be unconsciously encouraging bias and discrimination in their pupils.[2]

2. That the pupils as they grow older shall build a clear understanding of what democracy means, historically and ethically—what Jefferson and Franklin and Lincoln stood for; how democracy means respect for human personality wherever found; how equality of rights and of opportunity is an essential part of democracy; how America has in historic fact helped to spread democracy as an ideal throughout the world—and that all shall learn to

---

[2] In some public schools it has been noted that teachers separate at lunch time according to their religious affiliations—Protestant teachers in one room, Catholic teachers in another, Jewish teachers in a third. That such a separation among teachers will foster separations and antagonisms among pupils seems inevitable.

accept such a democracy in very fact as the American way of life and learn to live it personally.

3. That the pupils shall increasingly understand that freedom in a democracy is always limited by the requirement of equal regard for others. One is free to act only as his acts help, and do not hurt, all affected by them.

4. That pupil groups shall increasingly learn and use the method of conferring—the method of basing group action on group discussion and decision. This is the method of intelligence, of acting on thinking, applied to group action. It is precisely the method of democracy.

5. That the pupils shall really grow, grow in all the good ways possible to man. Just as this is an inclusive aim of education in general, so it is in particular an essential aim of intercultural education. If that aim be not so met that the whole being of the person grows—grows in thinking, grows in feeling, grows in bodily movement, and all three in fullest interaction—then shall we not treat others as we should. We must understand what others do experience in contrast with what they might experience; we must feel with them in what is, and for them in what might be; and we must in our acts live up to our best understanding and highest impulses. It is this kind of real and full growing which is here demanded.

The school of an earlier day failed in this regard. Merely to learn from books in order to recite to teachers will by no means bring the needed conduct effects. At best, success in mere book learning builds the mind only; too often the practice gives mere wordiness, mere verbalism. A different kind of education is needed, an education in life for living. Facing actual situations with appropriate thoughts and feelings and acts is necessary in order to effect any adequate education; it is essential to inter-cultural education. We seek here, then, a kind of living which will bring the fullest possible educative growth to all—growth in mutual understanding, growth in mutual regard, and growth in action appropriate to such understanding and regard. Only such full growing from full living will suffice to correct the evils of bias, prejudice, and discrimination.

6. That the pupils shall learn increasingly to act on the basis of thinking and not on that of mere habit or custom or of mere impulse. Only through action founded on thinking can we hope to obtain the effective growth just discussed. Only on this basis can we hope that the individual and the group will properly treat all others who are affected by their acts.

7. That each pupil shall, so far as the school can effect it, build the invariable habit of acting on the best that he has found, of living up to the highest insight that he can gain through searching. To build this trait effectively is to follow the moral path of duty.

8. That each group shall come to know and respect the cultural contributions of other groups. Wisely managed, this works doubly—it builds respect for others, and it upbuilds respect for one's own group.

9. That our pupils shall understand and appreciate the composite character of the American population and its consequent advantage to our civilization.

10. That teachers and older pupils shall study the various historic causes and supporting rationalizations of group prejudices. If these are clearly understood and properly acted upon, the future may be better. For in the long run, men tend to act according to evidence.

11. That in particular the older pupils shall, under guidance, study out the problems of race and the evidence against racism. Only thus will the use of rationalizing defense mechanisms yield to facts. For a belief in racial superiority is perhaps the chief defense mechanism of racial discrimination.

12. That pupils as they grow older shall come to understand the international aspect of inter-group prejudices and discriminations—how the white race is a minority in the world, and how discriminations within our country are not only wrong here but hurtful to peace and order in the world at large.

New Conception of Learning Needed for Intercultural Education

Among our first basic questions was this: How shall we so "teach" intercultural education that children will truly learn? Really effective learning in the area of inter-group tensions is so difficult of wide attainment that extended discussion of the problem seems desirable here. The need for this special consideration is made the greater because the school conception of learning hitherto prevalent, and still widespread, was confined principally to the acquiring of the written content of books. The school method generally used has been to assign to a class a lesson in a book and require the pupils to learn it so that any one of them called upon could recite to the teacher what had thus been assigned. Any conscious process of character building, except that furnished by admonition and punishment, was conspicuous for its absence. Because most people still think of school learning in this fashion, it becomes necessary for us here not only to see the inadequacy of such learning for dealing with the intercultural bias-tension-discrimination problem but also to get insight into a better learning conception.

"Learning About" Differs from "Learning to Do"

First of all, we must see how *learning about* proper conduct is essentially different from *learning to do* the desired right thing. When as a child in school the writer of these words first studied English grammar, he learned to repeat the rule: "The words I and O should always be written in capital letters." The hope of those charged with educating me and my contemporaries was that, if the pupils would so learn the rule as to be able to recite it on demand, then when the right time came these two words would be properly written. But, alas, neither school nor life gave me at that time any actual situation in which such writing was called for, and I regret to report that a childish diary which has come down from those days has toward its beginning the pronoun I written as i and not I. Learning the rule did not suffice to effect the proper practice.

The same principle holds in more serious matters. Many young people used to learn the catechism, but learning to recite the catechism did not make them behave as the catechism demanded. Something more and something else is needed. Learning to *say* rules and learning to *obey* rules are two quite different things.

Modern psychology increasingly recognizes the fact just noted. For example, we read such statements as these: "What one learns is a reaction" (Gates). "It is essential that the student be led to do what is to be learned. . . . We learn only what we do" (Guthrie). "A student does not learn what was in a lecture or in a book. He learns only what the lecture or book caused him to do" (Guthrie). In fact, our keenest observers have long noticed the essential principle here involved, that people learn what they truly live. Plato said that "the penalty of wrongdoing" is "not stripes and death, which evil doers often escape, but a penalty which cannot be escaped," namely, the penalty of building the evil pattern of behaving into one's very character—men become what they do. Emerson spoke to the same effect: "He who does a good deed is instantly ennobled." William James, from a slightly different angle, said: "Nothing we ever do is, in strict scientific literalness, ever wiped out."

Alexandrian and Modern Education Contrasted

The old type of school, dedicated to "learning about," originated at Alexandria in the third century B.C. to teach the wisdom that had been written down at Athens. This type of school was carried to Rome to teach the accumulated wisdom of the Greeks to the Romans. When Christianity formulated its authoritative creed, it used the same procedure for maintaining its creed unimpaired. The Revival of Learning used the same procedure for teaching the revived classics. During that period of fifteen hundred years, this conception of the school and its process of learning established itself practically without a rival. Only with the coming of Pestalozzi (1764–1827) did the Alexandrian outlook begin to be seriously questioned.

The new conception, which since Pestalozzi has been much developed, stresses behaving as the basis of learning. We learn those responses we make as we face a situation. The whole organism, we now know, is involved in each significant response. Therefore we learn responses "all over." Thinking, feeling, and bodily movement are thus all three interrelated in each response, and all three together are accordingly being learned during all behavior.

The Alexandrian point of view was different. Its learning was intentionally limited to the mind, and the mind largely to memory. To learn to recite or to answer examination questions is, as we saw in the instance of my childhood diary, quite different from learning to behave.

In the newer outlook, to say that one has really learned a certain thing (a thought or a feeling or a movement)—learned it so that it will actually work when needed—means (1) that one has in a true situation responded that way, has done that thing (has thought that thought, or felt that feeling, or made that movement); (2) that the response when thus made does not simply pass away with the doing of it, but somehow remains with one, remains as the tendency to behave in that way again; hence (3) that when a suitable situation shall arise, one will be likely to behave so again.

Basic Principles of Learning

With this understanding of what to "learn" means, we can now state more explicitly the following principles of learning:

A. We learn our responses, only our responses, and all our responses.
B. We learn each response as we accept it to use, as we accept it to live by.

In a small New England village, Cabot Wendall, an "old stock" American boy in the senior high school, one day sees a new boy in his class and learns that his name is Abraham Cohen. What will

Cabot do, and what will he learn from so doing? Cabot may say to himself, "A Jew! We already have too many. I'll show him what he can expect here." If that is Cabot's response, and if he accepts it in his heart as his way of behaving, then his so responding helps fasten this attitude into his character as a habit. Each such succeeding act builds it the stronger in him. But, on the contrary, Cabot may say, "A Jew. I'll make him feel at home, for I'll stand for none of this anti-Semitism around here if I can help it." If this is Cabot's response, and if he accepts it as his way of feeling and acting, then he builds this attitude into his character.

For many purposes, it will help to restate A and B in the following words:

C. If one is to learn anything (as a thought or a feeling or an act), he must respond with that thing to some actual situation.

The next statement applies to all three of the foregoing principles:

D. We learn each response in the degree that we live it.

The degree of learning and degree of living are important to consider.

As to the degree of learning, we all know some things which "we shall never forget" no matter how long we live. We also realize that some things simply insist on coming to mind even though we should like to forget them. Any one thing, be it a thought or a feeling or a movement, is better or more strongly learned than another if it stays with us for a longer time and/or if it tends more strongly to get back into the stream of life.

As to the degree of living, some responses mean so little to us that we hardly think of them at the time and seldom or never think of them again. Others mean more. Of the latter we are more keenly conscious at the time, and we see and feel their importance. Thus it is that those responses that we live most consciously and count most important stay with us longest.

E. We learn any response, especially a thought or mental image, in the degree that we have ready a mental scheme into which to fit it.

This was the Herbartian principle of apperception. If my friend moves next door to me, I shall more easily remember where he lives than if he moves to some region I know nothing about.

Response by the Whole Organism Brings Concomitant Learnings

Today it is well understood that the whole organism is involved in each significant response. Not only do we move physically, but we also think and feel as we move. We used to believe that each part of one's being acted, as it were, separately. We now know that this is not true. For example, the knee-jerk reflex seems to act entirely on its own, but to grit the teeth or clench one's fist at the time of the test will increase the knee jerk. In this matter of acting or responding all over, older people have learned to conceal in large part what goes on inside. But watch a child and see how his thoughts and feelings show themselves in facial expression and bodily movements. He obviously responds and acts all over.

Our principles of learning have shown us that we learn our responses. If we respond all over, we learn then all over. No matter what a child is doing, he is—in the degree he is living it— thinking about it, feeling it, and acting physically all over about it. Any significant instance of living, and consequently of learning, thus includes in one single sweep all parts of the total response—thought elements, feeling elements, and movement elements. All these elements are inextricably interrelated, and all are thus being learned. Concomitant learnings are thus going on throughout all the waking time of active experience.

Character and Cumulative Learnings

To have a definite character means to have fairly settled ways of thinking, feeling, and acting. A person with a proper character thinks before he acts in order that his act may properly fit what he knows and thus accord with his tested principles. The act of such a person is dependable, in that another person of equal intelligence and knowledge can see and understand why it was done. He responds, not mechanically, not to the surface but rather to the deeper insight of what the situation means.

Now these settled and reliable ways of seeing and judging and deciding are composed of well-built cumulative learnings—conceptions, attitudes, methods of study, standards of judging, principles of action. Each such, let it be repeated, is an instance of cumulative learning.

Take one's conception of a horse. This is the organized result of all one's cumulative thoughts regarding horses as one has met horses in personal experience, has read about them, and has heard about them. Two successive experiences will have something in common but will still present differences. The common elements one compounds to help constitute the nucleus of the conception; the differences one joins appropriately to the nucleus to show the various differences to be expected. Keeping this up through the years, one will, if he has a sufficient variety of experiences and cares enough about the matter, build in time a fairly dependable notion of what to expect of horses, both of all horses and also of different kinds of horses and different behaviors of horses under different conditions. All this aggregate of cumulative learnings about horses constitutes one's conception of horses to tell one what in reason to expect of them.

At the same time that one is building his conception of horses, he is also building his attitude or attitudes toward horses. For, in accordance with his different conceptions of different kinds of horses, he will have built correspondingly different attitudes to fit the different conceptions—one attitude toward a big plodding work horse, another attitude toward a spirited saddle horse.

In the same cumulative way one will build methods of study from one's different experiences of studying different types of situations. Again there will be common elements and differentiating elements. In the same cumulative way one will build one's standards of excellence, one's principles of action, and one's defensible habits of acting.

The fact that the whole organism acts on each particular occasion gives us the constituent elements out of which these conceptions, attitudes, habits, and so forth are built. Successive experiences will have elements in common with certain preceding experiences. It is the cumulative organization of the like and unlike elements of experiences that presents us with our important cumulative learnings. It is out of the aggregate of these and all other learnings that one's character is formed.

We are now ready to see more fully why intercultural education cannot depend on the old Alexandrian type of education. That older school thought of education as giving to the empty mind the thoughts contained in the book or lecture. It thus *talked about* life, but did not have the learner *actually face* life situations. His responses were as purely mental, and mental only, as could well be conceived. And his mind, as stated earlier, was itself largely reduced to memory. In other words, the learner did not, through the school, live in any very active or full way. In particular, no behavior was involved—other than the behavior of "study" and obedience. There was no facing of actual situations, no active participation in purposeful endeavor, no shared efforts, no responsibility—except for reciting. In a word, there was very, very little chance or need to build character. Intercultural education, however, must actively build character both *for* meeting life situations and *by* meeting life situations. Merely to read about a situation cannot and will not build the needed character.

Personality Maladjustment

Just as the motor car cannot run well unless its engine is in proper internal adjustment, so is it with man. He cannot meet life's demands unless he is in good internal adjustment. And he can build habits and attitudes that mean bad internal adjustment, habits and attitudes that interfere with meeting life's situations in a healthy, happy way.

Take, for instance, the matter of courage, of morale. Some people so mistrust themselves that they will not even try in situations where they might, by proper effort, succeed well. Others, on the contrary, are too sure of themselves and so rush ahead into unnecessary trouble. To have built habits either of too little trust in oneself or of unwarranted trust is to increase one's proportion of unnecessary failure and trouble. Each is a case of maladjustment.

Each such instance of personality maladjustment is an instance of cumulative learning. Chiefly it appears where an emotion has repeatedly failed of proper discharge. An inferiority complex may thus come from repeated instances of humiliating failure. Insecurity may come from distressing upsets where one had in vain expected or sought safety. An abiding grudge may come from repeated instances of experiencing unjust treatment.

Some characteristics based on maladjustment are difficult to distinguish from plain immoral traits, as for instance bias and discrimination against a minority group. But there will usually accompany such attitudes, as intimated above, some rationalization or other maladjustment defense mechanism. One of the worst of these defense mechanisms for inter-group relations is the disposition we call scapegoating, the tendency to transfer a grudge or grievance from the situation where it was built and "take it out" on some innocent third party or group.

Intercultural education must especially concern itself with all those personality maladjustments which foster and aggravate inter-group tensions. It must deal actively with maladjustments that lead a person to discriminate against members of other groups, and also with the maladjustments which naturally follow from experiencing discrimination. When we consider the extent to which discrimination abounds in our midst, we can only marvel that the resulting maladjustments are no more numerous or serious.

Teachers must be especially sensitive to the existence of hurtful maladjustments on the part of both the persecutor and the persecuted. They must recognize what maladjustments may lead to and aggravate bias and discrimination as well as what maladjustments normally follow in greater or less degree from experiencing bias and discrimination. And teachers must know how to deal with such maladjustments—how to deal in ordinary classroom procedures so as both to prevent and to cure the lesser kinds; how to recognize those which call for more expert consideration and treatment.

CHAPTER II

PARENTS [1]

Intercultural relations means relations between people. If we wish to see the contribution of family life to intercultural education, then we must look at how the home builds into the child his capacity for human relationships.

Does the life the child leads within his family teach him: I feel good about myself. . . . I am able. . . . I can do.

Or does it teach him: I doubt myself. . . . I am not sure. . . . I am the kind of person who fails.

For from such feelings must certainly come their social counterpart—either: I trust other people. . . . I believe in them. . . . I like them and accept them . . . or: I wonder about others. . . . I suspect them . . . . People make me fail more and more, so I must watch them ever so carefully.

Here is the key kind of experience which the family gives in inter-group and intercultural education. For as one learns to feel about himself and about the individuals in his world, so must one inevitably feel about himself in relation to the groups those individuals comprise or the groups which symbolize those individuals.

A prime question, then, for intercultural education becomes: How does a child grow up so that he feels good about himself and so that he feels trusting of others?

[1] This chapter was written by JAMES L. HYMES, JR., Co-ordinator of Early Childhood Education, State Teachers College, New Paltz, N. Y.

The answer lies in the way the child's needs as a person are met at each step in his growing up. If the child lives a successful life from the standpoint of being provided for and satisfied when he has a want, the child then has the basis on which good, trusting feelings can be built. This is a promising life basis for intercultural education.

If at each stage in his growing up, however, the child's own growth creates needs which his particular world ignores—the world of his family, their ways of doing things, their standards, their values, their habitual responses—an unpromising basis exists. The basis is similarly unpromising if the child's particular world places demands on him—expectations, standards, goals—which his growth does not enable him to meet with comfort and ease and inner satisfaction. Such a basis makes the teacher's job harder but by no means impossible.

From the one kind of life the child learns that this is a good world; it is a world where he has a place and a welcome, and an agreeable one at that; it is a world not full of threats and fears and deprivations but one in which he is able and where, feeling able, he can accept others as they are. No need to fight them; no need to keep them down; no need to cast them out or to fear them. Such a child, satisfied within himself, can accept others; he has a feeling basis on which democratic intercultural relations can be built.

From the other kind of life the child learns that this is a hard world; it is a world where he has to fight to hold his own and where he never gets enough of what he needs; it is a world where there is not enough to go around. He has to fight others; he has to keep his eye on them. With no real confidence in himself, he cannot afford to let the other fellow have a chance. Such a child, unsatisfied within himself, will probably fear others; he has a feeling basis for hating or excluding or hurting or—at best— merely tolerating other groups.

How do families build these feelings in their children? Let us look at five families. Each one "teaches" some form of inter-

*cultural relations. It teaches through the adequacy of how it meets
its children's needs.*

The Reuthers

Dr. and Mrs. Reuther are well-read, active, professional people,
leaders in their community. The doctor works through his
medical societies; he is also on the Board of Directors of the
YMCA. His name is a familiar and a reliable one that is used in
supporting a wide variety of drives and campaigns for good
causes. Mrs. Reuther, a former nurse and teacher, is a vigorous
and bustling person, equally able and equally busy. She is president of her church's Woman's League and a past president of
the League of Women Voters, and she is active in the Century
Club and in a number of smaller groups.

On both sides of the family the Reuthers go back to German
soil. Paternal and maternal ancestors left the old country in the
middle eighteen-hundreds in search of more personal freedom.
To have been hurt and to have been cast out because you
believed the wrong things, or because you were you, is a his-
torical part of this family picture.

This old story made the Reuthers especially sensitive to the
evils of the Nazi regime. They were early spotters of the rise of
racism; they spoke soon and clearly against the Nazis; they
warned from the very start that this meant conflict, that it touched
all of us, that we cannot let others be hurt without hurting ourselves. From deep within them, from all they knew to be moral
and true and right, they rebelled against the rising tide of hate.

The Reuthers have a baby. The world they want to see ahead
for him is one where man accepts his fellow man; where no one
is excluded because of what he is; where people have the right
to be different, and where everyone benefits because they are
different. It is this kind of world to which the Reuthers lend their
political support, this they talk for among their friends and to
whoever else will listen, this they have in their unspoken dreams
and hopes as they watch their baby grow.

The Whitesides

This family group is genuine early American. Roots on both sides also go back to the same source, but in this case to New England—to Plymouth Rock—and before that to England.

It almost seems that the Whitesides were fated to be married. Their fathers belonged to the same clubs; their mothers attended the same teas and were active in the same societies; as children the Whitesides went to the same Sunday School, way back in something they only dimly remember now as the "primary group." There was great overlapping among their families' friends. Same church, same neighborhood, same school, same recreation, same newspapers and magazines in their homes, same people dropping in on Sunday afternoons and coming to dinner parties—a circle of similarity has surrounded the Whitesides from far back in time. The boy and girl growing up did not know it then; the man and woman do know it now, and they like it and it continues.

The Whitesides have a baby, too. They are not politically conscious people. They read little except an occasional novel, the fiction magazines, a few leading news accounts, and the departments of their newspaper of special interest. They almost never discuss national and international questions. If you asked them what kind of a world they want for their son they would be surprised. If they could put an answer into words they would tell you about a world peopled with 1970 editions of the Bradfords, Wadsworths, Brewsters—the people like themselves.

The Waldos

The Whitesides seldom say things which might directly color a child's growing point of view. The Waldos are a different lot. Hardly a day goes by without Mr. Waldo having some kind of explosion.

His newspaper keeps harping on the Reds—the threat they are nationally, how obstinate and pigheaded and menacing internationally. Mr. Waldo buys this paper because he loves it. He

pounds the table when he reads of a particularly dastardly maneuver (and everything *is* a maneuver); he worries visibly
whenever his paper views with alarm (the paper's type goes up
into capitals and Mr. Waldo's eyebrows and temperature rise
with it); he gloats so that everyone hears him when those Reds
are foiled again.

It is this way in his business too; Mr. Waldo's world is peopled
with enemies. "Labor" tries to put him personally out of business;
"the Jews" have singled him out to take some of his pennies away;
"niggers" exist solely to do annoying things which upset him
(and they do it on purpose, to hear Mr. Waldo tell it).

At any meal, on any evening at home, and on Sundays the air
may be filled with Mr. Waldo's verbal wrestling with all these
threats. Mrs. Waldo has heard all this a hundred times. She is a
housewife—patient, easy-going, accepting; things do not bother
her much. She takes life in her stride, even her husband's
growling.

The Waldos also have a new baby. The child is still very young;
he does not yet hear what goes on in the living room after the
news broadcast or over the supper table when Mr. Waldo tells
whom he defeated today. Children grow up, however, and it is
not very likely that Mr. Waldo will grow up any more.

The Sallaks

Mr. Waldo does not know he is dealing in prejudice; that is
something the other fellow has. The Sallaks, however, are much
more aware of prejudice in a world in which they have been on
the receiving end.

William Sallak and Rose, his wife, were both born on the
other side. They have a small store—fruits, vegetables, and staples
—long hours, ceaseless courtesies and agreeability, no vacations,
no holidays, tired feet, colds. It is much less than they each
hoped for when, years ago, they so bravely and eagerly set out.

The Sallaks know how the neighborhood thinks of them: "The
Wops." (The Sallaks came from Bohemia, but no one has been

interested enough to find that out.) You go to "The Wops" when the other stores are closed—early in the morning, late at night, Sundays, holidays.

They live in the back of their store. A bedroom, a living room and parlor, a kitchen, a bath, a place for the child—except that it is all in two rooms. And that is all they can look forward to. For one thing, the store never brings in enough. There never is money ahead to make a move possible. For another, where would they go? And so they stay.

This is their life in America—a hard life, but it is a life. The church is their one comfort. There they can go and be like others. The church frightens them a little; their God is so powerful, so stern, so all-knowing. Yet He is that way for everyone, and there is comfort in that.

And Arthur, their baby? What of him? Is this to be his life, too? He was born here. He is an American. What is the way to get him ready for what lies ahead?

The Sallaks have their answer. Arthur will get ahead by being tough; he has to learn to take it. A foreign boy—no, a boy whose parents are foreign-born—he cannot be a sissy. It is good to learn that early because it is the one big thing to know.

The Sallaks have another point: Arthur will get ahead if he acts good enough. The church says this, and it will be important in the store. The greatest sin is to be fresh to the wrong people, to speak out, and to talk back. Smile when the people come in, be polite and cute, do favors; they like you that way. And be nice at school. There it really counts. Be on time, be quiet, be neat. Be tough on the one hand but be soft and gentle on the other.

The Resses

This mother and father answer the same questions in a different way. Prejudice is a familiar problem for them, too. Their family —a grandparent, some uncles, cousins—had been in Europe. The war and the pre-war period wiped them all out, every last one of them so far as is known . . . killed for no reason except being

Jews. And killed not prettily but nastily, hurtfully, degradingly. This was the culmination of a long history of hurts and wounds for being what you are.

Alex Ress is a college graduate. He was an independent at college; he said then that he liked it that way. He had to like it—none of the fraternities pledged Jews. He had lived off-campus, but at least he had received a college education. You had to fight to get even that. His marks had been good in high school—he knew that; the school knew that. But try to get into a good college. Just try. His seventh application was accepted.

Sylvia had found it equally hard at college. She was one of a small clique of girls. Together they had a good time, but they had to make it themselves. You knew you were different and there was no point fighting against it. You never could be president of your class, president of a club, editor of the college paper. But you could get marks and you could have your own fun.

The hurts did not actually start in college (although you felt them more then perhaps), but they did not end with college either. Alex Ress is a lawyer. He is a good one, but there are certain cases he does not take, certain judges he does not argue before, certain clients who are shifted to one of the Gentile partners (even though the case is in his specialty and he does most of the spadework on it).

When you stop to look at it, childhood is the only happy time. Life is a sad thing once you get to know it. Childhood is innocence; childhood is fun; in childhood you get what you want and need. Those are the happy times.

The Resses plan to say nothing to Sonny about his being a Jew for a good long time. Let him have some fun while the having is good.

What can you predict about these children?

As teachers we must share the goal that the Reuthers have: to help children grow so that they are capable of enjoyable inter-group relationships. This is our moral responsibility; it is essential if our society is to be democratic. How successfully do these different families lay a foundation for the achievement of that goal?

The First Thing a Child Needs

As soon as the child is born, he has very great needs. They are needs so real that, unfilled, they hurt him; they are needs so great that, satisfied, they result in a peace and composure that can actually be seen. This is where the first steps in the foundation are laid. Learning feelings about oneself and feelings about others starts with the baby's first feedings. Not fed when he is hungry, the child suffers contractions of his stomach—hurtful, unpleasant contractions; fed, the child has what he needs and with food comes the sense of well-being and comfort.

There is even more to feeding than this. For not only does the hungry baby carry inside him unpleasant and aching pangs; he is also unable to do anything directly about them. The adult can go to the icebox; the adolescent can stop for his bottle of coke; the woman in her living room can nibble her piece of candy. But the child is impotent. Impotent except for one device: his cry—an exhausting, energy-expending device and one that is so often ignored. We have, in fact, built up rationalizations to support our ignoring of his need: crying is good for his lungs. . . . And we have built up fears to support our ignoring of his need: if you give in you will have a spoiled child on your hands.

But what happens to the baby's feelings when he wants something desperately, when he is impotent to get it himself, and when it hurts him because he cannot get it? Much of our planning for infant feeding has been done on the basis that nothing happens to his feelings. Food is the only thing that matters, we say; no other learnings are involved.

A whole body of procedure is based on this idea: feed the child every four hours or feed him every three (keep him on a schedule). If he cries because he is hungry, let him cry. Drop out the early morning feeding at four weeks (or three, or five—but drop it out at some set time). If he cries because he is distressed, let him cry. End the suckling at nine months (or at six, or eight, or ten); offer a cup, and break the bottles if you are afraid you will be tempted to give in. If he cries, let him cry.

In most families the adult knows best; the adult sets the schedule. The child has no feelings, and his language has no meaning at all; the child, in fact, has a devil inside him determined to persist in evil ways. If once you give in, if once you let the barriers down, you are doomed. With this approach comes consistency—"the hobgoblin of little minds," but in raising children the golden virtue. Whatever you do, stick by your plan. Never waver. Children are like horses and they must be broken. Stay by your guns.

Here in feeding, in the way the child gets the very first thing he asks of this world, the feelings start. Is he fed when he is hungry? Does he get all the food he needs to end his hunger, or is there a watch that knows better than he when he has had enough? Does he get his food in the way he wants it, in the way he knows, in the way he is biologically prepared to take it? Does he get the kind of food his stage of growing can manage? Or is what he wants constantly being taken away and something new and harder to swallow offered in its place?

If the feeding goes one way, the feelings are nice ones: I get what I want and the world is good. If the feeding goes another way, the feelings are hostile: I cry and nothing happens; I hurt and no one cares; you ask more of me than I can do.

Dr. and Mrs. Reuther want a world where people accept one another, where people can work together and enjoy one another, where friendliness and not hostility holds sway. This is what they will teach their child when they know they are teaching him something. The doctor and his wife are health-conscious, however. Food has an extra importance to them.

Their Bobby is fed on a four-hour schedule. He is awakened to be fed if he is sleeping; he is allowed to cry if he is awake. Bobby is allowed fifteen minutes for a bottle. It is taken away if he is slow and the bottle not emptied; the bottle is teased back into his mouth if the time is not yet up. Bobby is fed on schedule. He will be weaned on schedule, and new foods will be pushed into him when the books say they should be. Good food habits are the most important thing. Unfortunately for intercultural education the Reuthers act as though that were all that is involved in feeding.

Fortunately for intercultural education the Waldo baby does not yet hear what his father says; more fortunately, however, the Waldos hear the baby. When he cries, they feed him. They pick him up and hold him, and Mrs. Waldo puts him to her breast. She is president of nothing. She is going nowhere and has time on her hands. The baby can suck as long as he wants to. The Waldos' doctor once mapped out when certain things should happen according to the book, but Mrs. Waldo does not take instructions too seriously. The baby will be weaned "after a while"; if he spits out his vegetables today, "he'll take them tomorrow or the next day."

Three Things Go Together

Eating happens often in the baby's early life; whatever feelings come along with it are practiced and learned time and time again. And tied in with food and related to it are two other activities: sleeping and eliminating. What touches one activity touches all three, and together they make up almost the whole of the child's early life.

Through each of these the child has the chance to get what he needs, to be satisfied, and thus to learn from his own good feeling that he is an all-right person and that the world is a friendly place. Or the opposite feelings can come: that the child cannot do what he wants, that he cannot do what the others want, that he is a not-right person in a world of demanding people.

Sleeping offers such opportunities from the very start of life. All children want and need sleep, but they want and need it in one particular way: they want it when they are sleepy. Yet in forcing patterns on children's feeding we also force patterns on their sleeping. Following a schedule, a man-made schedule and not the baby's own, in some homes sleeping children are awakened because now it is time for food. The thing that is giving them very deep satisfaction is taken away and in its place comes something which they do not ask for or want at the moment.

And then, having done this, day after day for several early months when the babies' feelings are first laid down, some families proceed in the opposite direction. They become devotees of sleep. They think there is something golden in sleep itself. From awakening babies before they are ready, they spend several years trying to get children to go to sleep. The child is left in his room; the room is darkened and the house kept quiet. The child cries; he does not want quiet now. He wants life, companionship, something moving and responding. But the adult says he needs sleep, although the surest sign that could tell us—the child's reactions, his body state—says so clearly that he does not.

The battle starts in the first year. Some parents persist in looking for a morning nap and try to force it long after the child's own body has given it up. And the battle continues into the third and fourth and fifth year as, in home after home, that precious institution of the regular afternoon nap is upheld by parents and overthrown by children.

Out of the conflict between the pressure the family brings (what its culture considers right) and the pressure within the child (his own rhythm and state of growing) emerge his basic feelings toward himself and others—either: I feel good; I get what I want when I want and need it; people are good; they give you what you cannot get yourself . . . or: I don't feel good about myself; my way of doing things must be wrong; I get mad at this world with its people who hold out on me and make life so difficult.

Running a store keeps you on your toes; someone is always coming in. You do not have time to follow all the rules and bring up babies the way the books say you should. The best that Rose Sallak can do is to put the baby on his own. Sometimes he sleeps past his feeding time, particularly if his mother is busy with customers. Sometimes he skips his nap because no one is free to keep after him and see that he goes to sleep.

With Mrs. Ress the baby comes first; he is going to have a good childhood if the mother has her way. Everything that is good for children will be his . . . and sleep is good. The doctor says so and the books do too—thirteen hours a day for a baby his age. But it certainly is a struggle getting Sonny to see it that way; he just will not stay asleep.

One Battle Comes Later

The conflict over elimination is postponed a while. No one teaches the newly born baby about elimination; no one makes him change his ways. What gives him relief, a more comfortable feeling inside, a lessening of tension—this is accepted whenever and wherever it happens. But, as though to make up for the time lost in giving in to the youngness of the child, the battle is picked up with great intensity later. There are strenuous efforts, all too soon, to control the time, and to set the place, and to determine the way.

There may be no shaming, no scolding words spoken. The child is carried to the toilet; it is the time when a movement often comes. On this particular day the mother is successful—the movement does come—then *this* is the time to teach. She shows her good feelings by praise, by an extra hug and an extra kiss, by the big smile on her face, and by the tone of her voice. Yet why?

The child must wonder. For this is not something that is his work. This is not something that he tries to do and then succeeds; it is mother who has succeeded This is an accident, a happy business of timing which on this day just came off. Here is a beginning for dangerous self-doubt. For is this how you win approval? Is that what makes for acceptance? Is this how you get those nice-sounding words and the holdings and the special looks? Through luck? Through chance? Through nothing you can do yourself to deserve them?

And many times, of course, the mother is not successful. The movement comes too early or the movement comes too late. When this happens, then the scoldings and shamings often do come or there is a disappointment which the child clearly senses. Again, why? From the child's standpoint, it is merely because he has eased a very real pressure inside him, because he had done what he had to do, because he has done the thing which now makes him feel content and pleased and at ease.

This is his real self—and yet it is not good. What makes him feel so content is somehow a wrong thing to do. And the right thing? Something he cannot do; he has not grown enough.

The Whitesides live in a protected, isolated shell; they are under-educated because of the life they lead . . . and their child will be under-educated too. It will take much exposure to books and ideas and people and work before he will know that the world is broader than his family sees it, and still more before he will be able to learn to like it in a broader way. For in one area the Whiteside baby has already had a thorough education. He has built up feelings about himself; these will be harder to change than will the scope of his ideas. In the Whiteside scheme of society you must do things right and be correct— whether it is in serving tea or the stationery you choose, in keeping your car polished, or in training your baby. The Whiteside baby was toilet-trained early; his mother and a maid kept after him, trying and trying until they succeeded. There were slip-ups even after they thought they had won, but a few good scoldings soon fixed that: "You are a bad, bad boy." The age at which your child learns to keep dry and clean is a crucial test, and it is the subject of many a conversation.

Affection Counts, Too

In intercultural education we are concerned about how the family can give to the child, through the very life he leads, the feeling that he is an able and good person. One further way that children can get this feeling—or its dangerous opposite—is through the amount of cuddling, fondling, and affection-tempered handling they receive in infancy.

In each of the five families we are looking at, the child was a wanted child. He was planned for, eagerly awaited; he was no unwelcome threat to family income or health or fun. Each baby was wanted for his own sake, not as an excuse to hold the family together or to give a parent something to do or to add new luster to a fading family life.

Not all children are born this lucky way. Some are not wanted, consciously or unconsciously. And the strange thing about children is that they have their ways of knowing. No amount of going through the motions of love, no amount of substituting gifts or things or rewards can make up for a basic lack of feeling. Children sense what is going on.

Unwanted children start life with a very real handicap in intercultural education. For from the very start they never get their fill of the good feelings that being wanted brings. No matter how much of other things they may get, they do not know enough of the inner satisfaction that comes when one is loved and accepted and welcome, and when the whole language of their parents' behavior tells them that this is so.

But even when children are wanted, some families do not always capitalize on this and exploit it to the fullest. Some children do not get the maximum satisfaction that they could from their potentially good start. The same old process operates:

our culture—our way of doing things—steps in to deprive them of what they need.

We have only to look at children's behavior to see what it is they want. There is a child all tense, his every nerve ending tingling, his muscles arched and taut, his body stiff and tight, with the tears flowing. The child is picked up, held, talked to, comforted. The tenseness goes, relaxation comes—a peace, a repose, an at-rest feeling. Just as the kitten purrs, so children's posture and muscle tone and their whole physical response tell us that these outward signs of affection (growing from an honest feeling) are something they thrive on. These go deep with them and strike a very responsive chord.

The presence of affection shows in one way (children like it and ask for it); the absence shows in another. We learn the importance of outward signs of affection from the happy behavior of children who have known it; we learn their importance also from the sadder behavior of children who have never had enough. We see children in foster homes, institutions, and orphanages— foundlings, deserted and abandoned children, those deprived of parents. Here are children brought up in an institutional atmosphere where, sometimes for sheer physical reasons, there is not enough of this important playing, laughing, singing with, holding, comforting, talking to, cuddling. The result is a quieter child, less responsive, less outgoing toward his world.

Breast feeding (or close holding when the child is bottle fed) is one excellent way that children can get the good feelings that help them. The child is born with almost no chin and thus he can get close to his mother, snuggle when he feeds, make his body and his mother's almost one in closeness. Yet some children do not get enough of this; our culture—what is considered right and good— steps in.

Mrs. Reuther, the doctor's wife, would have nothing to do with breast feeding. To her it was almost "peasant-like." Furthermore, it would have tied her down, kept her away from meetings, upset her whole schedule. And the Reuthers are up-to-date, scientific, modern. Their baby, Bobby, was fed from a bottle stand. He lay on his crib and the milk dripped when he sucked. Both bottle and baby were "untouched by human hand."

In some families our modern concept of the great importance of time gets in the way of children getting what they need. The opportunities that could be exploited to give these good things to children are by-passed because "we have to get the job done." Feeding is rushed through—a watch sets the pace. Bathing is not play time; it is a quick wash and out.

Mr. Whiteside is a businesslike man; Mrs. Whiteside runs a well-organized home in a quiet yet efficient way. Their social schedule, business appointments, and dinner parties all come off as they should. In this family it makes good sense to feed the baby on schedule, to have a set time limit for the feeding, to put aside a certain number of minutes for the bath. After supper each night there is even a time scheduled when father will play with the baby. It is a little disturbing to him that the child does not seem to know when to stop.

In some families the little sprinkling of knowledge that we moderns possess is the barrier that keeps children from the good feelings they might otherwise get.

Mrs. Ress had a good obstetrician; then a pediatrician took over. The doctors knew all the answers. Who was a lowly mother in such scientific company? At the hospital the nurses wore white, and all visitors were given a mouth mask. Wasn't a mother really a menace? The women's magazines Mrs. Ress reads are full of stories on the faults of mothers, the mistakes they make, of how schools could do a good job were it not for the home, of how easy it is for children to be spoiled. . . . Somewhere deep in Mrs. Ress an important decision is made:

she will keep hands off that precious baby; she doesn't know enough.

The children in all five of our families are boy babies. For boys one cultural rule is clear: boys do not cry. The extent to which families follow this rule strictly is one more determiner of whether children get the comfort they ask for in a way they can understand. Children do get hurt or worried or distressed at events in their growing up. They fall, and it pains, and they cry; they lose a toy and it bothers them; they are denied something and the distress goes deep. How these events are handled—whether the children get the solace and support they need—is another way that feelings of being good and right and able, or being bad and naughty and inadequate, are built into children.

Mrs. Sallak has to leave her baby alone a great deal. Sometimes he cries in the back room and she can hear him. Perhaps he is wet, or the bed is rumpled or his position uncomfortable, or perhaps his arm is caught in the crib bar. There are times when Rose can go back to see; other times she is busy. But children should not cry. God made this a hard world, and children have to learn not to give in to what hurts. That is the way you get ready for the bumps, the bigger bumps, that lie ahead . . . as Rose sees it.

The children in all five of our families are the first-born. In each family, before long, a second child comes. This can be one of those events which worry children: Why this change? Where does it come from? What does it mean to me . . . and to me and mother? And, to make it a more complicated event, the cultural pattern in some homes says: This must be a secret; the child must not be told. The way each family handles the advent of a second child again builds into the first more feelings about himself and about the people in his world.

Some parents set out to lessen the worry—they prepare the child ahead of time, let him in on the "secret," help him to see that it is no threat to him, give him extra love and more privileges. A new baby is a giving-up time for the first-born; these parents see that it becomes a getting time too. Other families stand by what their culture says—keep it a secret and ignore the feelings built up inside.

The Reuthers had their second child when their first boy was three. With a medical background on both sides of the family it was easy for them to accept and answer questions about sex. They talked openly in the family about the coming baby, and they answered Bobby's questions simply as they came. It was easier for Bobby, being in on the coming event, to accept the new baby as partly his and to see her as less of a barrier between his precious mother and himself. For a while Bobby wanted more hugs from his mother, but this seemed natural enough to her and she was glad to give him as many as she could and as much extra time as she could fit in.

Mrs. Sallak is very moral about sex. She has seen newspaper headlines about sex and the trouble it gets people into. The church has taught her this too. The Sallak boy was also three when the new baby came. The baby girl came and that was that; one day she was not there, the next day she was. Not knowing why, not expecting anything new, the Sallak boy now demanded a lot. He wanted to be held whenever Rose came near, he cried over every little thing, he asked for help on jobs he could manage, and he even wet his pants again although he had stopped that some time ago. In his mother's eyes he was just "bad." He was older now and "he knows better." In the boy's eyes, perhaps his mother was right. He must have been naughty or this new baby would not have happened to him; Arthur felt less good about himself.

An Inner Force

As muscles grow, and bones strengthen, and nerve connections become better established throughout the first year, the child is compelled by an inner force into still other behavior that as inherently represents him as did his earlier wanting of food, wanting to sleep, wanting to eliminate, and wanting of love.

The child is ready now—his internal growing makes him ready —to touch, to handle, to move, to crawl, to stand, to walk, to run. This is the child at a new stage. These are the activities into which his growing propels him. There are tensions inside him which his very growing creates; his one way out is to do those things which release the tensions and which, in their release, bring him satisfactions. He must crawl, he must handle, he must touch.

This is the child. But parents also are propelled into certain kinds of behavior. Either they have learned to side with the child, to give him the chance to do the things that mean good living for him; or they have learned to set up blocks, to put barriers in the way, to try to change the child quickly into something they consider nicer. And, depending on their choice of behavior, the feelings inside the child develop—either: I am good, I can do what I want to do, I can do it as long as I want to . . . or: I am bad, what I like to do is not allowed, what is me is not right. The foundation feelings for intercultural relationships—for good or bad— thus continue to be laid down.

Either the child can touch and handle—thumbs, toes, genitals, toys, ash trays, dirt, pots and pans, pianos—or the child grows up surrounded by "do's" and "don'ts" and by "You are naughty" and "You are bad."

The child can mess around and feel—food, textures, sand, mud, dirt—or the child grows up surrounded by "must nots" and "Keep clean."

The Whitesides have a really nice home. The furniture is tastefully chosen, and it is all expensive. There are deep rugs, costly bric-a-brac, surfaces that are highly polished and easily scratched. It is the kind of home where people are apt to call. It is embarrassing if the house is upset. Mrs. Whiteside usually dresses up in the afternoon—just in case—and she likes her boy to keep dressed up too.

At the Waldos' life is quite different. The furniture is second-hand and not too good at that. Once a week Mrs. Waldo gives a thorough cleaning; the rest of the time things just get picked up. The only person likely to drop in is Mrs. Rousch, the neighbor downstairs, and then just for a cigarette and a cup of coffee; she does not care how the place looks.

Either the child can experiment with sound—babbling and cooing, repeating words, nonsense sounds, loud sounds and soft ones, queer made-up words, "dirty" words—or the child grows up surrounded by "Hush" and "Don't yell and shout so" and "Mustn't say that."

The child can use his large muscles to crawl and walk and pull up and climb and balance and run and jump—in the house, on furniture, down the steps, across the floor, up in trees, on the street—or the child grows up surrounded by "Don't climb on that" and "Walk, don't run" and "That's dangerous, mustn't do that."

The Reuthers like a sound mind in a strong body—it is one of their favorite slogans. Bobby's first steps were a real thrill for them, and they have never got over how well he uses his body. In their back yard they have big boxes for him to climb on, boards he can walk on from one box to the other. Bobby jumps down from them, he does daredevil tricks that tickle his parents —he can even hang by his knees from a bar!

Mr. and Mrs. Ress had all their thrills early. Crawling, sitting up, standing, walking—these were exciting so long as they were safe. But one thing leads to another. The stairs in their house are a menace, and Sonny wants to jump down from them! There is a stoop out front, and Sonny does not seem to realize how high and dangerous it is; he keeps climbing up on it and his mother can hardly keep him off.

Only those who have confidence in themselves can in turn have confidence in others. Yet some families fail their children. They do it in two ways, and neither way is good preparation for enjoy-able intercultural relations. The first way to failure is to push chil-dren ahead before they are ready to go, to put pressure on them for behavior they are not capable of. The second way to failure is to keep children from trying.

Children want success, but they want it through their own ef-forts. They want the chance to do the hard thing—that is, the hard thing as *they* see it—and they ask for this chance at every stage of their growing up. The toddler takes a few steps and falls; he stands right up and walks again. The two-year-old tries to feed himself; he spills and messes and tires, but he keeps on trying until he succeeds. The three-year-old wants to button his buttons; he works at it, pushing, trying to find the hole, pulling until the but-ton comes through. "I want to do it myself" is the war cry of children. This is the way the good feelings grow.

It is not easy to run a store and to raise a baby. And if you have two children it is that much worse! Mrs. Sallak has always had to keep after Arthur to get him to do all she thinks he should: take his own baths, get dressed by himself, button his buttons, tie his shoelaces, fix his straps. Arthur keeps running to mother for help. "It is just because he doesn't try, he doesn't stick at it, he gives up so easily." She always turns him away.

Mrs. Ress, on the other hand, has time on her hands. Her Sonny tries to button his buttons, but they are so hard for him to do. Mother is glad to do it for him; that is what mothers are for. Sonny wants to serve himself at dinner, but he spills, of course, and it just goes better if Mommy does it. Mrs. Ress is glad she has so much time. The messes that children can get into! Just riding his tricycle, Sonny can get the wheel caught, or some toy is in the way—you have to be on your toes to be a good mother and straighten all those little things out.

The child can have a chance to do the things which make him feel good, which most truly express his growing state, which give him outlets that lead to inner satisfaction. Or the child grows up feeling that the things which mean him, his way of doing them, are bad or dangerous and not to be done. Either he learns to feel that he can cope with his world, or the feeling grows that the world is too much for him. One alternative leads to confidence and satisfaction; the other to suspicion. Either he learns gradually to change his ways as his growing makes him ready to do so, or there is pressure on him to change before he is ready. Either we accept the child as he is and provide safe channels for his expression, or we set out early to dam up his energies, to deny them, or to divert them into the culture-right ways.

The Feelings, Too

Such choices are continually being made in all the activities, the doing-things, of early childhood. They are being made, too, in the way we handle the emotional responses, the feeling-things, of early life.

The young child has feelings. He gets angry and wants to get even; he knows jealousy and he wants to hurt; he feels frustration and he seeks a way out. These feelings are himself; they are his responses. Either we accept them and provide a safe channel for their expression, and thus build up more reason for his feeling right inside; or we deny them and threaten when they come out, and thus build up more reason for his doubting inside.

The two-year-old cries because he wants something deeply. The family has two ways of responding: one is sympathetic, through slowly explaining and explaining over again; the other is abrupt—"Stop your crying or I'll spank you and then you will have something to cry about." The one method accepts the child's feelings as real; the other denies that what he feels is right.

The three-year-old hits. The family has two ways of responding: One method accepts the fact that three-year-olds do not yet have the self-control that will come later. Accepting this, it explains and interprets: "Hitting hurts. I can't let anyone hurt you, and I can't let you hurt Johnny." The other method punishes the child for feeling what he does: "You are bad to do that. Hitting is naughty. I'll hit you if you don't stop."

The four-year-old says "I hate you" when he cannot have his way. He has learned enough control to substitute words for an actual deed. One way of responding acknowledges this, is glad for at least that much progress, and accepts what the child feels: "It is all right to be mad, but I can't let you go out now." The other way shames the child for feeling what he does: "It is naughty to say that and you are a bad, bad boy. If you say you hate me again, I'll go away and leave you and I'll never come back."

The Whitesides have a maid; she has a lot to do with the children. When the parents are around, Sally is rather strict; her job depends on teaching good behavior—she can take no funny business from the children. On her own, however, Sally has a different way. She knows how children feel—she has felt angry and hurt herself at times, and she knows how hard it is to keep the feelings in. And Sally has a feeling for children; she knows that they do not always mean what they say in the way it sounds. There is a great cushion here for the Whiteside babies. Sally is getting in some good innings for intercultural education, although she would be surprised if you told her that.

Children must learn. They must take on the ways that are right in our world. They must learn what can be said, and what can be done, and when and where and how. The question is one of timing. With some children the pressure comes too early, the change is made too abruptly, the penalties are too severe; there is too little regard for where the children have come from, how far along the road they are, and why they act now in the way they do. And, when the timing is off, the feeling built up is: This which I feel, this which I do because I am me, this is bad and I am bad.

The Lessons Learned

Learning never comes through clearly. In all of us the learnings are mixed; the slate is not pure black or white.

Only in the deeply disturbed do the feelings come through heavily weighted in one direction; only in those have all experiences built toward one single end; only in a few of us do all these events of early life teach one kind of feeling and that alone.

For most of us the result is a mixture: a getting here, a losing there. We have the chance to find most of what we want in one set of experiences, but from one set we do not get all; in another group of actions we lose a great deal of what we want, but we do not lose all.

The particular children we are following show us that these things are true. Bobby Reuther comes through his growing up with many feelings of defeat from his early feeding and toilet training and the interruptions in his sleep. But, to offset this, he comes through the experience of acquiring a baby sister with good feelings, and he adds to these through his freedom to use his body and his growing skills, to do more and more and to develop. Sonny Ress gets less handling and fondling than are necessary to give him good feelings; he has too little chance to know success through trying out and experimenting; his way of doing things—sleeping was an example—will be cut across whenever the books say something else is good for him. But Sonny is a wanted child and he lives in a warm and friendly home; his parents want happiness for him, and all this goes to build him up.

In only a few of us are the feelings all those of satisfaction or all those of deprivation; it is the normal thing to have some of both. But, to whatever extent our feelings are those of dissatisfaction, to that extent we are unreliable. We can know the facts of biological inheritance, and we can know the intermixture of races. We can be fully aware of the contributions of different nationalities. We can see day by day the evidences of our actual interdependence. We can know by heart the phrases singing the equality of man. Yet in the crucial actions of our life, if we have suffered early from deprivation, one compelling motivation must remain—our personal sense of unworthiness. This we carry within us, and from this must always flow some measure of hostility to others and some fear of them because of the threat they are to our feeble selves.

When he was almost four Bobby Reuther attended nursery school. He was a terror in his group. He kicked other children, pulled their hair, hit others a good deal, knocked down blocks. At first the teachers were not surprised—three-year-olds do these things, and particularly a child who has had little companionship. But Bobby did not change much by the end of the year. He still knew which children he could make cry; he knew which ones he could make run away. Lack of experience was not his trouble so much as angry feelings inside.

In our homes we may never hear the verbal expressions of prejudice. The jokes that sneer or the jokes that lie may be no part of our lives. Our parents may be people of good will toward others; they may have dreams of a friendly society for us. We may know people that are different from the stereotypes, some of them may even be our families' "best friends." Yet, to the extent that the feelings of dissatisfaction inside us are many, we stand ever ready to become—despite all moral exhortations and all intellectual education—the all-too-ready followers of the disrupters and dividers who would hurt the weak.

What Does This Mean for the School?

It is important for teachers to know the family lives of their children. One reason teachers must know home backgrounds is that the home teaches some things better than the school does. Sometimes we say this with sorrow. We recognize it ruefully, despairingly: "What are you going to do with a home like that?" . . . "You can not get anywhere if you can not get the co-operation of the parents." The family's amateur way, unblessed by academic degrees and by professional study, has a potency of its own.

Yet we need not despair; the school can learn from what the home does. In lieu of moaning and groaning, in lieu of charging off our failures, we can try to see just why the home is so effective in shaping children for good or bad and can take leads from what it does.

There is a second reason for teachers to know what the home background is: family ways can change. Parents, too, can learn. No inexorable educational determinism is at work there, except as we let it work.

If we as teachers abdicate in despair, the parents will inevitably continue as before. If we abstain from praise, good ways unthinkingly pursued may drop out—and hurtful ways, equally uncritically adopted, may creep in or persist.

Change never comes overnight. It comes only as we work at it slowly, gradually, and over long periods of time. But few families will ever consciously change in an improving direction unless we as teachers lend our support and our approval to what is good and unless we make available our friendly guidance in what seems less desirable.

There is a third reason, too. Some homes cannot change; others can change only so slowly that real harm is done in the meantime. Attitudes and ways of proceeding which are built on them, techniques grounded in long and habitual practice—these do not quickly disappear even where there are good intentions on the part of the family.

Where, over long periods of time, hurtful attitudes have prevailed in the home, there is a special make-up task for the school to do. The school needs to know two things: Who are the children in deepest need of a turning of the tide? Which ones need a special chance for a new way to look at themselves?

If we know what goes on in the home the stage is set for one important part of our endeavor: We can spot those children who most need help, and through the school's program we can immunize them against the threats-from-living which they have long known and will long continue to know.

Lesson 1: A Nourishing School

The family produces non-compulsive, accepting personalities when it gives children to the full what they want, when and how they want it, and when it wards off unnecessary and man-imposed failures. Only rarely, however, do the schools operate on this principle. But perhaps educators and others who see how crucial the well-nourished personality is to good intercultural relationships will help the schools to do this more generally.

Like life within the family, school can be a defeating experience or it can have a rewarding, fulfilling effect. Just as the good home does not expect more from the child than he can comfortably give or expect it earlier than he can give it and just as the good home does not wean the child too early or toilet-train him too early, so the good school will not push for reading achievement too early or for sitting still too early or for drawing on small pieces of paper too early. For in the school setting those are some counterparts of the cultural pressures which the good parent ameliorates in the home setting.

Unless the pressures on children in school are softened by an understanding of what makes children feel good, it will matter little if smart teaching techniques are used in units on intercultural education at some one point or at many points in the child's school career. Unless his total schooling and his total living build up in some particular child a sense that he is an important person capable of doing many good things, that child inevitably must remain a poor bet in his intercultural behavior.

Schools which wish to learn from good homes, then, can take this first lesson: They must seize every opportunity to build up in the child a faith in himself. By so doing, they will build up in him a trust of other people. In doing this big job every teacher, regardless of the subject and regardless of the age group concerned, "teaches" intercultural education. It is the total program of the school which counts.

Such a school will have none of the defeating emphasis on formal drill and rote learning before the child is by maturity and experience ready for it. It will have none of the insistence on pinpoint quiet and motionless sitting before the child is physiologically ready for it. Such a school will have a wider, broader program—beyond symbols, words, books. For at no age do these alone give to all children the success which they need, and at some ages those narrower avenues keep from almost all children the success they want.

A school with this broader program will have a different concept of what is good behavior. For sometimes, from the child's standpoint and because of the growing he has done, good behavior means running, shouting, pushing, noise. Schools cannot remain a suppressing force in children's lives and at the same time build for sound intercultural education on the basis of fully satisfied personalities.

A good school will have more expressive activities: the arts, drama, crafts, building, games. It will have smaller classes where children can be known personally and where they can have the dignity of being real people. And, lastly, the school will have teachers—warm persons themselves—who are emotionally ready to go out to children, unplagued by fears that the children will take advantage of them or become spoiled, undisciplined, and "unable to draw the line."

Lesson 2: Some Children Need More

A program along these general lines will help all children; there are some, however, who need even more of such help. There are some on whom the cultural impact within the family has been too severe. In countless situations—in feeding, weaning, sleeping, toilet training; in touching, handling, noise, and language—prohibitions and behavior beyond their capacity have been imposed on them. One urgent job for the schools to do is to spot such handicapped children.

This will not be easy for the schools to do. Some children of this type will be too good, and the school's tendency will be to overlook these. Some will be too bad, and the school's tendency will be to punish such children more. But if all these children can be spotted, the schools can make up to them specifically for the fulfilling experiences they have missed.

Every opportunity must be sought and new opportunities created so that such children can find success. They have had enough of deprivation, enough of trying yet not succeeding, enough of falling short and not coming up to scratch. These children need school experiences where they *can* come through. In reading, in writing, on the ball field, in social relations, in art and music, and in the shop the children's doctor has written his prescription. There is a specific medicine which will be the antidote for the slow poison of self-doubt that is in them. That medicine is approval, belonging, achievement.

With these children all teachers must go out of their way to be friendly. They must take every chance to show warmth and to give approbation. For this is a medicine which cannot operate through weakness and faults; if it is to work it must capitalize on strength.

It may even be necessary for the school to blind its eyes to faults. For the pressures inside these children are such as to make them show many faults. Some of them do the wrong thing not because they do not know it is wrong but because of the more compelling motivation of having someone notice them. Their life has taught them to sell themselves short. They have learned that they cannot do the good things, their things, and win notice that way; they can, however, become a nuisance, and that has the same value—it makes people pay attention.

Those who are concerned with good intercultural relationships will overlook some misbehavior in such children. They will make allowances. They will not see every mistake the children make; they will not set out persistently to instruct and correct and improve them. For, first of all, these children need a boosting up. They cannot accept improvement until they first accept and feel good about themselves.

If the schools can spot these children, they can do one thing more: they can give them many safety valves. For a life too filled with dissatisfaction piles up the feelings inside. Unless some safety valve is found, these are the very feelings which blow off the top in intercultural hatreds. The fellow who is different, the fellow who is out, or the fellow who seems weak becomes the safe person for those children to hit.

Schools can help such children by guiding them into as many activities as possible where it is legal and truly safe for their feelings to come out. The arts, in particular, have a major contribution to make here. Work with finger paints, free painting on large sheets of paper at the easel or on the floor, work with clay, a chance to hammer and pound at a work bench—all these can be "school work" and safety valves at the same time.

Children with severe handicaps of this kind will benefit by being allowed in their athletic games and in their free time to play as roughly as they want to. They will benefit by a real chance to get dirty—to dig in sand and mud and dirt. They will benefit by whatever chance the school can provide for them to destroy and to damage where it does no actual harm. With young children, for example, knocking down blocks is fully as good for this purpose as building up with blocks; ripping paper may be better for them than cutting with scissors on a straight line; hitting dolls and spanking them and being bossy in doll play may be more healthful than playing in a "nicer" way.

Lesson 3: The Open Channel

If we want to understand a child's background, which is at the base of his intercultural attitudes, we cannot learn all that we have to know by talking once and briefly with his parents. There is no one thing we are after—no one happening, no one experience, no one event. The child's background in intercultural relationships involves all his past living, his total life. This takes a long time to learn, and we must be prepared to learn it slowly. There is no one way we can learn it, no way we can learn it all at once.

This fact has a direct bearing on the school's relations with parents. For it means that there must be the closest possible relationship, and one that extends over the longest possible period of time. Home-and-school relations cannot be confined to one open-school week a year, to one meeting for the whole school a year, to occasional and formal gatherings where one person talks and the others listen.

In place of these there must somehow be developed a continuous and open channel with a flood of give and take. For only so can a teacher, bit by bit and piece by piece, listening and learning, build up a picture of what growing up was like for the child and what feelings he took from it. And it is this which the teacher has to know.

CHAPTER III

THE PRIMARY TEACHER [1]

*School can be a friendly place, a satisfying experience. It can be
a dull, frustrating, or lonely place—even for 1A's. School can
help children to grow, gain confidence, get along with others. It
can intensify feelings of anxiety, inadequacy, and failure.*

*This chapter tells how a teacher of very young children began
to help them to accept themselves and each other—a fundamental
step in building intercultural attitudes.*

*The case studies of children reported here (as recorded by
teachers) and the references to teacher activities are based on records from the Philadelphia Early Childhood Project. The actual
names are of course changed, as are certain other details for purposes of illustration.*

Miss Wheeler and "the Eels"

Miss Wheeler walked to her desk and sat down wearily as the
music supervisor took over her first graders. It had been one of
those gray Mondays—yard duty, assembly, and monthly report
cards due at the office in the morning. In addition, the children
were more than usually wriggly, perhaps because of the uncertain
weather. Even the old reliables, the "good" children, seemed less
dependable, and the "problems" were particularly irritating—
Eugene Howells, for instance.

Miss Wheeler glanced over in Eugene's direction. Though the

[1] This chapter was written by HELEN TRAGER, Director of Age-Level
Studies, Bureau for Intercultural Education.

others were alert and sat up eagerly, he was slumped in his seat. Listlessly he mouthed the words of the song. Against the side of his desk his little fingers, as if unrelated to the rest of him, tapped out the rhythm. Even that much participation was unusual for him. Thumb sucking and a complete withdrawal from the on-going activity were more characteristic—or little aggressive acts like tripping children as they passed, throwing tiny gobs of wet blotter down the back of Bessie's dress, hair pulling, pinching, pushing in the lines.

Particularly the thumb sucking upset Miss Wheeler. It was re-volting, and she often avoided looking at Eugene so as not to see it. If only he were more like Bessie. It was a blessing that of the three Negro children in the class, she had only *one* to really com-plain about. She supposed they could not all be so nice as Bessie, who was an exception. She was polite, neat, and diligent and car-ried herself so proudly—there was not a nasty habit in her wiry little body.

The second verse of the rain song concluded, the children mer-rily scrambled for other seats so they could play "orchestra." Caroline stayed at the back of the room, hands clenched. She seemed to be deep in an argument with Dorothy and Myrna. They were probably getting the best of her as usual, for Caroline was too much of a little lady to be able to handle them. They knew how angry they could make her and never missed an op-portunity. Caroline, flushed and unhappy, glared at Dorothy, as Dorothy and Myrna walked away, giggling together.

Myrna looked like a cat who had swallowed a mouse. She de-lighted in a fight—especially when she won. Her beribboned blonde curls bobbing up and down contrasted sharply with Dor-othy's straight, unkempt, stringy red hair. Dimpled, doll-fresh Myrna, with every curl of her hair and every fold of her dress in place; Dorothy, dressed carelessly in hand-me-downs. What did they have in common? Dorothy—gaunt, serious, a rather dreamy child, given to tall tales; Myrna—demanding, bossy, always brag-ging about her money or her father, "the Doctor."

Miss Wheeler could not help feeling that she had somehow never established a real line of communication with either of the two girls. Every class, she thought, seems to have a few youngsters like these who manage to elude all your efforts right up to promotion day. Each day you struggle anew. They resist. You lose. In spite of her skill, Miss Wheeler had spent many restless nights in her fifteen years of teaching wondering over "the eels," as she called them. "The eels" were the children you could not catch hold of, the children who either seemed to be struggling against you or who were almost indifferent to everyone outside their private worlds.

The warning bell buzzed for afternoon dismissal. Each child pushed his way to his own seat. The music supervisor said goodbye. Miss Wheeler explained about order in the hallway and the importance of good lines on the stairs. She asked for someone to tell the others "why we have lines on the staircase." Most of the class, anxious to tell why, strained to catch her attention either by waving hands wildly in the air, or by sitting bolt upright, hands clasped, eyes fairly popping out of their sockets.

But Frank sat quietly, absorbed, apparently miles away. He started when Miss Wheeler called on him; he was confused and embarrassed. Stephen tried to prompt him *sotto voce*. Miss Wheeler was sorry now that she had startled him. Poor Frank— bright, earnest, well behaved. He either did not listen or did not seem to understand much of what went on in school. Maybe his afternoon Greek school just tired him out so he could not concentrate in her class. He too might be grouped with "the eels," though his slipping away seemed to be due more to helplessness than to indifference or struggle.

Miss Wheeler watched the youngsters pull on their wraps. The music undoubtedly had a good effect on them. There were fewer mishaps than usual, and everyone, including Eugene Howells, was ready and on line when the dismissal gong clanged.

They chirped, "Good afternoon, Miss Wheeler," and scampered out of the big front door.

Report cards were waiting to be marked and stacked neatly in the top middle drawer, next to the little yellow mark book. Miss Wheeler set to work on the cards. Place a letter next to Conduct, Work, and Effort on each of the forty-one cards and the day's work would be done. Simple—yet not so simple. Is Frank "B" in Effort and "A" in Work? That does not make sense. How can anyone know how much effort a child makes? Myrna always makes an effort, but is it the kind of effort to receive an "A"?

Miss Wheeler's head ached. The air in the classroom was stale and chalk dry. A mounting sense of inadequacy and frustration swept over her. She hastily sorted out the cards of the less troublesome children and marked those. The others she placed in her brief case; she would consider them after some supper and rest.

Maybe she was taking her job too seriously, she thought. There is a limit to what one teacher can do—or, for that matter, what school can do—for some children. Particularly when the children were so different from what they used to be. Over the years the neighborhood had been slowly losing its old families and absorbing new ones; middle-class Americans now comprised a smaller proportion of the residents. In place of the diminished middle-class group had come lower-income people—less "American," from many nationality backgrounds, and of different faiths. The few established Negro families also had new neighbors, but they consisted of less "desirable" colored families.

This new mixture and all these new elements meant many adjustments for the teacher. It meant more work and often less satisfaction. For, although the school standards with respect to subject matter stayed much the same, the school requirements were more difficult for these new children to achieve. Individual problems, disciplinary and scholastic, kept increasing. The job of teaching was becoming more and more exhausting. Under the circumstances Miss Wheeler thought she was probably doing very well indeed.

So Miss Wheeler mused as she locked up and walked to the office to hang up her keys and sign out. But somehow her rationalization did not lighten the weight of her self-dissatisfaction.

Fastened to the Time Book by a large paper clip was a note that read:

Don't Forget, Our First Meeting
Tomorrow, Tues., Nov. 16
at 2 P.M.
Teachers' Study Group

Another meeting! She wished she had not volunteered when the group was proposed. Work just never stopped. Something new always turned up just when you thought you could take no more. She pushed open the side door impatiently and started home.

Children and Their Relationships

The teachers' study group was an idea of the district superintendent, Dr. Robins, an old-timer who loved teaching and had great faith in what teachers could do if given the opportunity. For sometime now Dr. Robins had been pushing hard in the councils of top administration for establishment of the policy of school time for in-service education of teachers—and he had won. "Teachers need time to sit down together to discuss professional problems, as doctors do. It should be part of the job."

Not all the principals of the district agreed with him—nor did all his teachers. One principal, when the announcement was made at the principals' district conference, said, "It's just a waste of time. They won't get anything out of it. Just more time to do nothing. Teachers love that!" But that reaction was an extreme one.

Some principals were a little skeptical because the subject matter of the group meetings was to be "Children and Their Relationships." "Talk and theory," they said; "let's be practical!" They felt that their teachers could use their free time to better advantage in learning new skills in remedial reading or in the more modern approach to arithmetic. Why this new wrinkle? Dr.

Robins referred to it as the Fourth R—Human Relations. Always something new!

A few principals endorsed the idea enthusiastically. "Our teachers need time to think, exchange ideas, work together on common problems. They need a chance to learn about children. All their training has been centered on subject-matter. Skills have been reduced to a formula and treated as all-important. Children have been put through a mass-production kind of education. The human factor has gradually been ground out, especially in the large urban schools. A study of human relations sounds pretty important."

One member of the group felt so deeply about the importance of human relationship education that he urged the others to continue the discussion into their next meeting. "There is nothing more important in education today than to teach children to live together with mutual respect. We cannot afford the luxury of another world war. We must learn how to get rid of hate. Look at this community—full of misunderstanding, fear, and prejudice. What do we do about it in school? Nothing. We go home at three-thirty to our own neighborhoods. We are shirking our responsibility as educators." His remarks were not well received; there were some violent objections. The chairman succeeded in restoring order and urged the principals to attend to the matter at hand—plans to make teacher study group meetings a reality.

Dr. Robins stressed several points as minimum essentials in the planning. The meetings must be made up of small groups of teachers so as to allow for maximum participation and free expression of ideas. The teachers in any one group should vary as to age and experience, as far as possible they should come from different school neighborhoods, and several grades should be represented among them. The teachers' study group program was to be started experimentally on a small scale. Leadership was to come from the teachers themselves, with special help from outside consultants. The principals agreed to accept Dr. Robins's proposals, and the next steps were then outlined.

The Teachers' Study Group

Miss Wheeler felt that the first meeting of the teachers' study group was a little strained. When Dr. Robins explained the purpose of the meetings and then left the teachers to plan their work, there was a general feeling of uneasiness and some skepticism. Miss Wheeler rather liked the informal atmosphere, the idea of refreshments, the circular grouping of chairs, and the non-competitive atmosphere. Yet the meeting itself seemed undirected as compared with the regular faculty meetings run by her principal, Miss Scroggins. No one told the members of the group precisely what they were to do, and they struggled first to elicit opinions and then to reach decisions as to group preferences.

Discussion was limp until one of the colored teachers from an all-colored school spoke. Nothing limp about her. She had dignity, and she spoke with conviction. Apparently she thought analyses of all books used in school would be invaluable. She was startlingly frank in her criticism of the readers her 1A's had to read. She pointed out how consistently the stories represented only a white world that automatically excluded her youngsters. When there was a rare reference to the Negro, she said that it was usually so much a stereotype as to be offensive. The pictures of Negroes were as caricatured as the references in the texts. Too often Negroes were portrayed only as kerchief-headed, childlike, happy slaves of the Old South.

Some of the teachers were shocked by her directness, and there were a few icy stares. But not Miss Wheeler. She decided to get acquainted with that teacher. She recalled her high-school friendship with Martha Wilson, a colored classmate, and how angry her father had been when he heard about it. This Negro teacher somehow reminded her of Martha. During the recess, when some of her colleagues appeared cliquish, she went over to the colored teacher and introduced herself.

A good part of the rest of the meeting was given over to a discussion of the kinds of records they might begin to keep that would help them understand their children better. Some of the younger teachers had proposed this idea. Miss Wheeler and several others did not take too kindly to recording behavior. It seemed pointless, they said. If they were inexperienced teachers, perhaps yes. For, as Miss Wheeler put it, "My trouble is I know too much about my children, not too little." Yet, though dubious of records as "busy work," she agreed to do some observation and recording before the next meeting.

As her first subject she chose Eugene Howells, the little colored boy who was always sucking his thumb or tormenting other children. (When the teachers compared notes later, one of them observed that they had all chosen "problem" children rather than "normal" ones.) As she wrote up what Eugene did, Miss Wheeler became dimly conscious that she was persistently generalizing about Eugene, interpreting his behavior but rarely merely recording it. When she studied her records in the cold light of day before the next meeting, she became particularly annoyed with herself, because they revealed not what Eugene did but how she felt about him. And her feelings were clearly and consistently hostile. She looked for those characteristics that she disliked most and usually found them.

When teachers in the second meeting of the study group asked her questions about the boy, she mentioned his perpetual thumb sucking. One remarked that it was not a part of any of her records, even though she now told them it was a persistent habit.

After the meeting Miss Wheeler tried to understand her own feelings. She decided that Eugene's habit of sucking his thumb was very disturbing to her; that her revulsion ran through all of her relations with Eugene. She could not tell whether Eugene's being Negro made any difference in her feelings. She knew she had given up trying to work with him. If he had been a white boy, would she have given up trying?

Although she had protested that she knew him too well, she now decided that she needed to learn much more about him— more, too, about his relations with other children. She planned small group activities into which Eugene could be absorbed without too much effort on his part or on the part of the group. Miss Wheeler felt sure that Eugene could not face failure at this point —that he needed desperately to succeed, and often.

She began to observe him in his relations with other children. She could now see certain positive characteristics, some small glimmers of interest and patience here and there, under certain circumstances, where before she had seen only aggression or withdrawal. She painstakingly recorded the circumstances and his behavior. She found that Eugene was far from clumsy, as she had at first supposed. In outdoor play on the roof he showed the greatest improvement. In fact, he showed good physical co-ordination when he had a chance to test his skill against other youngsters. These others showed an interest in him and also admiration, at first mixed with surprise, as they became aware of this new side of Eugene.

In the meantime she tried to reach Mrs. Howells, Eugene's mother, and make an appointment with her. After several un-successful efforts, Miss Wheeler arranged a meeting. From Mrs. Howells, a tense, self-assertive little person, she was able to get a few more pieces of information that fitted together in the puzzle of Eugene's personality.

Eugene has a sickly younger brother upon whom Mrs. Howells' entire universe centers. Grandma, who is charged with care of Eugene, also dotes on the sick little boy. It took little prompting or probing for Miss Wheeler to recognize that both mother and grandmother are very critical of Eugene and impatient with him.

An inadequate income for two adults and two children makes the home a squalid place, with constant deprivation and bicker-ing. The absence of a father is an even more serious lack. Now Eugene's "taking it out" on other children, his thumb sucking, and his frequent self-isolation seemed more intelligible. Although Miss Wheeler did not yet understand what to do about the thumb sucking, she was confident that it could be handled.

Here was a child who needed desperately to be accepted by somebody, a child who needed to find self-respect. The fact of his color gave him an additional burden. She had not helped the other children to accept him, but, once she herself did, they might too. School could be one place where Eugene might find his self-respect and some happiness. As an experienced teacher she knew that she could not expect much for a long time; she knew that she had to build a new relationship with Eugene.

Now she felt hopeful and strangely relieved. Her first reaction of guilt because she had been rejecting Eugene, seeing only his bad impulses, disappeared. Not so easily resolved, however, were her guilt feelings that she had perhaps treated him with indifference because of his color. A long, frank talk with her new friend, Miss Thompkins, the Negro teacher whom she had met at the first meeting, helped her to get perspective on her own attitudes. Gradually she was able to see Eugene not as "her failure" but rather as her challenge; not as an "eel" who withdrew and resisted her, the teacher, but as a youngster who had never known how it feels to be liked and wanted and therefore had not yet learned to like others—a child who met hostility every day and so retaliated by little acts of aggression, or else by retiring to his own private world where he could be free from hurt, free of the people who made life difficult for him.

The Child and His Setting

Several of the study group discussions centered around the question, "How does the curriculum meet children's needs?" Each teacher set out to analyze her group and her program. Each used her own point of departure. Some turned to books on child development to learn what are the needs of children at particular stages of growth and how their present course of study ignored or met these needs. Others studied the community to understand better the different culture groups in it, the values held by parents of majority and minority groups, and how these values are reflected in the life of the school.

The community approach immediately presented a problem to the teachers because of the official school policy of not inquiring into the economic, religious, racial, or nationality backgrounds of pupils. One teacher had set out to collect these "vital statistics" on her class, and she reported on how little she could learn through regular school records or channels. The group discussed the problem and agreed that direct questions by teacher to pupil were to be avoided because of the ill will or misunderstanding that might result. Some proposed sending questionnaires to parents on some general theme such as health or safety. The questionnaires could then include other questions about the family cultural setting which would supply the necessary information yet would not antagonize the parents. Where good home-and-school relations had been established, interviews with parents seemed proper and might be fruitful. Again, group members cautioned against the use of direct questions unless mutual confidence between the parents and the school existed.

Still other information-getting procedures were proposed—procedures which would fit into the regular school routine and seemed less difficult or less likely to meet with opposition than the direct questioning method. Simple courses of action were suggested, such as conferring with the school nurse, the counselor, the kindergarten teacher, the truant officer, the principal. Facts about the family setting which each had gathered at some point of contact with the child, the parent, or in the home might then be pieced together by the teacher.

The Community and Its Resources

Out of these explorations for "vital statistics" came more than mere tables with the headings Age, Race, Religion, Nationality, Father's Occupation, Mother's Occupation, Physical Disability, and so on. There emerged instead a picture of real children in particular settings, youngsters whose lives were shaped by the circumstances and relationships in each environment. The school neighborhood, to which the teachers had been strangers, took on a more definite shape. And in the neighborhood there were rich human resources, all kinds of people who could be invited to school to talk with the children, obscure people as well as neighborhood leaders to visit and get to know.

As the teachers worked on individual and group problems between meetings, interest in the meetings themselves increased. Suggestions which the teachers made for the agenda genuinely reflected their interests and were more truly related to the immediate concerns of the group as the months went by. A regular system of reporting developed as individuals felt that they wanted to share with the others a particular activity, plan, or problem.

The atmosphere was markedly different from that of the first meeting, where there had been so much holding back. The members of the study group were finding that it helped to talk over problems, get the other teachers' suggestions and viewpoints, and not be afraid to ask for aid. Most of all it was good for each to find that she was not alone—that other people had the same problem.

It was Miss Wheeler's experience with Eugene, more than anything else, that made her decide to work on her first-grade program so that it would suit the needs of her particular class and children. She found three questions to which she needed answers. First, she needed to find ways by which to understand the children better. Second, she had to learn ways of helping individuals as well as the whole group. Third, from the 1A program she had to begin to eliminate activities or procedures that were waste motion and to substitute vital experiences that would have meaning for the children.

Miss Wheeler Gets to Know the Children

She spent some time in trying to decide how, within the framework of the requirements for the grade, she might develop for the children activities that were real, that would give them opportunities to be themselves and to express themselves. She became increasingly conscious of the excessive routine and restriction, the limited freedom and opportunity for initiative, in her accustomed procedure.

Painting and clay work immediately suggested themselves as releasing types of activities, and she included liberal time allotments for them in a revised program. Until now they had been squeezed into her schedule only spasmodically. The arts served the twofold purpose of more "outgo" for the children and more opportunity for her to see the meaning which experiences held for them.

She wondered whether the art work would be too "individual" and not socializing enough. To avoid this she planned to relate a good bit of the art work to trips or other group experiences. There was to be pupil-teacher planning before trips and a great deal of "doing" and talk afterwards. During the planning stage it was the children who proposed the idea of group painting and so helped solve one of her dilemmas. Several children still preferred to work alone, but they too, in one way or another, shared with the group.

Slowly, over a period of months, the school day became more related and satisfying for both teacher and children. At the same time a new pride in *their* class, in *their* activities, grew to such proportions that it was almost as if the 1A's were becoming exclusive, special, and a closed group. To overcome this tendency Miss Wheeler encouraged her class to invite children of other grades to visit or share in these activities, and the 1A's in turn began to explore the school and become aware of and friendly to children not in their own room.

Painting and talking about shared experiences led to acting out what they saw and how they felt about it. In spite of themselves, even the children who were formerly very much on the fringe of the group became involved.

Talk sessions on "what I'd like to be," or just talk while making boats or playing store helped all of them to know one another better. As the children felt free to talk at play, they became more concentrated and silent at work that required silence. Discipline was less and less adult-imposed, and Miss Wheeler had more time, more energy, and more opportunities to study her children, to find out what they were really like, to learn what made them tick. She was free "to work with" them and relieved of the task of "making them work."

The children now had many opportunities to win a place in the group. Planning stressed the importance of everyone's having a chance to succeed in different ways. In the process each child's differences emerged and added to the richness of the whole group. Each child's faults and talents were increasingly accepted without special emphasis, yet with understanding.

The old, uniform standard of achievement Miss Wheeler relinquished with a great sense of relief; she saw now that it was impossible to attempt to make the achievement of all alike.

It would be hard to say who learned more in those first few months—the teacher or the children. Miss Scroggins, the principal, was delighted, for the achievement of the skills she prized did not suffer in a class that worked with gusto. The principal noticed, too, that Miss Wheeler's 1A class in comparison with the other 1A in the school seemed to be much more mature and at the same time more relaxed. They talked more than most children did in the other classes, but it was not uncontrolled, uncontrollable talk. As a matter of fact, most of the talk served some basic educational purpose.

The Fantasies of Dorothy

For instance, for Dorothy Coners, the gaunt waif with the stringy red hair, bosom friend of Myrna, talk was both a personal safety valve and a way of developing a sense of belonging in the group. Dorothy, timid when not with aggressive Myrna, was a born storyteller. The children delighted in her stories and at every opportunity encouraged her to spin a yarn. This had been something of an irritation to Miss Wheeler in the days when she was struggling with "eels" and trying to get a maximum of coerced work and imposed order in 1A. Now she too encouraged Dorothy to tell stories.

They were strange stories which often mixed fantasy, reality, and humor. Miss Wheeler took down bits of them whenever she could and always found rereading the transcript of the stories a rewarding experience. Halfway through one of her yarns, Dorothy said, "My mother picks up our baby and she says all the time, 'You're the best one of all my children. You're the best baby in the world.'" Then Dorothy added as an aside, and without self-consciousness, completely forgetting her role as storyteller, "I guess she's only kidding." Another time, during a conversation period, she said, "I dreamed our whole house was a beautiful garden full of flowers. All over flowers. Everything was made out of flowers, but not the house. It was made of cake and candy and ice cream. And my mother was turned into a witch. A real one!" Then she looked at Miss Wheeler, and around at the children, and said, "Kids are scary—don't be scary, kids. It's only a dream." On another occasion, she told them, "So we went on a picnic—and we had a lot to eat, and my sister was real jealous—and we had soda, and my sister was real, real jealous." And again, "So my mother gave me twelve dips of ice cream and chocolate syrup—all for me and I ate it all up." (Hesitatingly) "She likes me, I guess." In her fantasies, Dorothy's wishes and fears came pouring out.

Her "stories" helped Miss Wheeler to understand something of Dorothy's home problems, her feelings of rejection and guilt in relation to her mother, her jealousy toward the baby sister, and her mixed-up fears even about the Catholic church. Looking at Alberta's drawing of a church, Dorothy said, "I'm scared to go into a Catholic church. O-o-h, it's real scary. The Sisters scare me. I was even scared the first time I went in my own church." (And all along Miss Wheeler had assumed that Dorothy was Irish and a Catholic; only now did she learn that she was a Protestant, of Slovak parents.)

The opportunity to tell stories gave the otherwise retiring Dorothy status in the eyes of the group. It served as an outlet for her pent-up emotions. It gave Miss Wheeler insights she could not otherwise have obtained.

Dorothy's expressed fear of the Catholic church was something Miss Wheeler wanted to talk over with her next-door neighbor Miss Murray, for Miss Murray had an ease in talking about religious questions that seemed to Miss Wheeler enviable. In addition to Miss Murray there was little Mary Walker, who had come from St. Joseph's Parochial School and might help Dorothy with her number work. Friendship with a Catholic child like Mary might be a very good thing for Dorothy.

The Teachers Discuss Child-Study Techniques

Not all the children were so articulate in an audience situation as Dorothy Coners, and at the study group the teachers discussed several techniques they could use to help shy children express themselves. They agreed that, at least through the second grade, dramatic play in a completely permissive atmosphere was richly rewarding to both children and teacher alike. (There was a long and interesting discussion of what is a "permissive atmosphere," and several teachers frankly admitted that they would not "give over" to the children completely even during the play period.) It was suggested that careful records of the roles assumed by particular children during play, together with the interaction and the exact dialogue, be kept systematically and analyzed over a period of time. Teachers who had recorded conversations during the play period—fragments of just plain, unhampered, un-self-conscious talk—gave illustrations of some of the insights to be gained by this practice. Fears, wishes, myths, and confusions were expressed by the children; the patterns that sometimes emerged pointed up the source of a child's feeling of security or inadequacy. It was such data that Miss Wheeler gathered and on which she tried to develop activities and relationships that would help her children to grow and live happily in school.

Dependable Stephen

Take Stephen in Miss Wheeler's 1A. No fantasy about Stephen. He had a fund of information as inexhaustible as his patience. All the children liked Stephen and learned from him.

Play periods permitted exchanges like the following. Stephen: "My brother has a new bank. It's blue and has a Jewish star on it." Someone said: "Mine's yellow." Stephen: "This one is blue, because Jews like blue, because it's a sky color, and the star is because we're saving for our holiday." Jane asked, "What holiday?" and Stephen replied, "Jewish Christmas." Later Stephen told the children about gifts he received for Christmas. Someone asked, "Did Santa Claus bring them?" and Stephen said, "Oh, no, we don't believe in Santa Claus. We have a different Santa Claus. We have a Rabbi!" He told about the Chanukah play and the celebration in Sunday school. He made an illustration of the candelabrum on the blackboard. Mary said, "It looks like a Christmas tree." Charles wanted to get one. Jimmy wanted to play Stevie's story. Stevie explained that Jewish people have candles instead of Christmas trees. Jane asserted, "So do Catholics." Mary said, "Catholics have Christmas trees." Caroline said, "So do Christians." Then Fred said he'd like to have both. Barbara said, "They're both pretty." "Anyway," said Dorothy, "they both have lights." Fred: "It's like having two Christmas trees."

Miss Wheeler had always liked Stephen—depended on him, in fact. She had not stopped to think about him much or tried to analyze him. Early in the term she had decided that he was a very stable child with more than average assurance and poise. Then, since Stephen was "no problem," she had done what most teachers would—she did not think too often about him.

She now remembered how surprised she was to find that he was Jewish, because she had always assumed that Jewish children were either diffident, hypersensitive, and anticipatory of rejection, or were aggressive and at the same time anxious and insecure underneath their aggressiveness. Stephen just did not fit either pattern. Though of a different cultural background than most of the other children and of a different religion, Stephen's own assurance, his interest in and acceptance of his group, and his satisfaction communicated themselves to the other children. His background was a bridge rather than a barrier. With a good adjustment at home, love from his parents, a sense of pride in his own culture, Stephen was well equipped to take part in democratic group life in school.

The Children Are Resources

Miss Wheeler developed ways of using Stephen's wealth of information so that the whole class might grow in their understanding of things Jewish. Holiday observances afforded a good opportunity for growth in understanding. She planned a program with Stephen and a small committee of children of different faiths just before Passover. Stephen's mother helped her to find a few good source books.[2] The other 1A class came to see the exhibit and learned to sing an ancient folksong which Miss Wheeler played for them on the piano. Together they ate matzoth and learned what the symbols on the package meant.

Thus the process of maturing, learning, and relaxing went on in Miss Wheeler's 1A. Helping the children to be unafraid became a major goal—a difficult goal, for most of them had been trained to be ashamed of their fears and to push them aside. In Miss Wheeler's class fear came to be regarded differently. You could talk about what bothered you and the things you did not understand. Nobody laughed, or told you to stop talking nonsense, or scolded you for being bad. You could feel good in school; you could have real friends in school; you could tell the teacher when you were scared.

Working with Frank's Fears

Frank Mussalas was often afraid and troubled. At long last he began to confide in Miss Wheeler, who already knew simply that

[2] *High Holidays* (New York: Department of Interreligious Cooperation of the Anti-Defamation League, 1946).
Getting Acquainted with Jewish Neighbors, by Mildred Moody Eakin (New York: The Macmillan Company, 1945).
The Story of Jewish Holidays and Customs, by Dorothy F. Zeligs (New York: Bloch Publishing Company, 1942).
Jewish Holidays: Do You Know Them? by Elise F. Moller (New York: The Woman's Press, 1945).

he was a devout Greek Catholic and an attendant at the Greek afternoon school. His good-looking young mother was a former teacher in a Greek school.

One morning, on entering the room, flanked by his sister and her girl friend, Frank said, "A big colored kid hits me every morning. When I come to school he won't let me in." His sister said, "We were gonna get a gang after him. But he's got a colored gang." Frank added, "Colored gangs are strong."

On still another day Frank came in excited and breathless. "We was playin' Chinese Stoopin' Tag. A colored kid bothered us. The same one. We don't like him. We don't let him play. So he gets mad and jumps on our feet."

Coming into the room before the others one morning, Frank said, "I didn't get to New York. Do you know why? My mother was afraid on account there's a strike, because niggers throw bricks and they stop the trains, and they might hurt you."

Frank's preoccupation with conflict situations, real or imagined, and his association of conflict with colored people as aggressors, seemed serious. Yet Miss Wheeler decided that it would be better not to discuss Frank's anti-Negro attitude or his general fears with Mrs. Mussalas. Since it appeared that Mrs. Mussalas shared and shaped Frank's attitudes and fears, contacts with her by Miss Wheeler seemed essential, but any direct or immediate approach to the family's prejudices appeared inadvisable.

In a conference with Frank's mother, Miss Wheeler learned that Mrs. Mussalas exerted considerable pressure on the boy to attend Greek school after three every day and that the Greek language was spoken at home exclusively. Frank's playtime was negligible. His own efforts to make friends outside his church group were discouraged on the one hand by his mother and on the other by the public school children who ridiculed his speech. Miss Wheeler suggested that the boy needed a chance to play with his schoolmates and an opportunity to learn English.

It had never before occurred to Mrs. Mussalas that she was depriving Frank of anything. She was concerned only that he retain some cultural tie with her homeland. She admitted to exerting pressure on the boy but seemed genuinely anxious to help him in school. She spoke of her family in Greece and how they had suffered during and since the war. "Frank must not forget about them," she said bitterly; "he must remember his people."

Miss Wheeler, now managing an increasingly flexible schedule, arranged that Frank be excused from number work and writing, both of which he did with relative efficiency. She helped him to get special lessons in English and reading during school hours. She carefully avoided prodding him and remembered guiltily how much she had done of that before. Her new tack was to encourage him whenever she had the least opportunity.

The matter of his fear of Negroes she tackled at the same time but in a less direct way. One of the trips of her 1A's was to the neighboring Morris Elementary School, where they visited the class of Miss Thompkins, the Negro teacher with whom she had become acquainted through the study group. This class was a 1A of Negro children. The two classes shared a story hour and rhythm period and had a wonderful time. The Morris 1A's promised to repay their visit.

Miss Wheeler's children had planned an afternoon tea party for their mothers to take place during the same week as the Morris School visit. They cooked apple sauce and churned butter, spread them both on gingerbread (made with the help of the sixth-grade cooking class), set tables for tea, and decorated the room. The program committee was headed by Frank Mussalas. Miss Wheeler suggested that it would be nice if the parents as well as the children entertained. Bessie Miller said her mother played the organ in her church and knew how to play the piano too. So Frank told Miss Wheeler what to put in the letter to Mrs. Miller. Bessie's mother accepted the invitation and when the time came she played easily and well.

It was only natural that Frank's mother and Bessie's mother

should meet at the tea, for Miss Wheeler used several good "get to know your neighbor" techniques.[3] Miss Wheeler felt that the afternoon was especially successful when she saw Bessie and Frank trotting out together just ahead of Mrs. Miller and Mrs. Mussalas, who were talking together. Mrs. Mussalas had spent years studying music. She had not had a chance to talk about it with anyone for some time. Miss Wheeler hoped fervently that the experience with Bessie and her mother would begin to make a change in Frank's and Mrs. Mussalas's attitude toward Negroes.

Exchange Visits Can Help to Change Attitudes

After Miss Wheeler's 1A's visited the Morris School she reported to the study group about it. She read them some of Frank Mussalas's pre-visit records and explained that she planned to continue to expose the whole group to pleasant experiences with children different from themselves. Miss Thompkins, the 1A teacher from the Morris School, spoke enthusiastically too about the value of exchange visits when the children do more than just eye each other as if on exhibition. She confessed that she had been skeptical at first about this kind of thing, too; it did not seem worth the effort. Miss Thompkins added with some hesitation: "Maybe it doesn't sound like much when Miss Wheeler and I suggest interschool visits, but the day after Miss Wheeler's class came to see us, Jessica came to me and said, 'When are those children coming to play with us again?' Not a very remarkable question, but it was significant coming from Jessica. I'd like to read from a record I did of Jessica before the visit:

"One morning while I was getting out work materials for the children, Jessica said, 'Miss Thompkins, you don't mind me following you around like this, do you?' I said, 'Of course not, Jessica, in fact you can help me with these materials if you will.' Jessica then said in a serious tone, 'In the other school the teacher didn't like me to follow her around like this. She would always

[3] *Get Together Americans*, by Rachel Davis DuBois (New York: Harper & Brothers, 1943).

send me back to my seat. She was a cracker.' I continued to stir the paste I was making and said casually, 'A cracker?' She answered, 'Yes, a white cracker.' Alice overheard Jessica and said, giggling, 'What do you mean, a white cracker?' Laughingly, Jessica answered, 'A white cracker chews tobacco.' She then frowned and said, 'White people are crackers. I hate white people.' "

For a few moments there was a dead silence in the room. A few teachers looked shocked and squirmed visibly. Miss Wheeler glanced around at the others and then watched the thoughtful expression on Miss Whitman's face. Miss Whitman taught at the Whittier School in the best part of town.

Overprotected and Disadvantaged

So far in the study group Miss Whitman's role had been to point out that they had no problems of relationships at the Whittier School. Falteringly at first, and then with more assurance, Miss Whitman spoke: "My children, everybody knows, have everything. They come from good homes and are well trained in every way. Yet I felt, as Miss Thompkins talked about her children and how they enjoyed meeting white children, that at Whittier School these offspring of the town's best families are really deprived of a chance to know what life is really like. At the Morris School, Negro children are segregated from white children. In Whittier, our children, for different reasons, are separated from everyone different from themselves. Although I have not heard any child speak as frankly about his hate for 'the other kind of people' as Jessica did, I have seen symptoms of it in a hundred forms. If the home overprotects Whittier children, at least the school can teach them about the real world, can give them a chance to understand their fellow Americans."

Miss Whitman paused, quite out of breath and flushed. They could not know how it hurt her to say this, because she had always declared that at Whittier they had "American children" and had no problem.

Myrna Bribes to Win Her Way

As Miss Wheeler worked on curriculum revision she turned more and more to the individuals and groups in her class for leads to program. She was coming to regard the needs of both as important in planning. For some time she had been collecting records on Myrna Berman, the perfectly groomed, becurled, and dimpled child who was the good companion of Dorothy-the-waif. Just as with Eugene, Miss Wheeler's annoyance with Myrna had prevented the teacher from seeing anything but her undesirable traits. She had seen only Myrna's aggressiveness, her claim to the center of the stage.

The day-by-day records, however, presented irrefutable evidence of the child's pathetic insecurity. Unlike Stephen, Myrna does not have roots in her own Jewish culture. Nor does she appear to feel secure in the dominant culture group. Her need to have more than others, to be better than others, and to be boss emerged in the records. So did the rejection of Myrna by other children.

One morning Myrna told the group that she was getting a "Hollywood doll" for Christmas. Stevie said, "I'm getting a gun for Chanukah." Myrna answered, competitively, "Chanukah is my holiday, too, but we only call it Christmas." During the conversation period Myrna said, "My father bought two Christmas trees. One for the office and one for Benjy and me. They're only little trees on account of we're Jewish."

During a general discussion on how to aid the "graduating class" bazaar, Myrna said, "If I don't find something to bring, I'll bring a hundred thousand dollars. I've got that much. We're rich." Caroline answered her, "Goodness, Myrna, you're an awful liar. Nobody's got so much money."

In one of her confiding moments Myrna leaned against Miss Wheeler's chair. Her head was down and she was looking at her feet and scuffing one foot against the chair leg. She spoke in a very low tone. "I have no more friends. All my friends got somebody else because I didn't bring no taffies today. My daddy has to keep the rest for his patients. Now they don't like me."

A conference with Mrs. Berman and the beginning of a more friendly relationship between Miss Wheeler and Myrna helped to throw a little light on one source of Myrna's insecurity—a cause perhaps of her contrariness, bossiness, and aggression. Mrs. Berman talked freely about marital difficulties. She expressed resentment against Myrna, who evidently won attention from papa though mama failed to. Money loomed large to the family and was considered a cure-all by Mrs. Berman.

Myrna in many ways mirrored her mother's values and attitudes, yet at the same time she resisted the control that her mother tried to impose. For instance, she showed her strong, independent will when she approached Miss Wheeler's desk arm in arm with Bessie. "Bessie is my friend. I'm going to visit her every day at visiting time. My mother says why don't I choose white girls."

As Miss Wheeler tried to fit all of the Myrna pieces together, they added up to this: Myrna's stress on money, her boasting about papa's professional status, the taffies that money supplied, and the clothes—none of them were really helpful in the achievement of status for Myrna. She had fair-weather friends because she had, in six-year-old terms, the "luxuries" they wanted or envied. Myrna appeared to be aware of the transient, temporary basis of these friendships, felt more insecure because of them, and therefore literally pushed herself to the fore in her anxiety to gain acceptance somehow. To be accepted was an urgent drive for her, particularly because mama rejected her—and papa did so too, in effect, since he was a busy doctor.

Miss Wheeler suspected that nothing would be gained if she, as a teacher, became an interested sponsor of Myrna, who was often referred to by the others as a "show-off" anyhow. Perhaps all that would be gained by this too obvious stratagem would be the addition of the name "teacher's pet" for Myrna. Somehow the children themselves must take Myrna in on her own merits. If Myrna could see that she did not have to "buy" her way in or push her way forward, she might stop bribing and pushing. Where to begin? This was the problem Miss Wheeler brought to the study group.

Friendship Patterns Help Explain Caroline

At a study group meeting, several others joined Miss Wheeler in requesting techniques for the study of the leaders and followers, the friends and isolates in their classes. How can one get an over-all view of groups, leaders, and friendships in a class? they asked. Many of them felt a need to check some of their own assumptions on the following points: Who is popular? Why? Who is friends with whom? What is the basis of a particualr friendship? Who is always alone? Why?

The members of the group discussed some of their own theories. Most of the teachers agreed that parent pressure, common interests, or the skills of children, or the proximity of children's homes to each other, and attendance at the same Sunday school or church were factors that influence friendships. Several teachers expressed special concern over snob cliques as well as over the way some children are rejected by the whole group. They felt that many teachers tend to accept these as "natural" groupings. They disagreed about whether or not teachers should do anything to "reshuffle" groups or help to create opportunities for new friendships. Some pointed out that many teachers are always unconsciously throwing certain children together and thus tend to strengthen undesirable relationships.

However they explained the basis of friendship, the teachers wanted to find out more about sub-groups and actual friendship patterns in their classes. As a beginning, each teacher made up a list of her pupils, arranging the names in the order of the most liked (at the top) down to the least liked (at the bottom). Having created this rough scale of teacher estimates of popularity or rejection, each teacher then set down the names of members of friendship groups, as far as she knew them.

Next came practice in the several techniques of obtaining and charting actual friendships.[4] The teachers worked on diagrams to determine how many satisfactory adjustments (mutual choices) there were in the class and to learn who among the children were rejected and by whom.

Miss Wheeler was eager to begin analyzing the friendship patterns in her class. She had been worrying over the fact that she was getting so involved in the study of individuals. She learned later that she had actually been seeing each child in his relationship to the whole or to a part of the group but had not too clearly understood the bases for these group relationships. She found that most of her ideas about who is friends with whom were borne out in observations and charting. In a few cases, however, new angles began to emerge.

For instance, Miss Wheeler had never been able to understand why Caroline Spencer seemed to have so few friends. In spite of her good grades, good looks, and pleasant manners Caroline got into difficulties with many children. In these situations she came off badly, was contrary, and sulked afterward. But charting did not show the anticipated almost total rejection. It showed that Caroline was chosen as a friend by some children and was rejected by an equal number. This puzzling information led Miss Wheeler to dig further for an explanation.

She learned that Caroline is an only child, of Anglo-Saxon, white, Protestant background. Both parents dote on her. She has had little experience in getting along with children, for she lives in an exclusively adult world. Her parents plan her time at home and rarely arrange for her to see friends. In her relations with adults Caroline always gets her own way. Therefore, when she is crossed or rejected by a child in school, Caroline resents it bitterly. She gets quarrelsome and contrary. Her experience in

---

[4] *Helping Teachers Understand Children*, prepared for the Commission on Teacher Education by the Staff of the Division on Child Development and Teacher Personnel (Washington: American Council on Education, 1945), pp. 275–363.

"The Improvement of Human Relations in the Classroom," by Willard C. Olson, in *Childhood Education*, March, 1946, pp. 317–325.

dominating adult situations gives her an advantage in some school situations, particularly when she hasn't much competition. In a competitive situation, Caroline is overcome with rage and is soon defeated. Observation showed that her friends are, on the whole, docile gentle youngsters in awe of Caroline's sophistication and assurance. She tends to run them, fuehrer fashion, as a genteel gang leader.

When Miss Wheeler talked with Mr. and Mrs. Spencer, she found them sensitive and resistant on the subject of their daughter. When they were told frankly that Caroline was not the most popular child in the class, they were surprised and skeptical. Only the battery of evidence which Miss Wheeler submitted to them succeeded in ruffling their complacency. Before the long conference was over they were suggesting how they might broaden Caroline's little group of friends and help her. Something Mr. Spencer said just as they were concluding their talk seemed most significant to Miss Wheeler. "Come to think of it," he said, "Caroline has had her way at home; she always comes out on top. We give in, we make everything easy for her. It's important that she learn that it's all right to fail." Then, thoughtfully, "Maybe we *have* spoiled her."

After that Miss Wheeler knew that she could count on the child's parents. Her big job was to help Caroline learn to accept failure and to deal fairly with others.

Bessie, the Good Girl

As Miss Wheeler worked on friendship charts, it was Bessie Miller who turned out to be a real surprise. When all her records and charts were analyzed, the child who always obeyed, was always neat, always eager, and always "A" in everything was no one's choice as friend.

Miss Wheeler observed Bessie closely for several days to see if any possible clue could be found. First she jumped to the conclusion that the others did not choose Bessie because she was a Negro child. But even Eugene Howells had been chosen by two white boys. Clara Jackson was a Negro and she had friends. No, the color explanation was too easy a rationalization.

The behavior records suggested another clue. There seemed to be a consistent strain of anxiety and tension running through all of Bessie's records, no matter what the activity. Miss Wheeler was amazed that she had not seen this before. A talk with Bessie's mother indicated that the anxiety had probably been there all the time but was now more apparent.

Mrs. Miller was as meticulously dressed as Bessie. She was a young woman with a determined, serious manner. Her concern for Bessie centered largely on Bessie's mastery of various skills and her grades. She asked anxiously about these at the beginning of the interview. When told that the teacher had not called to talk about grades, for they were fine, Mrs. Miller relaxed visibly. But it was difficult to regain her full interest from there on.

Miss Wheeler's report on Bessie's anxiety and her inability to make friends seemed to concern Mrs. Miller not at all. She stated with a certain stubbornness that marks were what counted in school, just as money and position did in the world, and that she would see to it that Bessie had good grades in school and then went to a good college. She herself had missed that chance, she said with a tinge of bitterness, and Bessie was not going to miss it too. As she talked, she became tense. Nothing, she said, would interfere with her daughter's success. Friends were important, but not now. "Our people have to work harder than anyone else to amount to anything. Bessie will amount to something!" When Miss Wheeler timidly suggested that the child had a right to friends and happiness now, Mrs. Miller did not hear. She described the careful routine at home every night, how Bessie reports on what she learned that day, and how mama coaches Bessie in preparation for the next day of school.

Miss Wheeler just listened and decided that at this point at least she would have to proceed alone. At school Bessie could be relieved of some of her anxiety. At school Bessie could have friends, particularly among the more easy-going youngsters. More frequent contact with Mrs. Miller might be helpful also, even if only the sending of a note to say how fine Bessie's grades were. Maybe that would decrease the pressure at home. It was worth a try anyway.

Miss Wheeler Sums Up

The study group was near the end of its first school year. Most of the original members were anxious to continue working together for another year. A few real friendships had developed between teachers from different schools, and it had become customary for small groups to get together socially between regular meetings or even to work at some special problem. In addition, inter-school visitation had begun.

A few new teachers had recently joined the group. One of these asked if they might hear a summary by the veterans of main points culled from the first year of work. There were a few efforts to summarize, but it was agreed that a small committee should prepare a full report for the next meeting. Miss Wheeler was appointed a member of the committee. A list of useful pamphlet material was requested also.

When the time to report came along, Miss Wheeler's part in the meeting was to sum up what she had been learning. She began, "Since Adam and Eve, it has been the men against the women; since schools began it has been teacher versus pupil. That struggle we feel should end, now!" Everyone laughed. The new teachers had already relaxed in the informal atmosphere of the study group.

"Seriously, though, this we must say and underline. We cannot teach you what we learned any more than you can show anyone how to swim without his learning step by step through the use of his own arms and legs. You can show him *how* to learn, then it is up to him.

"What have we learned? Here are a few things." Miss Wheeler turned to the summary she had written and read the following:

Good Relationships Are Important

A teacher begins to master her job when she stops mastering her children and begins to help them to help themselves. Then as the children gain self-confidence and self-respect they develop confidence in others, respect for others—in short, good relationships.

Often a teacher's reaction to a child prevents the child from learning and the teacher from understanding the child. Objectively recording child behavior can help a teacher to understand herself *and* the child.

Most teachers know much more about children than they put to use. What they know becomes a burden or a barrier rather than an instrument unless they can understand their own feelings, assumptions, and generalizations and can see a child not alone but interacting with others.

A Child Is What He Has Lived

Children bring to school the attitudes, beliefs, and behavior that come from their five or six years of living in a particular home situation in relation to particular parents and siblings. At birth a child is already a unique organism. From his earliest years his personality is taking shape. He reacts to his family and to all his experiences in his own way. His behavior in school, if it diverges from the school standard, should not simply be termed "bad." His behavior may not even be a reaction to the teacher or to the school (although again it may be). We have to remember that the child's behavior is his specific reaction because of what he is and what he has lived. The teacher can help him if she understands him not just as a bundle of behavior characteristics but as a person reacting to and with individuals and group situations.

Sometimes a group of children can help individual children where the teacher cannot. Understanding of group life in the classroom becomes a short cut to helping forty-five individual children.

The teacher who aims her "teaching" at a class in general hits no one in particular. The curriculum must be built on the needs and lives of particular children and groups of children if they are to learn anything from it. A teacher can learn to understand these needs.

No one technique can help a teacher understand children. Nor does merely teaching children help a teacher to understand them, any more than merely bearing children helps a mother to raise them intelligently.

Uniformity Creates Conflict

Standards set by the school or by the teacher are easier for some children to achieve than for others, because some come from homes where the middle-class Anglo-Protestant standards are identical with the school standards. These children automatically measure up to the requirements and in one sense have a position of advantage. The others, when caught in the conflict of school versus home standards, sometimes hide or deny what they are, try to measure up, and develop anxiety or feelings of inadequacy, or even self-hate. Those children are at a disadvantage.

Further complicating the educative process and impeding it is the fact that mass education often leaves unsolved the personality conflicts which children bring with them to school. Some children struggle visibly—the "eels." Others conform. In the process, new conflicts are produced.

The children, meanwhile, whether they struggle or conform to the school requirements, feel and behave toward one another as they have learned to do at home or on the street and as each needs to do for his ego's sake. They feel superior to or less good than this child or that, for good or bad reasons, relevant or irrelevant. They may feel inadequate in school because they have been made to feel inadequate at home, or because in school they never have a chance to develop their own particular talents, since the teacher is preoccupied with getting uniform behavior, uniform responses. Or they may feel superior to other children and actually may become less effective human beings than they might be, because of a false sense of superiority.

Uniformity Denies Freedom

Children in the first and second grades sometimes like to conform to rigid, uniform school standards. It gives them a sense of order, organization, and even security. Adults, too, can feel more secure in a regimented, restricted, authoritarian atmosphere, particularly when that is the only security they have ever had. This willingness to conform, though perhaps temporarily satisfying, actually is dangerous and self-defeating. It submerges individual creativeness, prevents development of independent thought and action, and, if permitted to become habitual, prevents the maximal development of each individual which is our democratic goal. Schools that discourage uniformity and value diversity help to develop an integrated, harmonious group life that encourages growth and respects freedom.

(Here Miss Wheeler put aside her paper and continued extemporaneously.)

"I can illustrate from my own experience this year what we are after. Some of the mistakes that I made about children in my 1A class are, I suppose, typical.

"I liked Caroline because she was ladylike and well dressed, came of a good 'American' family, and seemed to be the butt of attack of the children I did not like. I assumed that because she measured up to my standards she was a popular child in the class. I found, however, that she had very few friends, was something of a bully, and was unhappy. Over-indulged at home, she had been given an exaggerated idea of her own importance; she had no experience in how to win friends, but too much in how to influence people in the wrong way. She could not face failure.

"Eugene I did not like at all. He was a thumb sucker and I found that revolting. He seemed indifferent to work and play. His only efforts were acts of aggression of the most annoying kind.

He was a nuisance to me and to the children. I did not know what to do about Eugene, or did not care, so alternately I tried to discipline him or avoid him. Then I learned that he was used to precisely that formula at home. His mother preferred a younger brother even as I preferred others in the class to him. Eugene had an additional cross to bear: he is a Negro child.

"Dorothy was always telling tall tales. That and her red hair and, I suppose, her last name spelled 'Irish' for me. I thought there was not much to Dorothy except her blarney and I never got to know her until I found that she was not Irish after all. I began to listen to her tall tales and found that they were full of Dorothy's own life problems and her wishful thinking. She was a troubled six-year-old, that Dorothy.

"Myrna was Dorothy's bosom pal, and I suppose that would have made me at least a little antagonistic. But added to that was Myrna's boasting, her pushing, her showing off. I was ashamed for her and for her mother. She comes of a wealthy family and should know better. Myrna is Jewish and I just did not even think to do anything to help her, because I guess I just felt that that is the way Jewish children are; as in the case of Dorothy, I had swallowed a stereotype.

"Stephen is Jewish too. I did not think of him "that way" as he did not fit my stereotype. Stephen was O.K. All the children loved him, and I guess I did too. The thing about Stephen that we all admired was his self-respect, his self-assurance, his eager friendliness. Stephen was very conscious of being Jewish but was happy about it. The other children learned many things from him. I did too, because knowing him helped me later to know Myrna and to accept Jewish people. I decided that if Stephen could be like that, loved by us all, then maybe there was something wrong with Myrna as a person. Of course there was—plenty. Much of it I should have seen myself.

"Bessie was a 'prize pupil,' good, obedient, clean, hard-working. An A-A-A girl. I paid no special attention to Bessie. She was too good to need attention, I thought. Then I found that she was almost cracking under the strain and the standards set by mama and me. She had no friends and no fun at all. School and home were a grind for this six-year-old, and mama was putting her through her paces so that in twelve years she would get into the best girls' college. You see, Bessie was a Negro child and mama was going to batter down the walls of prejudice with a steel tank made of high grades from kindergarten all the way to college.

"I had no patience with Frank. He seemed to elude me. Every now and then I embarrassed him by calling on him unexpectedly. I found out that he actually did not understand what went on in my classroom at least one-third of the time, because his family spoke Greek at home. He was so tired the other two-thirds of the time that he might just as well have stayed at home. The poor boy went right from my 1A at 3 o'clock to Greek school for two hours. The children on the street and in school hounded him unmercifully, as I did in my own more subtle way. Consequently the boy was loaded with hostility, which came out in all kinds of ways but mainly in his antagonism toward and fear of Negroes.

"I'll conclude with one more real, live illustration. I had had enough practice, I thought, to ensure an almost automatic check on all the data available before I came to any conclusion about a child. Sometimes, however, my feelings were so unconsciously antipathetic that the logical, systematic procedure simply was not completed. I found that out last week when I studied a new child, Jane Slabey.

"I knew that the Slabeys are Polish Catholics; that Jane comes from a fatherless home where grandparents substitute for parents; that her mother is a by-the-day houseworker who leaves early in the morning and returns at 9 or 10 o'clock at night, after the children are asleep; and that Jane is a middle child in a family of six children. Jane is a plain child, a little on the heavy side. She comes to school poorly dressed and is often neither washed nor all buttoned up. My conclusion was that the odds were against her adjusting well in school.

"I accepted these family background facts about Jane and on

them I based my own assumptions as to her status and adjustment in the class. I had old records and more recent ones that could have told me fairly accurately where Jane stood in regard to the others—whether she was rejected, poorly adjusted, friendly with a limited group, or well liked by all. These records I had used dozens of times when analyzing friendships and group memberships of other children. But in Jane's case my own negative reaction to her home situation dominated my conclusions. I never even looked at the records.

"It was while I was planning group work for a half dozen children that I accidentally discovered that Jane was in fact the choice of a great many children and that her choices were, in almost all cases, reciprocal. I was astonished but still a little skeptical. I had sworn by those charts before, but somehow this acceptance of Jane just did not seem possible. So I spent some time observing her as she played with children in the lunchroom or as she worked in our own room. Without a doubt Jane got along, seemed happy, and was liked by the other children. I reexamined old anecdotal records, made sporadically months back; they reported Jane's even disposition and slow-moving, friendly manner. She was a child who took life in her stride.

"This sounds like a confession, and it is. I had been so cocky about 'understanding my own feelings,' and there I was, caught without a leg to stand on. The 'vital statistics' in this case sounded powerfully influential. They sounded so powerful that they influenced me to ignore Jane herself, right in front of my nose. And, as if to taunt me beyond endurance, this plump young thing told me in a confidential mood only yesterday, 'You know, Miss Wheeler, I like everybody!' "

Miss Wheeler concluded by distributing a brief mimeographed list of pamphlets which the teachers had found useful in their study of children.

Play: *A Yardstick of Growth*, by Clara Lambert, 3rd revised edition (New York: Play Schools Association, 1938).

Play: *A Child's Way of Growing Up*, by Clara Lambert (New York: Play Schools Association, 1947).

The Five to Eights and How They Grow, by Barbara Biber (New York: Bank Street Schools reprint from *Childhood Education*, Oct. 1941).

Children and You, by Eva Knox Evans (Chicago: Julius Rosenwald Fund, 1945).

A Pound of Prevention: *How Teachers Can Meet the Emotional Needs of Young Children*, by James L. Hymes, Jr. (New York: Teachers Service Committee on the Emotional Needs of Children, 1947).

CHAPTER IV

ADULT-SPONSORED YOUTH GROUPS[1]

The present chapter is concerned with youth groups organized by the more widely known national youth-serving agencies, such as the American Junior Red Cross, Boys' Clubs of America; Boy Scouts of America; Future Homemakers of America; 4-H Clubs; Camp Fire Girls; Catholic Youth organizations; Girl Scouts; Salvation Army; Jewish Community Centers, including the YMHA and the YWHA; various settlements; the YMCA and the YWCA; United Christian Youth Movement; and the youth programs of affiliated Protestant denominations. All these organizations serve young people by providing opportunities for the constructive use of leisure time. Each organization has a distinct ideology which affects its sphere of influence, its aims, and its methods. All, however, share many common functions and objectives. For instance, all include in their statements of purposes, either explicitly or by implication, the development of social responsibility and democratic citizenship.

This chapter indicates how such an organization not only can use the school but also can go beyond it in the interests of intercultural education. Because the experiences described here could take place through any of these organizations or through others not mentioned, it has seemed better not to name the several different agencies from which examples have been drawn. The projects described, however, are based on actual experiences; they repre-

[1] This chapter was written by BERNICE BRIDGES, Director, Youth Division of the National Social Welfare Assembly, Inc.

84

sent types of current activity which enhance the intercultural education of the participants.

Projects from several different agencies have been described as though they occurred in one group—a club of girls of junior high school age. This procedure is merely a fictional device to illustrate the group process and the program activities. (In a boys' organization the process would be much the same, though the activities would differ.) It must be emphasized that the projects did not all take place in one real group. Unless this fact is remembered, the experiences reported will seem unnaturally successful. Similarly, for convenience in telling the story, Miss Mason and Mr. Sigler are made the embodiment of the experiences, the insights, and the queries of numerous adult leaders of youth groups.

The Teacher and the Community

Marjorie Mason is a new junior high school teacher in Millville, a community nine miles from Central City, with a good connecting highway. Miss Mason arrived at Millville four days before the opening of school. Housing arrangements had been made previously, but she wanted to get herself settled and to learn something about the town. Acquaintance with a community, she knew, was essential to understanding the students in her classes.

On foot she toured the main streets and two neighborhoods of differing economic levels. She talked with Mr. Reed, the principal of Millville's junior and senior high school, and with two citizens to whom Mr. Reed had referred her. She held over-the-counter conversations with neighborhood storekeepers near the school. From these sources Miss Mason collected a useful introductory picture.

Miss Mason learned that the people of Millville were a representative American mixture of nationality backgrounds, religious faiths, and racial groupings. On the surface all was well. But the fact that all the Negroes, a few Mexicans, and most of the Italians lived on the side of the railroad tracks that had the poorer housing, plus a story told about the Negro veterans' resentment over the kinds of civilian jobs open to them, signified unfortunate intercultural undercurrents.

Thus far Millville had not looked upon recreation as a community concern. There were no supervised playgrounds. There was no youth center. There had been no adult education classes for three years. The schools were locked all summer, as well as after classes and over the week ends during the school year.

Mr. Reed, the principal, was concerned about the situation, but he had been new the year before and had felt that his first responsibility must be the teaching staff and the seventh-through-twelfth-year curriculum. As to the townsfolk, their interest in young people seemed to consist of gossiping about some teen-agers whose behavior was termed delinquent.

School Opens

When school opened Miss Mason had little time at first for anything but getting acquainted with names and faces. Gradually, as the classes became organized, she turned some of her attention to the business of learning to know individual students as persons. She began with her eighth-grade home room, because it obviously offered more opportunity for informal conversation than did the subject-centered classes. Miss Mason was not content with traditional and meaningless· educational gestures; she wanted to help youngsters with their life problems.

Millville had but one junior high school, in the same building with the senior high school. The home room, like the school as a whole, had students from all parts of town. Miss Mason knew the importance of the use of leisure time to the students' lives, so she began a casual inquiry in group and individual conversations as to what the young people did with their time outside of classes.

She learned that there were a few school clubs and activities (dramatics, music, and sports), but apparently only the more skilled students belonged. Two churches scheduled an activity one afternoon a week, but only the young people of the particular church belonged, even though officially the activity was open to others. Two Central City agencies had organized youth groups in Millville. One had developed two groups for girls; the first met in a church, the second met in homes. A boys' group, organized by the other agency, met in the library basement. None of Miss Mason's students belonged to any of these groups. What then did students in Miss Mason's home room find to do with their free time immediately after school? It appeared that a few had home responsibilities, but many of them went over to the drug store to sip cokes and talk, or ganged up on the streets in their neighborhoods when the weather was good.

How the Group Was Initiated

Miss Mason discussed the situation with Mr. Reed. They agreed that experiences in organized groups might make for the fuller growth and development of the youngsters. Clubs could provide opportunities for activities which not only were fun but also could help some with their needs and problems. With wise handling, club experiences might lead to a better understanding of social realities in the community and to the development of democratic attitudes and practices. Further conversation with the students made it obvious that many liked the club idea, though some of the boys, suspicious of adults, stipulated, "We want a club of our own."

Mr. Reed had known the X and PX youth organizations in other communities. He knew also that both organizations had able professional leaders in Central City. As a careful democratic administrator, however, he consulted the leaders of the two local agencies. He learned that they had no immediate plans for expansion and would co-operate in any way they could if the X and PX agencies organized groups in Millville. Miss Mason noticed that, before introducing a new agency into the community, consultation with established groups was apparently basic.

Responsibility for arrangements with the PX agency about a new boys' group was assumed by Mr. Reed, and he suggested that Miss Mason consult the X agency about the girls. Miss Mason talked with Miss Heron, the program director of the X agency, and found her interested and willing to co-operate.

Launching the Group

According to the program director, the first step was to find out whether the girls really wanted an X Club and then to find an adult adviser. There was no doubt that the girls wanted a club. As for an adviser, they had only one person in mind—Miss Mason. She was hesitant about taking the group. She was still feeling her way in her new job, her schedule of classes was heavy, and responsibilities were piling up. She thought of others. She did not yet know many women in Millville, except the teachers, and most of them had schedules like her own. Miss Webster had a light schedule, but she had not been very successful as adviser to the school newspaper staff. The students said she rewrote every article with which she disagreed, "so why bother to write for the paper?"

Miss Heron had mentioned some of the qualities desirable in an adviser: She should be a person who—

Is liked by the girls.

Respects and is willing to listen to the opinions of young people, even the less attractive ones.

Can be an adult in a youth group without dominating.

Has wide interests and is full of ideas that would enrich the group's program.

Can have her ideas rejected by the group in the same spirit she would expect group members to accept refusal of their ideas.

Is willing to give time not only for group activities but also for study of materials and attendance at leaders' meetings in order that she can be increasingly better equipped to do a good job.

Miss Mason did not think she could measure up to all the qualifications, but she recognized Miss Heron's list as fairly close to her own idea of what it takes to be a good teacher. She knew that the girls wanted her and that she liked them—an essential in any advisory relationship. She decided to accept the responsibility.

Miss Heron came out to the school and together they talked with Jane, Rita, Betty, and Sonia, four girls who belonged to no other group but who took some leadership in class discussions. These girls thought it a fine idea to have the budding club become a part of the X organization, and a brief meeting with all the girls in Miss Mason's home room confirmed that understanding.

Six girls, including the four who had met with Miss Heron, volunteered to plan the first get-together for those who might be interested in joining the club. They decided to invite all eighth-grade girls to a party at the home of one of the six leaders. Miss Heron had explained that X Clubs were open to any girl who wanted to belong. Apparently the explanation had had little meaning for the six girls, because a couple of days later while they were addressing invitations they promptly passed by the names of three girls. Miss Mason realized what was happening and asked why the girls were being omitted.

"Why, of course, we couldn't invite them," the girls replied. "Two are colored, and one is Mexican."

"But isn't this a party for all grade eight girls?" asked Rita. "We put a notice in the school paper asking all girls to hold the date!"

"Anyway, we couldn't come ourselves if we invited these girls."

"I bet they wouldn't come," another said, perhaps hopefully.

Miss Mason said, "Is it fair to organize a friendship club which excludes three girls who go to school with you day after day?"

"No, probably not," said they. "But after all a party is different from classes."

Miss Mason reminded them that if they really wanted an X Club, they were not free to draw a color line. Then she said, "Let's look at this from another angle. Would you like being one

of the three girls excluded?" "No," they agreed, "we wouldn't."
They talked together further and with some reluctance and
uneasy feelings sent invitations to all.

The party was a success, for almost everybody had fun, and
the club was off to an enthusiastic start. But the girls were not
really a group yet. There were several observable cliques. The
six girls who had prepared the party were one clique. They felt
possessive about the club, and it was difficult to get them to share
responsibilities with others. Two other small cliques were evidently made up of neighborhood friends, one from a section
representing greater economic security, the second from the
other side of town.

The three brown girls were present. They participated in the
games and other entertainment but stayed close together. Miss
Mason joined the three girls during refreshments. This led Rita
and Sonia to pull chairs into that circle. Despite this gesture, it
was doubtful whether the three girls felt completely welcome.

Out of the various cliques composed of individuals of diverse
backgrounds, Miss Mason's task was to help the girls develop a
group which had cohesion and unity of purpose. She knew that
neither pressure, such as she had felt it necessary to use in the
invitation episode, nor talk about group spirit would do what was
needed. Finding some program activities of interest to all was the
important step.

The Physical Setting

The girls decided to hold most of their club meetings in the
school. That took some arranging, because the custom had been
to close the building immediately after a brief period for extracurricular activities. Mr. Reed, however, was able to eliminate
this difficulty for the girls' group and help other activity groups
at the same time.

The first club meeting was something to remember. The plan
was to elect officers, choose a club name, decide whether any
rules were needed, and try to find out what the members wanted

to undertake as a club program. In advance Miss Mason talked with the temporary chairman (chosen at the party) about the importance of informal free discussion, with all the members participating. But she neglected to check on which room was being assigned to the girls for the meeting. It turned out to be a classroom with stationary seats and blackboards on two walls. The room definitely did not produce a feeling of informality.

The temporary chairman took the teacher's usual stand behind the desk and became a self-appointed disciplinarian. Business was accomplished with dispatch. They chose the name "Merrie Makers" for their club. Officers were elected with extraordinary unanimity. Miss Mason cautioned against rules until they were needed. In deciding about a program, the girls listened to suggestions made by the chairman and by Miss Mason. The response of the group members to almost any idea was an uncritical "yes."

Miss Mason knew that this response did not signify complete agreement. It was simply that the girls had had long practice in saying in the classroom what someone in authority expected them to say. If the girls were to be encouraged to think for themselves and to develop free and democratic participation, the physical setting would have to be changed.

They needed a room which was attractive and had some warmth of color. They needed chairs which could be pulled into a circle for discussions or pushed out of the way for games and dancing. They needed a piano for both group singing and games. They needed to have access to a kitchen for some occasions. They might need the craft shop and a place to store materials. Miss Mason counted on Mr. Reed's understanding of the importance of the physical setting in developing a program and a group process.

Clay Modeling

On the fourth Saturday after their organization the Merrie Makers went on a hike, taking a cook-out lunch with them. Down by the river bank where they made their fire some damp, sticky clay was discovered. It was not real modeling clay, but it was fun to fool with. Miss Mason asked if they would like to have a try at working with some real clay. Some said they would; others doubted if they ever could make anything.

Miss Mason said she did not know enough about clay to help them, but she thought she would be able to find someone who could. Miss Heron was helpful at this point. She recommended a young woman who had helped some of the X Clubs in Central City with crafts.

Miss Mead, the crafts leader, came out the next week and often thereafter. She was a very attractive young woman and skilled in working with people as well as in her craft. Even the girls who thought they could not make anything had a wonderful time under Miss Mead's tutelage.

Miss Mason was delighted with this progress for several reasons. She had feared that the group might have acquiesced in the clay idea too easily and that the temporary interest might not be abiding. But fortunately Miss Mead had been capable of helping the girls really to enjoy working with clay and to see its creative possibilities. Nevertheless, Miss Mason reminded herself, the girls must be encouraged to develop their own ideas for activities. The test of progress lies in whether the members steadily increase in ability to produce their own ideas and to manage their own affairs.

Another point which pleased Miss Mason was related to the group's intercultural education. The three brown girls had not been present since the first party, but all three returned the second week Miss Mead met with the Merrie Makers; Miss Mead was a Negro.

Miss Mason made two observations:

The use of carefully selected adult leaders of minority group background is one means of quietly fostering democratic human relations and the questioning of prejudices.

The occasional use of leaders representing the various ethnic groups of which the membership is composed is one means of helping all members to gain a comfortable sense of belonging.

The Play

In late November the girls decided they wanted to give a play. Six girls agreed to look up plays in the library and to talk with the dramatics teacher during the week.

At the next meeting the Mexican and Negro girls were not present. A rumor had spread that the club was to have a minstrel show. During the play discussion Miss Mason injected a question: "Would you really like to give a minstrel show with Negro students in the audience?" The reactions to this varied. "Oh, I know a couple of colored girls who would be swell sports and not care at all," said Sonia. This was accepted by the group until Ruth, a thoughtful, well-liked girl said, "Sure, I know those girls too, and probably they'd be swell sports about it, but I think it would probably hurt underneath." The girls turned this thought over in their minds. Then Rita said, "Well, if we don't have a minstrel show, what kind shall we have?" The idea of a minstrel show was dropped, but Miss Mason knew that it might not be easy to get the three missing members back into the club.

The club then talked over a few of the plays brought in by the six girls, but none of them appealed to the group. The girls were becoming discouraged when Miss Mason, risking the chance that she was leading too vigorously, spoke up, "Why not write and produce a play of your own?" She knew that in the process of writing a play people frequently introduce their own troubling problems and that the adult adviser thus learns more about the needs of individual girls and how to help them. Her suggestion seemed to offer exciting possibilities to the club members, and they agreed they would like to try. Their imaginations envisioned the final product before an audience of students, parents, faculty, and special guests.

Then began a discussion of what ideas the girls wanted to write into their play. Miss Mason suggested they make the play about things they had actually experienced. She asked, "What kinds of things are most difficult or disturbing to other girls you know?" The club members answered: "Parents," "friends," "dates," "school."

Now and then Miss Mason injected some question, such as, "Could you give us an example of what you mean?" or "Are all parents like that?" Her role was to use a few selected questions to push group thinking a little deeper, to urge specific comments rather than to allow the conversation to rest with generalizations, and to draw all girls into the discussion.

Finally it was agreed that many teen-age problems centered about families and friends, boy friends especially. Club members decided to write the play about a family and its children's friends. The characters were to be a father, mother, grandmother, son of fourteen, daughter of twelve, and their closest friends.

Then the question arose as to who would play the father, the son, and the boy friends. The girls thought that maybe the PX Club would help. This was the club of junior high school boys organized on Mr. Reed's initiative about the time the Merrie Makers club was started. The girls asked the boys, and Miss Mason talked with Mr. Sigler, the boys' adviser. The PX Club accepted and came to the next Merrie Makers meeting to help in the making of the play.

It took many weeks of discussion to work out the actual script. The combined group talked, wrote, refined, and changed situations again and again. Ultimately the characters were made to say some of the things about which the young people felt rather deeply: being too young for dates; late hours; allowances; the right to choose one's own friends. Dramatic situations in the play centered chiefly around parents' lack of consideration for children's opinions and parents who set for their children standards which they themselves do not practice.

Before long Miss Mason noted that some of the youngsters

needed more activity than they were getting through so much discussion of the play. It also seemed that the boys and girls with less talent were going to come out of the experience with little satisfaction to themselves unless some special plans were made for them. Needing aid to resolve these problems, she asked Miss Mead, the crafts leader, if she would join the group for the next few weeks.

When the discussion again turned to the question of who would take each part, Miss Mead asked the young dramatists if they had thought of making puppets to take the parts. Miss Mead said, "I'll show you what I mean." She brought out two attractively made puppets and put on a short demonstration for the group. Both boys and girls were delighted and thought the suggestion a wonderful idea.

From then on part of the group concentrated on casting the puppeteers and speakers and rehearsing the play. The others divided the responsibility for making the puppets, the stage, and the stage settings. There was sewing, stringing, hammering, sawing, and painting to be done. Committees were formed to arrange about the publicity, the lighting, and the many other details of managing a show.

The puppet play gave every member plenty to do; each contributed according to his own interests and abilities. All in the one project there was opportunity for creativity, dramatic expression, craftsmanship, physical activity, and social and business management.

The presentation of the play was a huge success. The puppeteers had become skillful. The receptive audience was all that could be asked, and the applause gave ample commendation for the weeks of work. Both club groups achieved a real feeling of having accomplished something important.

The guests were invited to stay for a cup of punch after the show. The lines of the play stimulated questions and comments among the parents; in turn the comments increased the advisers' insight into home situations. Miss Mason and Mr. Sigler agreed that they must find means of talking frequently with the parents. They must seek invitations to visit the homes, without which they could not hope fully to understand and truly to help the boys and girls.

Soon after the play the Merrie Makers received an announcement of an inter-agency hobby show to be held in Central City, for which one of the larger stores had provided space. The puppet show was entered in the exhibition, and the boys helped transport and set up the stage. The puppets received a blue ribbon, which naturally added to the whole group's satisfaction.

In reviewing this joint project, Mr. Sigler and Miss Mason recorded some observations for future reference:

> Boys and girls of this age would not have stuck to a project which took so many weeks had it not been for the final goal, in this case the play with an audience.

> Even with a stimulating objective some of the young people would have dropped out except for the reorganized plans (the puppets), which gave everyone something important to do which had to be accepted as a responsibility and carried through for the sake of the success of the enterprise.

> The group had been sensible in keeping most of the work periods brief enough that some time was allowed for active play.

> It had proved a good idea to interrupt the play making at the holiday season for a joint Christmas and Chanukah celebration.

> It was important that the advisers had tried to see that there was plenty to laugh about even in the midst of the more serious work on the play.

> Since the group members were so busy on matters which mattered to them all, with committees and work groups composed of representatives from various cliques, the sense of group unity had grown immeasurably.

Miss Mason and Miss Mead talked together about improving intercultural relationships in the group. During the work on the play each of the three brown girls had found something to do in which she could excel. The Mexican girl was clever at designing costumes for the puppets. One Negro girl was chosen for a speaking part, the daughter in the play. The second Negro girl had demonstrated ability in working with the publicity committee. Long before the play was over these three girls really belonged to the group from which they had temporarily withdrawn when the minstrel show was mentioned.

Then, too, the decision to have a joint Christmas and Chanukah celebration had given five Jewish girls and three Jewish boys an opportunity to share special knowledge. Each shared experience had increased the feeling that the club really belonged to all the members.

Miss Mason recognized that these weeks had meant real accomplishment in inter-group education. This, however, was but a beginning. There would need to be many experiences which widen and deepen understanding if permanent gains were to be achieved and to make themselves manifest in the students' daily lives.

Spring Fever

Spring had come by now, and the girls divided their time between outdoor activities and indoor meetings in which they seemed to want to do nothing but amuse themselves in desultory fashion. They played the piano, danced a little, and talked. Miss Mason and a few girls made suggestions of things that might be started, but the ideas were ignored.

At one of these meetings Sonia said the Merrie Makers ought to give a tea for their mothers. The approach of Mother's Day had suggested the idea. The girls agreed readily, and invitation, entertainment, and refreshment committees were appointed.

When the tea took place, only five mothers attended. No invitations had been sent, and the girls' verbal invitations either had not been delivered or else had discouraged attendance. The entertainment was composed of a piano solo and a vocal solo. There was supposed to have been a skit, but the group had not practiced and properties had not been collected. The refreshment committee had forgotten to provide napkins and cream, and someone had to dash out for them at the last minute.

Miss Mason liked good workmanship, and this poorly planned tea disturbed her. It would have relieved her feelings considerably to have criticized those who were responsible. Instead, she helped them meet their unforeseen emergencies that depressing afternoon and maintained her identity with the group. This was a case where, for the sake of the group unity, the failure must be accepted by all, including the adult adviser.

It was obvious that the girls were unhappy over the tea debacle, but Miss Mason wanted them to become consciously aware of why they had failed. Therefore at a club meeting the following week she opened a conversation about the tea. The girls were inclined to be defensive until they discovered that the censure they anticipated was not forthcoming; then a frank discussion ensued.

They had not really wanted to have a tea, they said, nor had they wanted to attend committee meetings when the weather was so nice outdoors. They admitted they should have spoken up rather than have accepted responsibilities which they did not carry out. In this frank discussion the failure became a group failure, not something to blame on one or two scapegoats. It also became apparent that the girls' pride in the club would contribute heavily to the avoidance of a repetition of such a disappointing occasion.

In this experience Miss Mason saw several implications:

After a long project which demands as concentrated attention as had the play, ample time must be allowed for relaxation before a group is ready to undertake another important venture.

If the group has had previous successes and can take the discouragement, there are rare occasions when it is better to let a club activity fail than for the adult adviser to save the situation.

When there is a failure, maintaining a good relationship among the girls and between the girls and the adviser is much more important than censuring the individuals most responsible for the failure.

A Camp Shares Accommodations

At Miss Heron's request Miss Mason agreed to be a counselor at the Central City X agency camp when summer came. Many of the Merrie Makers accompanied her to a camp rally in Central City, where they saw movies of camp activities and heard other girls tell of camp life. They talked about it, and the group decided to try to go to camp during the first week Miss Mason was to be counselor.

Camp fees posed a first problem for group solution. Not all the girls could afford them. Miss Heron helped out with some scholarships. Several of the girls earned money after school. A few had small savings. Some fathers put in extra money. A discussion of whether to pool funds or to return to each what she had put in involved broad social issues of income distribution and economic justice. Adopting the pool plan and the principles underlying this choice, the club got together enough to enable every Merrie Maker who could go to attend one week of camp. The Merrie Makers were to join X agency girls from Central City who were experienced campers.

The club girls not only learned how to camp but also learned many other things. Before the season opened, the insurance inspector informed the X agency which owned Camp Pinewood that the main building was not safe. As the agency cast about for a substitute, the director of a camp for a Jewish agency volunteered space in Camp Millbrook for two weeks.

At first the two sections of the camp were acutely conscious of differences which stemmed partly from camp customs and partly from religious practices. It was difficult for old Millbrook campers to adjust to sharing their camp. It was difficult for girls own traditions, and the Merrie Makers, camping for the first time, did not know what to expect. But gradually friendships developed and the fun of the camp activities surmounted strangeness. Shared experiences in an atmosphere of common purposes prevailed over differences recognized yet not allowed to separate friends.

The X agency girls ate the same food as their hosts. Millbrook was a kosher camp, and kitchen utensils and dishes were maintained on that basis. Several of the X agency counselors were interested in learning about the customs and were able to answer questions from Christian youngsters as they arose. Christian visitors learned that some Jewish girls were also novices at kosher food.

The entire camp participated in the customary Friday observances of the Jewish camp. After rest hour the campers came to the lodge for a "Shabbas treat" of candy. At supper the hostess led the beautiful family ceremony of "Blessing the Candles." A small group sang the Hebrew choral response. Christian girls and counselors learned the response, for they all wanted to take part. In the evening most of the campers attended the out-of-door services.

As the girls planned their own traditional "fire of friendship" for the closing night of camp they said, "Let's not choose the girl to light the fire according to her camp, because we're all one camp now."

This camp experience had contributed effectively to the intercultural education of the Merrie Makers. The camp included representatives of a variety of social and economic backgrounds. The inter-faith experience, plus the fact that the X agency campers and counselors were an inter-racial group, offered a rich opportunity for learning to respect and live with people of different cultural backgrounds.

The Second Year Begins

The Merrie Makers reorganized their group soon after school began. Almost immediately they proposed a dance to which they could invite the PX boys. After the meeting Rita and Ruth stopped to ask Miss Mason whether she thought Helen, Pat, and Marie (the three brown girls) would have a good time at the dance.

Miss Mason replied that she supposed they would know the answer to that question better than she. She did venture to say, however, that if they thought the dance was likely to leave any of the girls out of things they might wish to suggest a substitute plan.

Apparently some conversation took place in the intervening week, because by the next meeting the prevailing idea was to have a spaghetti supper. The boys liked this idea, and plans for the party began.

The supper was good, too; one of the girls brought her mother to supervise the committee of cooks. And, as a matter of fact, after supper the group did dance and everybody had a good time.

The Pioneer Parade

In mid-October another Millville group, one of the two girls' clubs which met in a church, suggested that the three organized girls' groups combine to put on a Festival of Nations.

The Merrie Makers entered into the idea enthusiastically. A joint committee from among the three groups made plans. Parents and community leaders who had special knowledge of foreign countries were consulted. Six nations were chosen to be represented, two by each club. Exhibits, folk dances, and folk songs constituted the program agreed upon.

One minister became so interested in the project that he gave hours of time to helping the girls work out their plans. Under his guidance the program idea changed from a folk festival to a Pioneer Parade. The girls learned about the contributions of various groups to the making of America. They wrote a script and planned a pageant which would dramatize their ideas. A verse-speaking choir was used for the spoken parts. The concluding thought of the Pioneer Parade was that "the pioneer task today is for all people to learn to live together with respect for and understanding of differences."

The pageant and the exhibits were staged at the school gym, and the public was invited. Again the girls had an appreciative audience. Mr. Reed's praises were especially pleasing to the group members.

The Merrie Makers had enjoyed the experience of working with other club groups. In addition, some important thinking had been done about "who is an American."

The Group Engages in Some Social Service

As the holiday season approached, the girls felt they wanted to give a basket to some "poor" family. Miss Mason thought the spirit commendable but she did not want to foster the Lady Bountiful attitude of the "haves" giving to the "have nots." She therefore suggested that they make an appointment to talk with Miss Meyers, the social worker at the local welfare office. Three girls went, and they ended their visit by inviting Miss Meyers to come to meet and talk with their whole group. Miss Meyers accepted. She started forthrightly by telling the girls how they could be most helpful to the welfare agency at the holidays. Then she talked informally about what conditions cause people to be poor, what needs to be done to right these conditions, and what the agency she worked with was doing to help people help themselves. The girls asked eager questions and, since the time had passed all too quickly, they asked if Miss Meyers would come again and talk with them about "what you have to do to be a social worker." After school and on Saturdays the club members spent several hours each in following Miss Meyers's suggestion that they repair and repaint old toys, which the welfare agency could then make available to parents who were unable to purchase new toys for their children.

Miss Mason jotted down the following points:

This was the first time the group had expressed and satisfied an urge to do something for others.

Referring the girls to Miss Meyers helped them to get acquainted with one more community resource.

Miss Meyers's suggestion about the toys helped the girls to learn to work through official channels in their giving.

The girls' interest in Miss Meyers's work opened up a new vocational possibility to them which could be further explored at another meeting.

Observation Trips

The group's interest in the work of the welfare office led Miss Mason to encourage the girls to learn more about other community services. They discussed various possibilities for finding out about such services in Central City as well as in Millville. After a group decision about what they thought it best to see, two Saturday trips were arranged, one to the hospital in Millville and the second to a well-conducted children's court in Central City. Arrangements for the trips were made by a committee of girls, but Miss Mason assisted by telephone calls which prepared the way. During the visits she further interpreted to the hospital and court officials what the girls hoped to see and to learn.

At the hospital they were shown examples of ward and private room service, the surgery and clinic rooms, the kitchens, and the nurses' home. One of the more experienced graduate nurses guided the tour. In an empty classroom the girls were invited to sit down and talk over questions in their minds. They learned something about nurses' training, ambulance service, the hospital insurance plan, and how the hospital was supported. Many questions were asked about the newly built maternity ward of the hospital. In answer to another question the girls learned that Negroes were not accepted in the hospital; if Negroes needed hospital care they had to go to Central City.

At the children's court a very understanding woman judge described for the girls examples of the kinds of cases which come before that court and talked about the home and neighborhood situations which contributed to the delinquent behavior of certain boys and girls. She explained how the court worked with the staff of a guidance clinic, with families, and with other community agencies in an effort to find the best solution for the needs of the individual boys and girls; she described how the court tried to effect changes in situations that caused juvenile delinquency.

After each of the two trips the girls talked with great interest about what they had learned. Miss Mason set down two observations:

> These two trips served to enlarge the girls' knowledge of community services, contributed to their understanding of some social problems, and introduced them to new ideas about vocations.

> There is a wealth of education possible through many other trips which might be arranged occasionally.

The Group Tries to Go Swimming

At the beginning of the spring semester the girls decided they would like to learn to swim. The group seemed to feel it was an important skill—and a social skill, as an adult might point out. There was a pool in the X agency in Central City.

While they were figuring whether each could afford the medical examination fee, plus transportation, plus the swimming fee, Miss Mason discovered that Negro girls were not admitted to the X pool. She brought this information to the group. The girls were indignant, but by this time they were so much one group that no one suggested going without Helen and Pat. An interesting point to the club was the fact that Marie, though no lighter than Helen and Pat, would be welcome. Marie was a Mexican-American.

"But Helen and Pat are members just like any of us," said the girls. "Why can't they go in?"

Miss Mason said, "Would you like to write a letter to the board of directors protesting a policy which keeps some of your members out of the pool?"

They would, and they did. They wrote and rewrote the letter. They wanted to make clear that they felt this an unfair policy, but they wanted to choose their words carefully so that the board members would take them seriously. The board president replied, thanking them and stating that the matter would be discussed by the board. Nothing happened for over a year. Then the pool was opened to the clubs which had Negro members. And another year later, a further step was taken and the pool was opened to the public without any restrictions. The girls had to wait a long time for results, but when the actions were taken Miss Mason reminded members of the group with whom she was still in contact that their letter probably had helped to get the policy changed.

Miss Mason was pleased with the progress of the club as indicated by the writing of the letter. One year and a half ago they were questioning the presence of three dark girls in their own group. Their present protest might mean simply that Helen and Pat and Marie were now their friends. Or, hopefully interpreted, it could be a sign of a growing sense of social responsibility and a consciousness of social injustice.

The Group Helps to Establish a Youth Center

At the beginning of the third year for the Merrie Makers, the girls were tenth graders. This proved to be the year in which

Miss Mason felt the greatest sense of accomplishment with and through them.

In the early fall the girls wanted "all co-ed activities." They gave a party and invited the PX members. The two groups decided that high school students needed a center of their own. Miss Mason and Mr. Sigler, the PX adviser, encouraged them to call together a selected group of adults and to ask their opinion. The adults became interested and agreed to serve as an advisory committee. One man helped to find a usable building, a former garage. Work groups spent hours planning, scrubbing, carpentering, and decorating. A few teachers and parents gave expert advice and some labor. Two adult community groups gave money.

The X and PX groups helped other students in the senior high school to feel that the center belonged to all. Many high school students were active in preparation; enthusiasm was high. But as the opening neared some mothers became disturbed about this center which was to be open to all senior high school students. No thought of racial discrimination had occurred within the clubs, for Negro members belonged to both the X and the PX groups and had as a matter of course helped work on the center. The race-conscious mothers, however, sent a protest to the principal. The young people were upset, and thoughtful action was needed.

A few members of the advisory committee were convinced that the open membership plan was right. Miss Mason and Mr. Sigler solicited their help. Calls were made on the leaders of the protest movement, and ample time was spent in interpreting why this was important to the young people. A carefully planned parents' meeting was held at which the X and the PX chairmen explained just why their members felt as they did about there being no racial restrictions. The X and PX clubs would consider such a restriction on the basis of race entirely undemocratic, and they did not want the center on those terms. Finally one father said he saw no reason why parents should impose their prejudices on the young people. Other parents agreed, some reluctantly. But the center opened to all.

The Group Discusses Segregation and Discrimination

At the meeting concerning the youth center one parent, in arguing for the exclusion of Negro boys and girls, stated that there was very little other activity open to Negroes, "so they would flock in in great numbers. They should have a spot of their own."

A few days later the X and PX groups met together. Before the business session began there was a good deal of talk about who said what at the parents' meeting. Ted, the PX chairman, asked, "What was Mr. Talbott's idea? What things are not open to Negroes?"

Jim said, "Well, for one thing, it's where we live. Why do you suppose a lot of Negroes live down by the tracks? Why don't they live on the hill? Nobody will rent them a house, that's why."

"And what about rents where you do live?" asked Mr. Sigler.

"Mostly it's a gouge," said Jim.

"It's not only the high rents," said Helen, "but it's the fact that none of the landlords want to paint or fix up the houses. It makes you kind of ashamed of your street."

"Of course," said Jim, "a lot of what's wrong down there is because our fathers can't get decent jobs—that is, jobs that pay anything much."

"Yeah, that's right," said Doris. "Why I know a man—a college graduate, who . . ." And thus the talk continued—impressions, first-hand experience, and some half truths, but the beginning of thought about important problems. The business session was forgotten. This talk was more interesting.

Finally Mr. Sigler asked, "Would you be interested in inviting Mr. Crawford to one of your meetings? He is chairman of the Millville Housing Committee. Asking questions of him might give us more facts. Perhaps we could then see whether there is anything the clubs can do to help." The group agreed. "After that we might make some inquiry about employment opportunities. Perhaps the United States Employment Service office could help us," added Miss Mason.

This discussion just "happened," but it was a beginning. Mr. Crawford, the housing committee chairman, came and talked about housing standards and about some of the reasons why housing conditions were bad for many people, but especially so for certain groups. Also, he made arrangements for a few of the group members to see examples of the kinds of houses in which some people, white and Negro, are forced to live by circumstances. The trip included a visit to examples of very poor housing and, in contrast, homes in a low-cost housing project which had been built two years before. The trip was carefully planned. Prior to the visit there was a group discussion on what should be observed and what kind of questions should be asked. After the trip the observers reported to the entire club, and there was a general discussion on what needed to be done in Millville and what the handicaps were to making good housing available to all.

In the course of the talk about housing the question of ability to pay came up. This recalled the earlier comments about employment, and the help of the USES was enlisted. The USES personnel understood the importance of this inquiry and invited the group to come to their offices at an appointed hour. Under the guidance of the director the group members learned about the general services of the USES and the problems encountered in the matter of restrictions on employment based on race or religious affiliation. Cases were cited of people with a southern European background, of people of non-white stock, and of those of certain religions who met with discrimination although they had qualifications equal or superior to those of the majority group in varied American communities.

After this visit the group members talked about the injustice of such restrictions. They were not sure how much they could do about so knotty a problem, but they agreed on two procedures:

To seek opportunities to ask adult groups for co-operation in protest against this injustice.

To talk with fathers and other employed members of their families to see how they really felt about such restrictions.

Mr. Sigler suggested that they ought to know their state law which prohibits segregation in public services. With the help of a lawyer father, two members looked up the law. This led the groups to make test visits to the local restaurants to see whether their Negro members would be refused service. They were not refused.

By this time the groups had accumulated so much data and had been given so much first-hand evidence of discrimination as well as of acceptance that they were eager to tell others what they had learned. The principal suggested that they work out an assembly program. Two church groups asked to hear their story. Through Miss Heron, the X agency program director, the Central City radio station learned of their efforts and gave them time to tell the story on the air. For each of these opportunities a committee of boys and girls worked carefully with the material. They wanted to tell their story in a way that would awaken concern and stir people to do something about the situation. These opportunities, together with the approval expressed by some adults whom they respected, gave the group members real satisfaction. They were especially pleased when the X agency asked them to write for its national magazine about what they had done.

The Group Tries to Go Roller Skating

One other thing of importance for the group happened late in the spring. A new roller-skating rink was opened in Millville, and the X girls decided to have a skating party. As they filed past the ticket window, the brown girls were in the middle of the group. Several white girls already had their tickets and were through the gate when a Negro girl approached the window. She was refused a ticket on the basis that skating this afternoon was for Skateland members only. Obviously this was a ruse. But the Negro girls asked for membership blanks, filled in their answers, and handed them in. They were never to receive a reply. When the Negro girls were refused, the entire club left without skating.

They sought help in writing a letter of protest to the owner of the rink. Miss Mason suggested that to be entirely fair they should test the situation again after making the protest. Three girls (two white, one brown) did this, but the results were as before.

One Negro girl's mother decided to take court action against the owner for violation of the state law. The X agency board in Central City and several Millville ministers and community leaders agreed to back the mother if she filed suit. The hearing was held. The judge praised the girls who acted as witnesses for their courage and fair-mindedness and not only lectured the Skateland owner on ignoring the principles of democracy but fined him $25 for breaking the state law.

Miss Mason observed that for the girls this experience was similar to that of the swimming pool except at the following points:

The girls saw results without having to wait long.

They had their first opportunity to observe the use of the courts in the protection of civil rights.

They shared responsibility with adult community leaders as they mobilized for action.

Mr. Sigler and Miss Mason agreed that:

Everything that had happened before in the way of good inter-group education was groundwork for this year's activities.

The discussion over segregation in the youth center stirred emotions which would soon have lapsed had not the succeeding discussion made it possible to start the group on the study and collection of data about the problems of segregation.

In working with the housing authority and the USES, the members increased their knowledge of community resources.

Out of all the discussion which had taken place in the group, the members had opportunity to clarify their own ideas and strengthen their convictions about injustices.

In order to accept the invitations to tell their story, the members found it necessary to formulate statements of principles and good practices and thus think through their beliefs in an orderly way.

Telling their story and seeing the court case through resulted in a sense of achievement and avoided the frustration which can come when a group gets excited about something about which nothing can be done.

The group had made real headway in developing a sense of social responsibility among the members. The young people were growing steadily in their ability to identify themselves with more and more people. First there had been cliques or sub-groups within the clubs; now the members had learned to work and play together as one group. Then there had been the experiences with other groups of their own age. Later came a concern for the whole school; one result was the youth center. And, finally, there was an effort to try to understand the special problems of one section of the community.

"That is growth," thought Miss Mason, "but a mere beginning." Now another year lay ahead. The growing must go on.

Conclusion

Basically, what contributes to a good youth group program? What are the significant implications of the foregoing story for other adult-sponsored youth groups?

1. *Good Facilities and Appropriate Equipment Are Assets.* The group in the story met in the school. In many communities the school offers the best space and equipment for the activities in which youth groups engage. But inadequate financing sometimes closes schools to after-school activities. The short-sighted-

ness of locking school doors at hours when youth need constructive activity should be vigorously protested.

Not all groups meet in schools. Some meet in youth organization buildings such as the Y's and settlement houses. Others meet in churches, community centers, civic halls, and homes. Some group workers believe that meeting outside the school strengthens the link between the young people and the community.

In selecting a meeting place, the important questions to ask are:

Can the group feel that the room belongs to them, preferably all the time, but at least for the periods they use it?

Can the group put up decorations or other symbols of ownership while they are using it?

Will they be free to carry on the kind of program they want and need?

Will persons in charge of the space place unfair or unnecessary limitations on the group?

Whatever the meeting place, good facilities and equipment are an asset to a good program, but they are not essential. For there are youth groups which have had a better time in an old, dilapidated store or a cellar furnished with cast-offs than in other buildings with the finest equipment.

2. *A Stimulating National Organization Can Advise.* There are several advantages in organizing a youth group with the help of a national youth organization:

The national organizations provide program materials, offer guidance on good practices, and share the successful experiences of other groups with the local agencies affiliated with them.

They provide advisory field staffs and arrange regional and national conferences for both leaders and youth.

They have adult citizen boards or councils wherever they organize, and professional staffs wherever possible, both of which serve as resources for individual group leaders.

Belonging to a city-wide, a national, or an international organization gives a sense of relationship with members elsewhere and provides a practical basis for discussion of national and international relations.

Several of the national organizations offer opportunities for continued participation by group members after school days are over.

No matter how helpful such a relationship can be, the fact remains that membership in a national organization cannot assure a satisfying program. A national office can and should suggest a variety of ideas. But each group must be free to work out its own program according to the needs and interests of the members.

3. *Interests Are Important in Voluntary Groups.* Boys and girls join youth groups because they choose to belong. There is never any sense of compulsion or necessity for joining. Similarly, the adult adviser chooses to accept responsibility for working with the group. Because of the voluntary character of the group relations, there is an eagerness and a readiness about the participation which is sometimes lacking in situations where attendance is required. The interest of the members and of the adult adviser in having a club is therefore a primary requisite to successful accomplishment.

The voluntary character of membership also raises questions as to the composition of the group. Sometimes groups are open to all of a certain age. In the case of the Merrie Makers, this meant that within the one group the members had an opportunity to learn to work and play with girls of different races, religious faiths, and economic and social backgrounds.

Some groups begin with a friendship group; this is called by some persons a natural group or a gang. The responsibility in this case is not one of creating group unity, as it was with the Merrie Makers. Rather, it is one of finding ways to introduce the group to satisfying experiences with other groups and individuals and so work toward the end of achieving a more inclusive membership.

4. *Democratic Objectives Must Be Maintained.* Most boys and girls join youth groups because they want to have a good time with others of their own age. Unconsciously they may want the security which comes from belonging to a group in which their opinions count. A leader knows that any group's wants and desires are expressed in the choice of things the members want to do.

In the adult-sponsored youth group the objectives of the adult adviser and of the parent organization also enter into the picture. Simply stated, these objectives frequently are to help young people become mature, self-directing citizens in a democratic society. This objective is the goal an adviser holds steadily in mind while helping a group to work out a program that fulfils the immediate wants, needs, and interests of the members. It is because of this ultimate objective that the adviser searches constantly for ways to stimulate the group to undertake program activities which are increasingly more significant.

To achieve that objective, each adviser needs to be consciously aware that real democracy depends on people who are secure, healthy, self-reliant, self-disciplined, informed, thinking, articulate citizens. It depends on people who believe in the essential human rights of every individual without regard to race, creed, color, or sex. There must be conscious awareness that young people do not suddenly become responsible citizens at the age of twenty-one. They grow that way gradually.

5. *A Democratic Group Process.* As was demonstrated by the story of Miss Mason and the Merrie Makers, the youth group members and the adult advisers work together. They discuss choices in kinds of program. They jointly agree (unanimously or by consensus when possible, by majority decision otherwise) what shall be done. They discuss who will be responsible. Committees or individuals carry out the responsibilities they have accepted.

A major event takes place, and the group evaluates the entire project. Then plans for the next undertaking begin. Or plans for several different undertakings may be carried on simultaneously; some may be earmarked for the more distant future, some scheduled for the immediate future. The whole group may tackle some plans together; for other activities, the work may be divided among the members.

The interplay of individual members with others in the group and with the adult adviser in discussing, deciding, acting on decisions, and evaluating is the group process through which learning takes place.

6. *A Skillful Adviser*. In the adult-sponsored youth group the adviser is the most important single factor in achieving a successful program. It is the adviser who makes or breaks the possibility for youth to experience the democratic group process at its best.

Other conditioning factors—such as the home, school, and church, community influences, and the natural youth group leaders—determine the group's readiness for progress. But within the group, regardless of the assets or liabilities inherent in the situation, the adviser has the important role.

It is the adviser who must know each boy and girl as individual persons, together with their unexpressed wants as well as their expressed interests. It is the adviser who must know what needs are fulfilled or not fulfilled for each boy and girl in the home and must consider, with the youngsters, what kinds of experience they need most in the club. This knowledge the adviser collects gradually while working with the group and out of it develops specific goals for each individual and for the group as a whole.

In the process of work with the group the adviser watches for opportunities to make suggestions in keeping with this knowledge of the deeper needs of the members. When the group shows no readiness for an idea, it is dropped for the time being. Later on another suggestion possibly related to the earlier idea is offered. Perhaps it interests the group, and as they work on this suggestion the interests are expanded, the thinking is deepened, and the sense of social responsibility is strengthened. It is even more desirable that the penetrating suggestions which meet real needs and foster the democratic way be made by group members.

The adviser's rights and privileges are no different from those of any youth member. The adviser's responsibility is the point of difference. It is chiefly the adviser, at least in the beginning of group experience, who keeps in mind the ultimate objectives toward which the group is working. As individuals in the group grow in their sense of responsibility for others and develop a social consciousness, they increasingly share with the adviser a desire to work toward more important objectives.

It is an important undertaking to assume the responsibility of advising a youth group; to become one of the group, yet one who is expected to contribute out of larger understanding and wider experience; to move the group gradually toward more significant and more socially desirable ends.

To help youth become mature, self-directing citizens in a democratic society, an adviser must *be* the kind of person here described, or at least be working toward that goal. An adviser must live a life of his own which steadily increases his intellectual and emotional maturity. An adviser must take every opportunity to increase his own understanding of social thought and major issues; in fact, the adviser needs to join other adult groups in working aggressively for a democratic society. The adviser's own attitudes, interests, experience, and convictions are the basis of his contribution to youth.

CHAPTER V

THE JUNIOR HIGH SCHOOL TEACHER[1]

*When children are growing from childhood into adolescence,
they must have about them adults who are willing to explore
honestly with them the area of human conduct and values. It is
often in these years that children first become aware of the part
which race and culture patterns—as well as income, family ideals,
and class differences—play in the degree to which they are accepted by their associates. Whether young people meet these dis-
coveries with antisocial aggression, with submissiveness and
eventual retreat from responsibility, or with an intelligent attempt
to understand social barriers and to work for their elimination
may depend upon the guidance given them in the home and in
school. The nature of their adjustment may also depend upon the
facilities which the larger community provides in the physical and
psychological environment in which young people must find and
test life values.*

*The following narratives describe some ways in which two
junior high schools in the same middle-western city attempted to
give children opportunities for increasing participation in the life
of their school and their community. Because the problems of
prejudice and discrimination are felt in widely differing environments, the schools represent two kinds of communities: one, a
community in which lower-income families need opportunities*

[1] This chapter was written by PRUDENCE BOSTWICK, Supervisor, Department of Instruction, and MYRTLE F. SUGARMAN, Supervising Teacher in the
Department of Instruction, Denver Public Schools.

117

*for personal and social development in a school district dominated
by middle-class values; the other, a community in which families
of various racial and cultural origins live in crowded neighborhoods encroached upon by an expanding industrial district.*

A "Really American" School

Mr. Sanders was lucky—he had been assigned to a school where
no inter-group or intercultural problems existed. At any rate, so
he was told when he began his teaching career in the Fremont
Junior High School. One teacher who had taught in the school
for twenty years enthusiastically assured him that Fremont was
one of the few "really American" schools in the city.

Since Mr. Sanders was young and critical and inclined to ask
questions about everything, he wanted to know what characterized an "American" school. His informants replied that most of
the children came from good, solid, middle-class homes—no ex-
tremes of wealth or poverty. Not only was the student body relatively homogeneous in its socio-economic status, but also most of
the children and their parents were native-born whites. There
were only two Negroes in the school, a very few Spanish-speaking children, three Japanese-Americans, and a sprinkling of children whose names indicated central and southern European backgrounds. The presence of these few representatives of minorities
caused no frictions. They were no threat to the security of the
majority, formed no solidly knit groups, were not conspicuous,
and were never belligerent.

In the weeks which followed, Mr. Sanders almost came to believe that he was indeed in a school where no intercultural or
inter-group problems added to the ordinary pressures of daily
living with adolescents. He was almost lulled into complacency
by the lunch-table conversations, which frequently consisted of
offering sincere thanks that the Fremont teachers were not facing
the delinquencies and aggression reported to exist in some other
junior high schools in the city.

Mr. Sanders liked to think about his 7B class and to plan for the three periods that he spent with them in a six-period day. Throughout the three years of junior high school he would be their teacher in a unified-studies or core curriculum. In Fremont, as in the other junior high schools of the city, the basis of the program was the common problems of boys and girls. Subject matter was to be presented not as an isolated body of facts and skills, but as a functional contribution to the study of problems related to children's experience. The three-hour block of time offered rich opportunity for engaging in varied activities and for becoming well acquainted with the group.

In getting to know his group Mr. Sanders was aided by the interviews, records, standardized tests of academic skills, interest inventories, and other diagnostic instruments already available. The children's autobiographies, written the first week of the semester, indicated something of the background, experience, and point of view of each child. To Mr. Sanders these autobiographies seemed far from "homogeneous." It did not require much reading between the lines to discover widely varying home backgrounds. Some children had traveled widely, were supplied with ample equipment for enjoying hobbies and home recreation, took music lessons, and belonged to organized out-of-school groups. By way of contrast, several autobiographies revealed a meager out-of-school experience, with few opportunities for enrichment. These autobiographies, along with other indications both in his own class and throughout the school, set Mr. Sanders to wondering if there were not socio-economic group problems that were being overlooked in the general acceptance of the "average American" label, so much a part of the school tradition.

When, at lunch, the conversation turned to changes taking place in the district, Mr. Sanders's ideas were confirmed. The greatest threat to the homogeneity of the school was the rapid expansion of an outlying section, Airy View, a haphazard outgrowth on the edge of the city.

Conflicts Appear

Mr. Sanders became more and more aware of the unstable emotional climate of his classroom. He began to see things which had not struck him before. There were certain definite though small indications of mutual disapproval. The seven Airy View children in his class differed more from the others than he had realized even after rereading the autobiographies. The most well-intentioned and democratic of the privileged youngsters talked casually of experiences which they took for granted and which Airy View regarded as bragging. On the other hand, even Joe, the most able and popular Airy View boy, used atrocious English in his oral reports and was criticized by the other group for his errors. There were complaints that all the Airy View boys, and sometimes the girls, used vulgar and profane language, particularly on the playground before school. When reprimanded for this kind of unacceptable behavior, these children were sullen and defiant. Their language, so shocking to "sissy kids" and teachers, was part of their home environment. "When you're mad, you got a right to cuss" was the unrepentant comment of one boy.

In studying the relationships in his own classroom in terms of group conflict, Mr. Sanders found that he had ignored many things; other things he had noticed but failed to interpret as significant. The voluntary grouping of children in the classroom, playground, lunchroom, and halls was clannish. The pattern of grouping persisted in many class activities involving choice of associates. The only exceptions to this pattern of group loyalty occurred when a marginal child with ambitions was in a position to choose from the group with which he hoped to be allied. The choice of squares for Wednesday morning square dancing followed an invariable pattern. The well-accepted children of both groups formed eights without a moment's hesitation. Then those who hated to dance or were unattractive or for some other reason were "fringers" formed reluctant squares and filed to the gymnasium for a joyless half hour. Three who were not permitted to dance because of religious restrictions at first went doggedly to the gymnasium and watched the others. Later Mr. Sanders cajoled the office staff into using them as messengers during activity period and spared them this side-line ordeal.

Just as Mr. Sanders was in the midst of his informal study of pupil relationships in his class, all 7B children were called upon to prepare an assembly program. Mr. Sanders's group was so busy getting its part of the program ready and, on the surface at least, so engrossed in the tasks of building scenery, learning lines, contriving costumes, and collecting properties that underlying differences apparently were forgotten. The friendly atmosphere was heartening to Mr. Sanders, who had been disturbed by the lack of enthusiasm generally shown in the class. Although the boys and girls had been together for six weeks, there had been little feeling of solidarity or of having fun together prior to the work on the program. On the other hand, it was encouraging to observe that, in spite of the lack of wholehearted acceptance, there had been no marked group hostility, even when certain individuals had tried to cause trouble.

Such an individual was Pat Yates, one of the Airy View boys, who showed resentment toward restriction and authority in any situation. He seemed to be a leader with considerable influence over the other Airy View children in the class. Pat was oversized and over the normal age in the group, clumping defiantly around the room in cowboy boots.

On Friday, the day of the 7B assembly program, while last-minute details were causing excitement and confusion, Pat began to scuffle with another boy. Ordinarily the inevitable pushing and shoving of junior high school boys had no serious effect on Mr. Sanders's poise. On that particular day, however, the added confusion irritated him to the point of rebuking the boys sharply.

By Monday, the program being over without mishap, Mr. Sanders had forgotten the incident, but Pat had neither forgotten nor forgiven. His parents came to school. Shabby in dress and defiant in spirit, they protested that the school was always against

Pat and the other "bus kids"—a phrase which Mr. Sanders had heard before and which Pat's parents insisted was derogatory. Though slightly mollified by Mr. Sanders's courtesy, they left still believing the school to be unfair. Their conversation had given Mr. Sanders a glimpse of the insecurities, rebuffs, and disappointments which were an integral part of the Yates family life. Lay-offs at the plant, during which Mr. Yates did odd jobs, made for periods of financial stress. Mrs. Yates had obviously worked hard all her life, taking care of a large family.

The Background

The visit from the Yates family made Mr. Sanders determine to see the Airy View district for himself. On a Sunday afternoon he drove across the railroad tracks and out toward the edge of town. What he saw was not a typical slum. He did not find the overcrowding, the lack of light and air, and the street playgrounds that he had in mind from the descriptions of tenement districts given in sociology courses. The houses were set far apart. The name "Airy View" was at least partially accurate. But the houses were small; some had not been finished, and few were painted. A number of the properties could be classified as small farms. The general atmosphere was one of making a living under difficulties, without much hope for the future.

Many things were becoming clearer to him. For example, he now understood why many of the Airy View children were sullen and rebellious whenever fees of any kind were collected. Most of them were too insecure to ask for assistance or to discuss the strain in the home that made the small fees a financial burden.

The religious backgrounds of the Airy View children added to inter-group problems and almost isolated some of them. A few were openly hostile to Jews, Catholics, and "foreigners." Airy View was peculiarly susceptible to the influence of fundamentalist groups, some of which were sincere but extremely narrow interpreters of Christianity. Others, immersed in the familiar fundamentalist creeds, were allied with sinister forces of bigotry, race prejudice, and "American nationalism." Some of the sects adopted distinctive styles of plain dress and forbade their children to dance, play games, attend parties, or associate with children of different religious beliefs. The effect of these restrictions was to set many of the Airy View children apart from the others and to make it extremely difficult for them to achieve that rapport with their peers which is indispensable to satisfactory adolescent adjustment. Through his special study of the Airy View district Mr. Sanders found that his friend Mr. Black, one of the science teachers, frequently offended parents in the district by statements of scientific facts which he assumed were not open to question; but many of those facts were contrary to their fundamentalist beliefs.

Although Airy View parents were more than willing to defend their children against real or imagined discrimination, they did not come to organized meetings of parents. The children either did not bother to take Parent-Teacher Association notices home or grew discouraged at having their parents show no interest in the meetings.

The shabby appearance of many Airy View children set them apart from others in the Fremont school. This segregation was not apparent among the boys in the junior high school, where personal appearance bothers the students little until they are in the ninth grade, and even then it is not a serious concern. Airy View shirt tails flapped with the same careless abandon as did those of boys whose fathers belonged to the professional and managerial groups, and there was a complete absence of stratification in the uniform dinginess of the corduroy trousers worn by most of the boys.

It was among the girls that clothes reflected different backgrounds and standards. One of the home arts teachers, Mrs. James, a discerning and understanding young woman, was eager to talk over the problems of the Airy View girls. According to her the clothes worn by the girls were indicative of differences in taste, standards, and out-of-school interests. She emphasized that

the differences were most pronounced in Grade 8A. By the time
the Airy View girls had reached this grade, most of them wore
conspicuous make-up, gaudy costume jewelry, elaborately curled
hair styles, dressy shoes often with high heels, and what were
obviously older sisters' cast-off silk dresses.

Mr. Sanders was inclined to scoff at the importance of these details, but Mrs. James went on to point out how the mutual disapproval of the style and taste of the girls of Airy View and of
those in the more favored districts reflected entirely different
points of view and made for disharmony. For instance, there was
the matter of dating. The Airy View girls chattered of their
conquests at public dances, borrowed lipsticks, and made great
efforts to copy hair styles from the movie magazines. These girls
scorned school mates whose major interests centered in Camp
Fire, Girl Scout, and other organized club groups, in hobbies and
sports, in music and dancing lessons, and in the simplest of social
occasions in their homes.

Many Airy View girls hoped to be graduated from the senior
high school, and a few had ambitions to attend business college;
but there was always the possibility that early marriage or economic straits in the family would necessitate their dropping out
of school. On the other hand, the middle and upper-middle-class
girls assumed that they would complete senior high school, and
many were already making college plans, even to the extent of
learning about the various sororities. Their parents looked upon
early marriage with disfavor and alarm, lest it interfere with
cherished plans for the future, and they believed in keeping their
daughters as unsophisticated as possible.

In contrast with these girls' pronounced lack of interest in or
extremely awkward and tentative attitude toward boys, the Airy
View girls displayed in their conversation and their attitude
toward the opposite sex an avid and fairly complete knowledge
of life. Overcrowding in the home, many babies, and lack of
inhibition in family conversation had instructed them early. They
paid little attention to boys of their own age, who as yet did not

share their precocious interest in the other sex. They "went with" older boys. Eternal vigilance was required on the part of teachers and office staff to prevent these girls from leaving school with alleged "brothers," young men in their late teens or early twenties, whose flashy cowboy-style clothes and sideburns represented Airy View's idea of glamour. Most of the teachers wearily admitted that the girls probably met these gallants somewhere else, but the school was obligated at least to see that the girls were safely started home on the school bus.

Such differences did not make for great conflict in Mrs. James's home arts classes. The Airy View girls rather admired this teacher's appearance, but they felt that her clothes were too plain. Even the giddiest, most boy-struck girls accepted without question the practical handwork in cooking and sewing. Discussion and activities related to grooming and the selection of clothing, however, were generally unsuccessful, because each of the two distinct groups of girls believed its own standards to be right.

Further evidence of disagreement in values was apparent in classes such as Mr. Sanders's, where the work was more largely verbal. Airy View girls and women read little, saw no reason for being interested in public affairs or world happenings, and had small faith in values that were not immediately tangible. Many of the other girls had no genuine interest in social studies or mathematics, but their parents insisted on their doing passable school work. The boys of the differing groups worked fairly well together, all being at the age when school effort had taken a decided slump. Some of the Airy View boys, indeed, had good abilities and ambitions in spite of meager resources in the home and lack of parental encouragement, but their hopes of advancement would probably be difficult to realize.

Although the disparity in background and interests made for a good deal of group conflict, Mr. Sanders felt that for the most part there were no serious personality maladjustments involved here. The exceptions were individuals like Pat Yates who were bitterly defensive but not ambitious, those whose religion set them apart, and those in the marginal group who must live in the Airy View environment but who wanted desperately to be part of the socially and economically privileged group. These marginal children tried to copy the manners, speech, and dress of those whom they admired and in doing so incurred the derision of the more rough-and-ready members of their own group. Having insufficiently satisfying contacts with their peers, they often sought the company of the teachers. To Mr. Sanders or any other teacher with an understanding of boys and girls, this unusual preference for adult society on the part of young adolescents was rightly interpreted as a symptom of unsatisfactory relations with others of their own age. Most junior high school pupils want adults when they want them, but for the most part they crave association with and acceptance by their contemporaries. And it is that kind of group acceptance which teachers need to help children to find.

The "Bus Kids" and the School

With his eyes opened by these indications of conflict in his classroom, Mr. Sanders began to see how right the Yates family had been when they insisted that the term "bus kids" had a disparaging and unfriendly significance. He therefore decided to analyze the school situation as a whole in order to find reasons for the isolation of the "bus kids."

First, he discovered that the term "bus kids" was used with varying degrees of emotion. Too often it became a stereotype denoting lower-class standards of behavior. Breakage, theft, or disturbance was frequently blamed on the "bus kids," even though investigation in many instances proved the assumption that they had been responsible for the misdeed to be untrue.

The mechanical details of their transportation to and from the school set these children apart. The bus arrived fifteen minutes before the official opening of the school doors. In good weather this early arrival presented no problem because the children played or strolled out of doors, but in bad weather they huddled in the front entry until the doors were opened. Naturally they yelled and demanded that the boy monitor assigned to watch the door let them in. Teachers entering had to push past the disorderly crowd and often unthinkingly made disapproving comments to one another in the office about the bad manners of the children.

After school the "bus kids" went to a classroom known as the "bus room" to wait a half hour for the arrival of the bus. Every teacher was assigned to bus duty for a week at a time about once in three semesters. The children were checked in at the bus room ten minutes after the dismissal bell; and if any late comer failed to produce an excuse the teacher in charge had the right to exclude him from the bus, thus making it necessary for him to walk home. While in the bus room the children were supposed to read magazines provided for them. When the "watcher" announced that the bus was in sight, they were to file quietly out the front door and be checked in on the bus. Actually, the half hour of waiting was one of fatigue and frustration to both children and teacher, and it required a formidable disciplinarian to keep the march to the bus from becoming a rout. This early after-school departure automatically prevented the bus riders from participating in any rehearsals or social events which took place in the school after school hours.

Another cause of frustration that led to an aggressive attitude on the part of the "bus kids" was the practice of some teachers of keeping children after school as a disciplinary measure or for making up work. This practice was not intended to inflict unusual hardship on "bus children"; but worry that the teacher would forget to write an explanation of the delay, which could be taken home to appease anxious parents, drove many a "bus child" to tears and angry words.

Mr. Sanders made an appointment with the principal to discuss the problems which to him had become so important. On behalf of the "bus kids" he was concerned over these practices, which in their results were so generally contradictory to the democratic philosophy stated in the printed objectives of the school. The principal, a sincere and capable person, was quick to recognize the value of Mr. Sanders's analysis of the situation. He immediately appointed Mr. Sanders, Mrs. James, and Mr. Black to present the problem to the faculty and to suggest steps that might be taken to give the Airy View children a better chance to participate in the life of the school.

Teachers Must Help

When the problem was presented graphically with all the re-inforcing data which Mr. Sanders and his committee had gathered from their careful observation of the life of the "bus kids," the reaction of the faculty was one of amazement. Although the teachers had been aware of personal antagonisms and frustrations in some of the children from Airy View, they had never stopped to think that the school had a "minority" problem. They had complacently assumed that inter-group problems could arise only in schools that had racial, religious, or national minorities.

The problem was twofold. The faculty agreed, first, that an extensive study of inter-group relationships was needed in order that the program of the school should meet more effectively the social and emotional problems of its boys and girls; and, second, that some immediate solution of the bus problem must be worked out.

The details of the proposed study were carefully planned and carried out. A more critical approach to the question of differing American socio-economic backgrounds and their effects on school groups was seen to be necessary—an approach in this case to be based on an understanding of the ways of life represented by the children in the school. The changing pattern of the district was accepted, and it was agreed that the school program should be geared to meet the change. A reading list of books dealing with class and caste conflicts in the United States was prepared and studied in faculty group meetings. Someone suggested that

Who Shall Be Educated?[2] by Warner, Havighurst, and Loeb should be included. Another cited parts of Margaret Mead's *And Keep Your Powder Dry.*[3] The boys' adviser praised Allison Davis's chapter on "Socialization and the Adolescent Personality" in *The Forty-third Yearbook of the National Society for the Study of Education.*[4] By the time the committee started to work on gathering materials for the faculty study groups, they had received many other suggestions, which indicated that some of the teachers had already been reading and thinking about the socio-economic implications of education. The thinking of these individuals, however, needed the stimulation of working with others on common problems.

In order to analyze the practices of the school as they affected inter-group relationships, the faculty agreed to work out plans for using sociometric methods in observation of their classes. Whenever instances of isolation were discovered, whether they were the result of socio-economic discrimination or of personality maladjustment, the teachers were to call upon all available resources to make the classroom activities contribute to the acceptance and satisfactory adjustment of individuals or groups who needed help.

The application of the scientific method of analyzing problems was not easily accepted by some of the faculty, who hesitated to admit that class distinctions were such powerful social factors in the life of the people of the United States. It seemed inconsistent with the ideals of freedom and equality, as stressed in the study of American history and government, to recognize the "bus children" as "lower-class," with culture standards differing from those of other groups in the school. Factual evidence, how-

[2] *Who Shall Be Educated?* by W. Lloyd Warner, Robert J. Havighurst, and Martin B. Loeb (New York: Harper & Brothers, 1944).

[3] *And Keep Your Powder Dry*, by Margaret Mead (New York: William Morrow and Co., 1942).

[4] *Adolescence*, Nelson B. Henry, editor, Part I of the Forty-Third yearbook of the National Society for the Study of Education (Chicago: University of Chicago, 1944).

ever, was presented to show that many practices of American education tend to perpetuate class consciousness, and to hinder rather than to encourage class mobility, by putting too much stress on narrow vocational training for all children for whom college training seems a financial impossibility.

Confronted by convincing evidence, the entire faculty realized that in this instance respect for individuals—an indispensable tenet of American democracy—would become a reality in the school more quickly if the attitudes and actions of the "bus children" were analyzed in terms of their background. It was not enough, they agreed, to hold up before these children and urge them to accept behavior standards which in many cases were next to impossible for them to attain. By facing the fact that the "bus children" were different, teachers would be better able to detect and change the practices of the school which had tended to emphasize the differences between the Airy View children and other groups, thus widening the gap between them.

Before the broader aspects of the inter-group study could be considered in any thoroughgoing fashion, the faculty insisted that immediate measures be taken to improve the bus situation. The administrative details of this problem, so out of keeping with the philosophy stated by the school, had certainly not been critically analyzed. Now the faculty were chagrined to learn that Mr. Sanders, a newcomer, had seen the situation so much more clearly than they had seen it themselves.

Steps were quickly taken to make the arrival and departure of the "bus children" less difficult for all concerned. In bad weather the bus room, under the supervision of the boys' adviser, was opened in the morning as soon as the children arrived. The organization of the room after school was made less restrictive and dull. To occupy the waiting time in the bus room, a plan for pursuing a variety of hobbies with more after-school appeal than reading was worked out by the children themselves. And when, in addition, knitting, crocheting, whittling, drawing, and other activities were permitted, the children suffered less from discontent and fatigue. They even accepted cheerfully the responsibility for tidying the bus room before leaving, and they worked out their own plans for collecting the hobby materials.

Rehearsals for school programs and activities were scheduled, as much as possible, before school and during the school day so as to give the "bus children" a chance to take part. In order that they might also attend school parties and socials, efforts were made to schedule all such affairs for the last hour of the school day. When this proved impossible, the "bus children" were given the option of providing their own transportation home from after-school socials. Formerly this would have caused the child to lose his bus privileges, the argument being that a child who could pay his way occasionally could provide for himself all the time. Under the new plan any child could use other means of transportation for special occasions without losing his status as a regular bus rider.

These first steps taken to solve the bus problem seemed inadequate and superficial to a faculty growing aware of the complexity and importance of the larger problem of giving underprivileged children status and self-respect. But the self-critical faculty members could see that even these changes represented sincere gestures of good faith toward recognizing the feelings of discrimination and rejection from which the "bus children" had suffered.

Other changes affected both the school life and the home life of the children. Through faculty planning, the orientation units in Mr. Sanders's 7B class, with which the three years of junior high school began, were expanded to include more material designed to make the incoming 7B child feel himself a part of a unified group. Plans for directing group activities away from clannishness were included in the source units for teachers. Through discussions of hobbies and interests, the 7B's were to signify similar interests and common ambitions. The 7B class party was to be held early in the semester, during school time, as a get-acquainted occasion, and each home-room group was to plan mixers and games and share in the responsibility for the success of the plans. All these plans were of particular help to new teachers who had had little experience with "groups" of children.

Through a suggestion by the principal of the school to the city's health and recreation department, recreation facilities in the Airy View district were expanded in order to give the children there some of the sports and crafts experiences enjoyed by boys and girls who belonged to clubs and went to summer camps.

Instead of having large monthly Parent-Teacher Association meetings, the Fremont faculty tried the plan of reducing the number of large meetings to three a year, the rest being informal group meetings in the home rooms with the home-room teachers. Airy View parents who had felt lost in the large formal meetings seemed to feel more free in the small groups.

The home arts teachers, and others who taught something of manners and grooming, directed their emphases away from the concept of one uniform standard of good taste. They gave much consideration, instead, to the varying standards of different people and to the appropriateness of adapting dress and manners to a given situation. In dealing with desirable changes in behavior, the fundamental emphasis was placed upon greater flexibility of attitude and appreciation of, if not agreement with, others.

Relationships Improve

From these small beginnings came modifications and additions which improved the relationships of the different groups within the school. With time allotted for special activities within the day, more children had the opportunity to take part and feel that they belonged to the school. Even Pat Yates entered the boxing tournament and made a good record. The informal parent-group meetings attracted a few more mothers with each succeeding month. The most important outcome for the faculty was the increased awareness of intercultural problems and a more critical approach to democracy as preached and as practiced. With every new development of the inter-group study, the school reflected in its practices the richer understandings that were being acquired.

When the groups within the school had come to look upon each other with more acceptance, Mr. Sanders and other teachers began to see opportunities for developing a larger, more outgoing acceptance of the community and the world beyond.

Because the children in the Fremont Junior High School had had little opportunity for face-to-face relationships with young people of many backgrounds, they tended to think in stereotypes. They were convinced that their school was the best junior high school in the city and made sweeping condemnations of racial, religious, and socio-economic groups in other schools. Mr. Sanders felt that a reasonable amount of school spirit was desirable, but regarded the complacency and isolationism of the Fremont children as little short of chauvinistic. Whenever another school was mentioned, children were quick with labels which dismissed any attempts to bring about a more thoughtful understanding. They would say of one school that all the students were Negroes or Mexicans and that they constantly engaged in gang wars. Similarly, all those at another were Jews. The most derisive epithets were directed toward a junior high school situated in an exclusive residential district. Mr. Sanders's class believed that all the children of that school were waited upon by servants at home and were conveyed to school in limousines by chauffeurs. Mr. Sanders had been a supply teacher in this school before his permanent assignment to Fremont and had enjoyed his brief experience with the children there. Although a few came from homes of great wealth, the majority represented moderately well-to-do families who had no desire to pamper their children. Mr. Sanders's accounts of his first-hand experiences with the "rich kids" made little impression on his Fremont class, who cherished their prejudices as being more colorful and interesting than the facts.

The year when Mr. Sanders's students were in Grade 8B an almost perfect opportunity for a study of the junior high schools of the community presented itself. The opening wedge came in the form of a minstrel show given by a music class in assembly. The program portrayed Negroes as black-faced buffoons speaking in the thickest of inexpert Southern accents. When the class returned to their room the members evaluated the program according to custom. Usually the evaluations were brief and conveyed appreciation. Surprisingly enough, it was the Airy View children who objected strenuously to the minstrel show on the grounds that the two Negro children who rode on the bus did not "talk funny," were not coal black, and did not wear odd clothes. Trying not to push his enthusiasm too far, Mr. Sanders pointed out that many people thought of all Negroes as they were portrayed in minstrel shows, just as they thought of all Englishmen as wearing top hats and monocles and of all Italians as organ grinders. The children, amused, added other illustrations of stereotypes. Mr. Sanders brought the discussion to a point by repeating some of the statements about other schools in the community that he had heard and jotted down in his notebook. The class thought it might be a good idea to find out something about the community and defer their study of other lands until they had tested some of their prejudices about their own city.

The study assumed ambitious proportions and involved a great deal of effort for Mr. Sanders and the class. There were bus trips to other schools, conferences were held with representatives of the various junior high schools, talks were given by adult speakers representing minority groups in the community, and films on minority problems applicable to the local situation were shown. Mr. Sanders took snapshots of children in all the schools, enlarged them, and had his class guess which school each child represented. Only a few were quick to pass judgment, the majority having learned from the study that it was unwise to form hasty conclusions from insufficient evidence.

Other teachers who had felt the need for such a unit but had not seen an opportunity for introducing a study of the community's junior high schools, joined Mr. Sanders on the unit. Each new class that worked on the problem of seeing the all-city junior high school picture devised new approaches and activities. It was decided that the study should be a permanent part of the curriculum, to be used whenever the need arose for expanding points of view. An important result of the study was the expansion of the teachers' thinking about schools other than their own. The faculty, by starting with their own problems, had moved forward to a more significant and professional appreciation of the work that other schools were doing.

There was ample evidence in Mr. Sanders's class that the study had changed behavior. When it was decided that a study should be made of other countries and their people, the children vetoed the "quaint costume" approach and demanded realistic, up-to-date information. It was agreed that Europe and Asia should be studied first and that these studies should be followed by a unit on Latin America. When the unit on Latin America was worked out, there was no opposition to starting with the Spanish-speaking group in the local community, then taking up those in the state and the region, before moving on to more remote Latin-American problems.

Although the children found new implications from day to day and participated enthusiastically, the course of procedure was not smooth. During the inter-school study, and later in the Europe-Asia unit, Mr. Sanders was more than once opposed by parents representing the "America for Americans" type of organization. The complaint of these parents was that foreign ways were being presented too favorably. They especially resented the attitudes of acceptance being built up toward such groups as the Japanese-Americans and the Italian-Americans in the city. A few parents were fearful about having their children make first-hand contacts with minority groups. Some familiar charges of "un-Americanism" were heard whenever a new or critical approach to American culture was attempted.

These experiences sometimes made Mr. Sanders wish that he had limited his teaching to ancient history or to college courses in calculus. The discouragements and setbacks, however, were outweighed by the enthusiastic support of other parent groups who had met and talked over the study in all its stages, who understood what Mr. Sanders and the others were trying to do, and who opposed attacks from uninformed pressure groups. The most satisfying reward of all was in watching all the children of the school learning to work together in solving problems so meaningful and challenging that the differences in the Fremont student body were forgotten.

The faculty members who not long before had failed to see certain problems that were right in their midst were now reaching out to make themselves and their classes aware of the problems of people everywhere. Through recognition of the inter-group problem in the school, these teachers had become more sensitive to the tensions and conflicts beneath the surface of many human relationships.

As Mr. Sanders walked down the steps to go home on the last day of school, the children were being checked in on the bus— by a student, not by a teacher. They waved and called out wishes for a good summer. He had a jumbled impression of plaid shirts and chewing gum, giggling and chatter, as the bus rolled away from the school toward the Airy View section of the city. "There must be more placid ways of earning a living than that of teaching in a junior high school," thought Mr. Sanders, but those placid ways were not for him. Already he was looking forward to the workshop in intercultural relations, where this summer he hoped to supplement his enthusiastic if not always successful struggle with group problems by discussion and work with experienced leaders who could give him fresh resources and ideas. And then? Mr. Sanders did not much care. He knew from experience that new problems would turn up in September. Why worry on the last day of school in June?

"One World" Microcosm

Jane Horton, a teacher of social studies and sponsor of the student council at the Longfellow Junior High School, was waiting in the office for the arrival of a delegation of sixth-grade children from the three elementary schools which contributed to Longfellow Junior High. The children were representing the student councils of their schools in a joint meeting with the student council at Longfellow. Miss Horton was not really anxious, but she would be glad when the children arrived and the meeting was under way. The elementary school children had been invited by the Longfellow Student Council to discuss ways in which all the young people of the district could work together for a safe and sane Halloween.

Story of a Failure

This was not the first time such a project had been tried. The previous year, when the All-City Student Council had originated the idea, the Longfellow faculty had been hopeful of its success even in their school district, where delinquency rates were officially the highest in the city. But the project had not succeeded in the Longfellow district, though other school districts in the town had come through extremely well, with property destruction by young marauders cut by 80 per cent according to police figures. In the Longfellow district, notorious for youthful gangs who seemed unable to distinguish vandalism from heroism, Halloween disturbances had persisted in their usual number and destructiveness.

Thinking back now to that dismal failure, Miss Horton could see that it had been plainly foreshadowed. She recalled the meeting of parents which had been held to talk over plans for the Halloween project. Only a handful had shown up in answer to letters sent out by the Parent-Teacher Association. Equally ineffective, and even more discouraging, had been the Longfellow Student Council meeting at which the project was discussed. The Halloween situation was one which the boys and girls felt unable to meet.

In spite of these discouragements Miss Horton had had no intention of giving up. Perhaps, she had admitted to herself, she could not immediately arouse the boys and girls of Longfellow to a sense of responsibility for co-operating with the All-City Student Council. But she had held fast to the belief that, if the children of the Longfellow School could actually experience the satisfaction of working successfully with other children of their district on such a project as the Halloween campaign, co-operation with children everywhere in the city might ultimately develop.

Testing Ground of Democracy

Jane Horton's job was not an easy one. The hours were long, the teaching load was heavy, and she worried over the economic and social struggles that were evident everywhere in the community. Nevertheless, after five years there, she was still glad that she taught in the Longfellow district. There were perhaps few places in which she could come to know so well and evaluate so truly the different contributions of the various racial and cultural groups that make up the United States of America.

Many of the families served by the school were in the marginal group which is the first to suffer from unemployment, depressions, or rising prices. With respect to racial and cultural origins, the people of the district were certainly heterogeneous. One section was occupied by a stable and generally self-supporting Negro population. Now a rapidly growing influx of Spanish-speaking families was pushing the Negroes against the eastern boundaries of their section, fixed through restrictive covenants. The economic status of these newcomers was generally lower than that of the Negroes, and, since their need for inexpensive housing had not been met, 85 per cent of them lived under substandard conditions. The war had raised the income level of the population, but living conditions were scarcely improved. The arrival of several thousand Japanese people from the West Coast increased the strain on housing facilities. The population changes had been reflected in the enrollment pattern of Longfellow Junior High; when the present school year began the students were approximately 30 per cent Negro, 25 per cent Spanish-speaking, 5 per cent Japanese, and 40 per cent Anglo-American. Included in the last 40 per cent were not only children of native-born Anglos[5] but also the children of Poles, Volga Germans, Russian Jews, and people from the Scandinavian countries.

In recent years the flood of books about racial and cultural minorities and about the need for "one world" had helped Jane Horton to become increasingly aware of the fact that the Longfellow Junior High School and its community were really a testing ground of the democratic ideal. Democracy had always seemed to her to mean respect for individual personality and the opportunity for all those concerned to share in the solution of common problems. She felt, too, that another right and obligation of people in a democratic society was to think together about what they were doing. Just accepting tradition was not enough; if the uncritical life is not worth living for the individual, it surely is not for a community.

These ideals were shared by other members of the school staff. Miss Horton particularly liked the attitude of Peter Arnold, the principal. His capacity for liking people seemed infinite. His kindness marked him as a valued leader in such a community, where people were frequently on the alert for slights and injustices. His strength and courage were good to see, but to Miss Horton his most important characteristic as a principal was his generous spirit. It was not enough for him that the law required children of all races and creeds to come to school; he felt that the school needed to make it worth their while to come. In the few years during which he had served as principal, he had awakened in the community a sense of his concern for all the boys and girls of

[5] This term is used in the Southwest by Spanish-speaking people to designate all English-speaking Americans.

the school and of his interest in all the parents—no matter what their race or creed or economic status. Mr. Arnold was clearly an artist in the field of human relationships, one who dealt successfully with all kinds of children—the shy and submissive, the hardened and arrogant, and the potential leaders of men.

The failure of the first Halloween program had offered a direct challenge to Mr. Arnold and his staff. They had felt that the most serious aspect of the failure lay in its implications of irresponsibility in both the school and the community. When the failure was made public and attention was called to the sad contrast between the destructive behavior of the Longfellow boys and girls and the improvement in other districts, the various groups in the Longfellow population had been quick to disclaim responsibility. Parents were inclined to blame the children of every cultural and racial group except their own. "It was the Negro children!" "It was the gangs of Mexicans!" "It was the Anglos—and then they try to blame it on us!" The larger community had said, "What can you expect from those children?"

A New Campaign

Intent upon building for future success, Mr. Arnold, instead of being disheartened by this situation, had used it as the starting point of a new campaign. Here, he saw, was an opportunity to get at some significant facts and make them known to the community. Accordingly he called together a committee of parents and teachers and invited a representative of the Juvenile Court to discuss with them the Halloween disturbances in the neighborhood and the general background of the boys and girls involved. The court referee revealed that among the young vandals had been members of every major racial or cultural group in the district except the Japanese-Americans. Anglos, Negroes, Spanish-speaking—all had been involved. Children as young as eight years, young people of high school age, and children of all the ages in between had participated in the destruction of property.

Here, indeed, was food for thought! When these facts, presented by a reliable and impartial witness, had been faced, the conclusion was inevitable—the problem was one for the district as a whole, not one for any specific group. It might be difficult to act upon this conclusion, but any other attack offered little hope of success.

It was Miss Horton who suggested to the faculty members who with her sponsored the student council that the elementary schools should send representatives to an inter-school planning session. In other parts of the city no attempt was made to bring the younger children into planning meetings at the junior high schools. But Miss Horton felt that the time for closer association among children in the schools of this community was long overdue. Recently she had been talking with one of the teachers at the Jefferson School who had said that, in studying ways in which the faculty might make the transition of children to Longfellow a happier experience, the faculty had discovered that the Negro children were afraid that as soon as they reached Longfellow they would be "beaten up" by the Anglo children from Whitman.

When Miss Horton discussed this problem with Mr. Arnold, he talked immediately with the principal of Whitman. Careful investigation by teachers unearthed the information that the children of Whitman were also afraid. Fears of going to a new school where for the first time they would meet comparatively large numbers of Negro children were easily elaborated into the anticipation of being "beaten up" themselves. These ideas on the part of the Whitman children undoubtedly sprang first from dread of the unknown, but chiefly from the cautioning of adults and older children in their community against any close association with children of "inferior" origins. Inquiry at the Tabor School revealed the same dread of the Anglo children at Longfellow. The friendly atmosphere of the Tabor School, where the Spanish-speaking children had largely overcome their social insecurities and gained a sense of achievement in reading and writing English, was in sharp contrast with what they expected in the large, crowded junior high school. Fears of being lost, fears of academic failure, fears of being hurt psychologically as well as physically by the dominant Anglo group—all these contributed to the dread with which the children looked forward to the next important step in their growing up.

The more Miss Horton and her committee talked this matter over, the more thoroughly they became convinced that the simplest and best way to help these fear-ridden children gain confidence in themselves and trust in others would be to set up a program of intervisitation and co-operative endeavor. The Halloween campaign seemed to offer an immediate opportunity to introduce such a program.

A Plan Is Born

"Here they come!" The news spread even into the social room across the hall from the office. In another minute Miss Horton was welcoming the representatives from the student council of the Jefferson School and their teacher sponsor. Two Negro boys, a Negro girl, an Anglo girl, and a Japanese-American boy made up the committee. They came from a school which had a Negro population of about 90 per cent. From the Tabor School, where the Spanish-speaking children constituted 80 per cent of the enrollment, there were three Spanish-speaking youngsters, one Anglo, and one Japanese-American. From Whitman, where the population was predominantly Anglo, there were five Anglos— two boys and three girls.

The courtesy committee of the Longfellow Student Council saw to it that the visiting children and their teacher sponsors were seated in a circle which extended clear to the edge of the social room. Only a small alcove, where a table was gaily set in Halloween colors for the serving of cookies and punch after the meeting, lay outside the circle.

Miss Horton could see that the visitors relaxed perceptibly as they looked around and recognized two Negro boys, one Negro girl, one Japanese-American girl, and two Spanish-speaking boys among the dozen members of the Longfellow council. How fortunate, she thought, that democratic election of leaders had produced on the council a good cross section of the school population!

The boy and girl presidents of the Longfellow Student Council opened the meeting with a report of the plans that were being developed by the All-City Student Council. They spoke from notes which they had taken at an All-City Council meeting the week before. There, as representatives from Longfellow, they had met boys and girls who had come from the seven other junior high schools and the four senior high schools in the town. All-City Council committees, on which representatives from both junior and senior high schools served, were being set up. One committee was to ask the city newspapers and the tramway company for publicity, another was to interview the police and fire departments, and still another was to ask the Radio Council for help in getting spot announcements on the local radio stations. A fourth committee was to request the Council of Churches to interest as many churches as possible in providing entertainment for their young people on Halloween.

The publicity for the campaign in each school district was to be the individual responsibility of the local school. The All-City Council, however, suggested that each of the senior high schools set up a speakers' bureau on which the junior high schools could call for assistance. The junior high schools, in turn, would train speakers and make them available to the elementary schools.

At this point in the report the Longfellow Council turned to the elementary school representatives. What did they think of this proposal? Was it a good idea? Would Longfellow speakers be welcome at Jefferson and Whitman and Tabor? What did the elementary school representatives think of having the Longfellow Dramatic Club prepare some skits to be given in each elementary school auditorium?

Brought into the discussion by this direct appeal to their judgment, the elementary school representatives forgot their shyness in the presence of their elders and soon began to talk freely. Their opinion had been asked. They were being given a chance to share in an impressively big undertaking which by junior and senior high students and by adults was held to be valuable. Certainly, they said, the Longfellow speakers and actors would be welcome on elementary school programs, but why couldn't the elementary school children themselves prepare skits to be given at Longfellow? What an excitement that would be!

By now the representatives from Jefferson were talking eagerly with those from Whitman, each group having entirely forgotten, for the moment at least, the reputation of the other for dangerous behavior. The circle of children and teachers, busily engaged in working out a civic project together, seemed to Miss Horton to symbolize the special brand of democratic human relations she so eagerly desired for all. In the eager fellowship which grew as the plans progressed, she rejoiced to see the end of an old era and the beginning of a new.

Co-operation Works

The later outcomes of the co-operative planning justified Miss Horton's faith. The talks and skits given by the Longfellow children at Jefferson, Tabor, and Whitman were a success. But even more delightful were the programs which the younger children brought to Longfellow. How they enjoyed the great stage, the auditorium full of enthusiastic teen-agers, the mysterious halls, and the promise of what life would be like when they had inherited all this for themselves in the next few years!

In the meantime, the parents of the children were by no means being left out of these new and exciting plans for a safe, sane, and happy Halloween. Their interest, stirred months before when they had listened to the revealing testimony given by the Juvenile Court representative, received a new impetus when they heard about the stimulating meeting at the Longfellow School. This time, when the Parent-Teacher Association sent out notices that a discussion of the Halloween project was to be held, an extraordinary representation of the mothers and fathers in the district responded.

No need to rehearse the tale of depredations on past Halloweens. The parents remembered all too well the broken fences, the spouting fire hydrants and the false fire alarms, the stolen gates, wrecked porch furniture, cut garden hose, punctured tires, soap-smeared windows, and all the rest of the vandal deeds. There was unanimous agreement that it was useless to suggest that the boys and girls of the community give up the excitement of terrorizing the neighborhood unless something more appealing were provided in its place.

Therefore the mothers and fathers in many parts of the district planned block parties for Halloween. Some parents worked with their churches to provide worth-while celebrations of the holiday evening. The teachers at the Longfellow School saw to it that there was an ample supply of games and fun books on the school library shelves, and they helped the children to discover in these books new ways of decorating their homes or churches or of entertaining their guests.

All during the month of the campaign the children at the Longfellow School followed the articles in the city newspapers with the greatest interest. They helped write radio scripts to be submitted to the Radio Council for production. Some of them were chosen by the council to be actors before the microphone. They prepared posters and signs of all kinds to remind the students of the need for conserving scarce materials and even scarcer labor through the abolition of vandalism; one of the posters from Longfellow was chosen to be reproduced for the tramway cards. They put unusual enthusiasm into the preparations for the annual Halloween party at the school in the afternoon and enjoyed it to the utmost when at last it took place. Everyone at Longfellow came to the party—teachers and pupils, all races, all creeds, all colors—eating, dancing, singing, and playing games together.

The following morning, when Miss Horton opened her newspaper, she read that not one school child in the Longfellow district had been involved in any vandalism. When she reached the school the children were already beginning to go into the auditorium to hear their principal, Mr. Arnold, announce officially what they already knew—that the Halloween campaign had been a success. Everywhere there was a sense of good will combined with justifiable pride. The co-operative program had worked. The months of thoughtful planning, plus the unstinted efforts during the campaign period, had brought forth good fruit.

Further Problems

Nor was this the end of the program. At a faculty meeting the next Wednesday afternoon Mr. Arnold remarked on how effective had been this attempt to solve one immediate problem of school and community by the teachers and parents putting their minds and hearts into it and by giving the children a real share in the planning. Would it be possible, he wondered, to continue in this same way, by these same means, to solve other problems in the school and community?

The faculty believed it not only possible but also highly desirable. They said so emphatically and forthwith began to map out a comprehensive survey of the community to identify the problems on which the school could work with the community to the greatest advantage. Thus it was that a project designed to prevent youthful vandalism on Halloween started a movement for community self-appraisal which in time led to a study of housing conditions in the district, a survey of recreational facilities available to children and to adults, a study of the activities of welfare agencies working in the community, a careful analysis of proposed health improvements for the district, and a summarized report of the employment status of the mothers and fathers of the children in the school. Longfellow School faculty meetings, while these studies were in progress, were devoted to reports of findings and to their interpretation by men and women from the community who were experts in the fields of housing, health, recreation, and employment.

A study of the characteristics and special problems of the various racial and cultural groups living in the district occupied the attention of another faculty committee. At the suggestion of this committee an anthropologist was brought in to talk with the faculty about the latest scientific information concerning race, with special emphasis on physical and psychological differences and likenesses. This scientist presented important facts about the intellectual capacities of racial groups—facts that controverted the common belief that race is a determining factor in mental superiority and inferiority. An objective analysis pointed up many determining factors in the physical, mental, and emotional environments in which children grow up.

Stimulated by their work as members of study groups, the Longfellow faculty began to build up a library of their own. Materials relating to the local situation were obtained from certain civic organizations; for example, the Bureau of Public Affairs contributed a study of the Japanese people, the town's intercultural council supplied a study of the Spanish-speaking people, and an illuminating study of the Negro people came from the local chapter of the Urban League. To give perspective to their thinking the faculty obtained such books as Gunnar Myrdal's *An American Dilemma*,[6] Bruno Lasker's *Race Attitudes in Children*;[7] Louis Adamic's *A Nation of Nations*,[8] Otto Klineberg's *Race Differences*;[9] Robert L. Sutherland's *Color, Class and Personality*;[10]

---

[6] *An American Dilemma*, by Gunnar Myrdal (New York: Harper & Brothers, 1944).

[7] *Race Attitudes in Children*, by Bruno Lasker (New York: Henry Holt & Co., 1929).

[8] *A Nation of Nations*, by Louis Adamic (New York: Harper & Brothers, 1945).

[9] *Race Differences*, by Otto Klineberg (New York: Harper & Brothers, 1935).

[10] *Color, Class and Personality*, by Robert L. Sutherland (Washington: American Youth Commission of the American Council on Education, 1942).

and Allison Davis and John Dollard's *Children of Bondage*.[11] These books were supplemented by subscriptions to such periodicals as *Intercultural Education News*, *American Unity*, and *Common Ground*.

New Attitudes Develop

It was inevitable that all this reading and discussion should produce new attitudes among many members of the teaching staff. Some of them even began to question the effectiveness of their school program in meeting the real needs of the boys and girls of the community. These teachers looked, as though for the first time, at the inadequate provisions made for vocational adjustment of some of the ninth-graders for whom the junior high school was to be the end of formal schooling. They saw how inappropriate for the children of the Longfellow School were many of the electives in the ninth grade. Formalized and verbalized quite beyond the experiences of junior high school children, these subjects had become proving grounds for intellectual acrobatics instead of resources for improving day-by-day living in the community.

From this point on the teachers began a conscious search for new ways of relating the curriculum to the personal and social needs of the boys and girls. They wanted to help these young people achieve a better understanding of their own and other racial and cultural groups. They wanted the children to know the great documents of freedom, not as they were presented in their eighth grade American history course, not as dead records of the past, but as living articles of faith upon which these young people could base their own present and future behavior; they wanted the children to realize that the duties of freedom are inseparable from the struggle for human rights. They wanted the school to make a difference in the way the children lived with other people, shared family responsibilities, earned and spent money, and chose their recreational activities. They wanted the school to help the

[11] *Children of Bondage*, by Allison Davis and John Dollard (Washington: American Youth Commission of the American Council on Education, 1940).

children find their place in their own social order; learn something about labor-management relations, labor unions, and the co-operative movement; and discover immediate opportunities for participation in the improvement of their own community. In short, these teachers wanted the school to help young people to develop their ideas about what is important in life and to translate these ideas into action.

Now that their creative imaginations were so busily at work, the teachers at the Longfellow School began to understand more fully the possibilities inherent in their core curriculum, which enabled a teacher to work with a group of children for a daily period longer than the usual forty-five minutes and to stay with them as their teacher and counselor throughout their three years in the junior high school. This organization of the work, which at first had seemed to some of the faculty simply an administrative imposition, now began to be seen in its true light as the instrument by which the school could develop a functional curriculum.

The School Becomes Part of the Community

Some of the parents who were accustomed to coming to the school, and others who had come for the first time to co-operate in the Halloween campaign, heard of the new interests growing at Longfellow and asked for the privilege of sharing in the faculty discussions. So pleased were they by the new insights into the problems of their community which the discussions gave them that they persuaded the officers of the Parent-Teacher Association to plan for a series of parent-teacher study meetings which would be open to all parents and would be aimed at clarifying issues of prejudice, race, and race relations. They wished especially to have parents and teachers, thinking together, identify the responsibilities of the minority and majority groups in building a better life for the school and its district.

Study, discussion, and plans of action made the year following the second Halloween campaign one of tremendous stimulation to the faculty. Jane Horton had supposed that nothing could delight her more than the success of that campaign. But now the broadening of interests and understanding which she was gaining through participation in a study by the whole faculty brought her a greater and much deeper joy. She counted as one of the really memorable occasions of that school year the afternoon when she sat in a discussion group of parents and teachers who were considering the nature of prejudice, its tragic effect on human relations, and how it can be controlled. Twelve months earlier such an open, frank discussion of this subject could not have been held by this group. But the cumulative effect of the shared activities and studies of the year just past had made a tremendous difference. Now every member of the study group was willing to try to discover his own bias and to recognize the fact that, although almost everyone indulges in prejudice, it can be reduced by honest thinking.

As Jane Horton considered the way in which this school year was progressing, it seemed to her that if one wants satisfaction in life—and who doesn't?—there is no better way to find it than by sharing in the solution of fundamentally important problems.

CHAPTER VI

GANGS[1]

The adolescent boy who drifts away from school and hangs out on a street corner with his buddies offers a direct challenge to those concerned with fostering better group relations—such a person often displays aggressive attitudes and behavior toward members of different groups. This chapter presents examples of this type of boy and investigates the reasons for his "delinquent" acts. The leadership qualities needed to redirect youthful energies into socially acceptable channels are listed, and promising endeavors in this field are described.

Why Boys Leave School

"My name is Anthony. My mother took me to three high schools before we found one that would accept me with my bad marks and truancy record. The third one took me but said I would probably not last there either. I stayed ten days, not long enough to learn much except where the typewriting room was located. Frank and me and some of the boys went back one night and grabbed a few of the typewriters. We knew a 'fence' who took them off us at twenty-five bucks apiece. That's when I really had money."

[1] The basic draft of this chapter was prepared by CHARLES E. HENDRY, School of Social Work, University of Toronto; the final draft was written by RUSSELL HOGREFE, Commission on Community Interrelations of the American Jewish Congress, out of whose experiences grew the material on a day in the life of a gang; the section on a year with a street-corner club and "A Constructive Program" were contributed by EDWARD HAYDON, Commission on Community Interrelations of the American Jewish Congress.

151

Many persons would respond to this authentic account by saying, "Nothing can be done with a boy like that—bad home conditions make boys like that impossible for the school to educate—this is a case for the courts, not for the teacher."

Why didn't Anthony stay in school? He says he had no trouble with school work but just could not stay interested in it. He had few traditional handicaps to success as a student. He reads rapidly with good comprehension and writes easily and well. In fact, when he thought he was to be sentenced to at least three years in prison he bought a new-type fountain pen which would write that long without refilling, as he planned to write a lengthy daily account of his experiences.

The meaninglessness of his school courses helps to explain Anthony's delinquency. So does his inability to find an adult friend among his teachers. This lack became especially important at a time when he was making his first emancipation steps away from his parents. He mentions his interest in chemistry but says nothing about the chemistry teacher. Maybe no one in the school could have got next to him; however, from personal acquaintance with Anthony, one of the writers of the present chapter can attest to how quickly he wins the friendship and respect of adults.

Anthony is a member of a street gang; Frank, who helped Anthony steal the typewriters, is also an experienced member who has been out of school for several years. In gang life he is several stages beyond Anthony. The following is another authentic observed happening, involving Frank.

One of the gang's favorite "hang-outs" is an all-night cafeteria. Frank is having coffee with his friends. He is a slender, almost sickly-looking boy. His face seems slightly flushed tonight, probably from drinking. Suddenly he leaves and someone says, "There goes Frank again." Everyone walks excitedly out in front of the restaurant. About sixty feet away Frank halts an elderly Negro whom he has seen pass the restaurant. As the Negro turns questioningly, Frank swings a long sweeping punch followed by two others. The Negro falls limply; Frank kicks his head viciously several times and walks away. No one moves for a few moments; then someone says, "What the hell, just another Jig." Everyone files back into the restaurant. There are several admiring comments about the nice punches. Several young men walk to the back of the restaurant to guard the telephone so that no one can call the police. Everyone resumes eating and talking.

In a few minutes Frank returns, accompanied by several admiring youths about his age. He glows with the recognition of open admiration and silent disapproval which he sees about him. He makes much of the congratulatory handshakes he receives at several tables, then returns to his table to finish his cake and coffee.

How about Frank's educational experience? He finished all but the last six months of high school. Apparently his motive for leaving school was simply that he had no motive for staying.

He enlisted in the navy during the war. When, as he says, the navy stuck him on the good ship Never Sail, he overstayed his leave. The guardhouse and solitary confinement convinced him he should get out. By studying in the library he acquired enough psychological knowledge to get an honorable medical discharge, or so he says.

While this boy has serious emotional problems, lack of intelligence is obviously not a factor. In contacts outside his immediate circle he is friendly but not aggressive or forward.

It is not enough to realize that the home, the church, the school, or any other institution has failed to help boys like Anthony and Frank understand and solve the problems involved in growing up. It is also necessary to know what positive attractions a gang offers to an individual. The behavior patterns of these two boys take on new significance when they are viewed as elements in a group situation rather than as isolated bits of individual "delinquency." Anthony had accomplices available in his gang when he wanted to steal typewriters; Frank had the approval of his gang for assaulting a Negro, and its members were at hand in case support was needed.

Youth groups which are self-organized are a common feature

in American life. Most such groups never become a problem for society. Many of them contain racial and ethnic mixtures to begin with, and a good relationship in the group evolves naturally.

One form of autonomous youth group, the street gang, frequently does not attain harmonious relationships with persons outside its immediate circle. Such gangs are a source of security to their members and reach their greatest strength in communities where unfavorable social and economic conditions make the need for security greatest. In the gang the members find support and protection and, not infrequently, a means of striking back at a society which they have consciously or subconsciously come to regard as hostile and unfair.

Studies of the nature and cause of prejudice and inter-group conflict have indicated that individual and group feelings of insecurity often underlie the clashes and tensions getween groups. It is not surprising, therefore, that the gang, built to provide security for the insecure, should be an important factor in many situations of inter-group conflict.

In many cases participation as a member or leader of a street gang is preferred to any other influence which touches the life of the individual. The gang then is meeting more of the individual's psychological needs than is any other influence. It may offer the only status, recognition, affection, friendships, and understanding to be had. These needs, however intangible they may appear, are apparently potent; often they are more important to the youth than a supply of physical goods. Food loses its taste amid bickering about being lazy. Even when shelter, food, and clothing are used by parents as a last resort to maintaining control, this too can often be escaped. Cases can be cited of young people who have come into a neighborhood where they had friends and lived for months completely independent of their parents. During this time they were given food, shelter, and clothing, "mooched" some more, stole a little, and worked even less.

Life, especially for youth, must have some sparkle. Few legitimate experiences offer them enough excitement; illegitimate

ones too often do much better. When a boy can have his excitement and some of the means for maintaining his relationships
with those most necessary to him, the combination is hard to
beat. Money from an exciting experience, such as stealing typewriters, makes it possible to be a good sport with the boys. It
eliminates the necessity of going home to meals to hear complaints
about not going to work. It makes it possible to buy clothes which
help him resemble those people he wishes to look like.

Yet educators need not despair of the possibilities of making
school life an exciting competitor to gang life. While a street gang
provides its moments of excitement, as a whole it is a drab existence. Perhaps the difference in the youth's status and recognition helps explain the accepted drabness of the street corner in
contrast to the rejected drabness of going to school. The following account is based on association with a gang for a period of
two years. It is not a record of any particular day, but rather a
synthesis of the kinds of activities that might make up a "typical"
or "average" day. The story is told from the viewpoint of a member of the gang.

7 A.M.

It's a swell day. Wonder if any of the gang are around yet.
Hey, there's Sam and Georgie coming out of the subway; they
sure look like they're still asleep. "Where you guys been?"
"Aw, we slept on the train last night. We started to sleep in a car
but a cop chased us, so we ended up on the train."

We're heading for the candy store now (that's our hangout).
We pass a car, and Sam says, "A couple guys started to sleep in
that car last night. Let's see if they're still there." We look, and
there they are, one on the front seat and one in the back. I give
them a couple of pokes, but they just grunt and curse and turn
over, so we leave them there.

Here comes three more of the boys down the street. They're
working on the docks this week, unloading ships.

Between a quarter and a half of our gang work. Most of us

quit high school in our second or third year and were supposed
to go to work. Our parents think this is a good idea, because
when they were our age they had already been working for
several years. You can't quit school unless you have a regular
job, so we get someone we know to give us a temporary job
and sign our working papers.

10 A.M.

We've had some coffee and walked around the neighborhood, and now we've been sitting on the newspaper box by the
candy store for a while. Some of the younger kids are starting
to show up now. Pretty soon we get into a real bull session.
We're talking about a fight we had three or four nights ago.
We do a lot of fighting, you know. We fight mostly with
strangers—Jigs, Jews, service men, or anybody—usually because
of insults. We're not fussy about what the odds are for or
against us when we fight. We don't worry about the rules, either. We throw punches, kick, use clubs, bats, and bottles, anything that's handy. We spend a lot more time talking about our
fights than we actually do fighting; sometimes we go back several months to hash over a specially good fight.

Right now two of the younger kinds are really going to
town. They're telling us how tough they are, and what they did
in this fight and that fight, and that they're not afraid of anyone; they keep saying that over and over. Several months ago
we wouldn't have anything to do with these young guys because they were just kids. Then we finally let them hang around
with us a little bit, and now they're with us almost all the time.
They're all right, but sometimes we have to put them in their
place. If one of these kids gets out of line a couple of us older
fellows will gang up on him, just to show that we're still boss.

12:30 P.M.

I'm getting hungry, so some of the boys have come with me
to this little restaurant to have coffee. It's time for lunch, but if

I go home my mother is going to kick like hell because I haven't got a job.

A bum just walked in. Frank knew him from before and shook hands with him, squeezing his hand real hard, and, of course, the old guy couldn't take it. We've been kidding the old guy and teasing him. We sometimes throw him a little money when he "touches" us for something to eat.

We've been here in the restaurant now for about an hour and the guy who owns the place is starting to give us some hints so I think we'll go back over by the candy store and see who's there.

2:00 P.M.

We just got back to the candy store. One of the boys found an old table top, so we got some boxes and we are all set to play cards. One of the boys just got a deck of cards; some of us are playing, the rest are looking on.

3:30 P.M.

"Hewer cewum thwa bewalls." Oh, that's right, you don't understand the way we talk. Joey just said, "Here come the bulls." We're going to keep on playing, we don't see nothing wrong with it. They play poker over in the station house all the time, but they never let us do anything like that around here. Yep, the car's stopping all right, and that son of a b— Sullivan, who knocked Frank around with a billy club a while back for no reason at all, tells us we gotta break it up. We explain we aren't doing anything but playing cards. We're not bothering anybody. He tells us toughlike that it doesn't matter, we gotta break it up anyway. As we start walking away, he tells us he doesn't want to see us around here when he comes back. We stop at the corner and stand there talking and by God they pull up and say, "I thought we told you guys to get moving." So we turn around and start walking again.

The law is out of sight now, so we start drifting back toward the candy store. Hell, we havta have some place to hang out. Where else have we got to go? We are all back now, but the guys are afraid to play cards, so we start fooling around. Some of us figure that kid Ralphie put on a big deal act in the bull session this morning, so Frank and I are gonna back him into the hallway and punch the hell out of him. We aren't gonna hurt him but we'll give him a good hint that he's not a big shot.

Boy, that was some workout. Now Jumbo, who's a little bit older and a heck of a lot bigger than Ralphie, tells us he'll take any four or five guys on. He's got a club about four feet long and he's swinging it around his head so we can't get close to him. We'll wait for a while and then we'll catch up with him, though, you wait and see.

If we keep on fooling around this way (we just threw a garbage can at Kid Ralphie and made a lot of noise), the neighbors will be calling the law and we'll be getting chased again.

5:00 P.M.

Willie just came along. He's been painting with his brother. He tells us how his brother gets these painting jobs and then how little work it is to make a lot of money. Then to make it real good he says there's a couple of nice girls in the house they're working on now.

It's funny how the guys who work always feel that they gotta come back and tell us how easy their job is and the big money that they make. Actually, I know Willie makes about $25 or $30 a week, and a lot of times he has to break his hump to keep the job because his brother's wise to him.

The guys that work on the docks just came along, and to hear them talk, they slept all day. I worked on the docks too. I know once in a while you can cut out and sleep for a couple of hours but sooner or later you gotta make up for it. On my last job we had a nice guy for a snapper, but his boss started raising hell because we weren't getting much done. I was sleeping in a lifeboat. The snapper looked in and the boss was right behind him so he had to fire me.

7:30 P.M.

Most of the boys are back here at the candy store. Buddy and Big Ralphie and JoJo are going to a dance with their girls. Kid Ralphie and Riff are going to the movies. The rest of us are just going to hang around.

I'd like to go dancing or go to the movies too, but when you're beat there's not much you can do about it. Kid Ralphie and Riff offered to pay my way to the movies, but of course I wouldn't go with them. I'd feel obligated to them and they're just kids. The rest of the guys in the gang'd think I was brown-nosing just so I could go to the movies. JoJo offered to pay my way to the dance, but I haven't got a girl right now, and any-way JoJo's given me a lot of money since I been out of work. Course, I do the same for him when he's out of a job or is broke, but you can't go on taking money off of your friends forever.

A couple of the boys who work on the docks got paid, so they are playing open-faced poker with an older guy here in the neighborhood for two bits a hand. By Sunday night they'll be broke. But that's the way it is when you work, it comes and goes pretty fast, and anyway money isn't important unless you can do what you want to with it and treat your friends right.

Jinx, the king of the bums, just came by and one of the boys gave him a dime and he sang a song and did a dance for us. Larry just gave the old man a rap because he thought he got a snotty answer to some teasing we were giving the old man. Larry is too handy with his hands. The old guy's just a bum, but he's an old man and you gotta have a little respect for him. Larry always wants to be sure the boys know he's a tough guy. Personally, I think he's afraid of some of the boys or he wouldn't put on such a big deal act to impress them.

Milly's coming up the street, she's a good kid but we like to tease her. We just gave Jinx another dime and told him to tip his hat to her and give her a fast line about her going out with him. She just walked by him like he wasn't there. She made some wise crack to us about our instigating.

A couple of boys got money so we had a soda. Kid Ralphie's brother sneaked some cookies off the counter and tossed them to one of the boys sitting at the booth. It's kinda fun to fool around because it's just like a game to see if you can keep from getting caught. We don't like Harry, the candy store guy, too well; he's a Jew and you know how they are. He bitches about our hanging around all the time. But when it's chilly outside, it's nice to stay indoors where it's warm. We don't steal too much on him.

Harry just caught one of us tossing something back to the guys in the booth and he put up a big holler about it. We gave him all the stuff back except a couple of packages and then he chased us out of the store, so we're back out on the sidewalk again.

8:30 P.M.

One of the boys just robbed a ball from the dime store and started a little baseball game in front of the tailor shop where the light is good on the sidewalk. You take a couple of sidewalk squares and bounce the ball back and forth and score just like in baseball. Sometimes people crab about us taking up the whole sidewalk, but we gotta have something to do and that doesn't hurt anybody.

Three or four of the boys are over on the newspaper box talking about girls. Sammy just told the boys that if a girl's been laid, there's no reason why anybody that knows about it shouldn't try to do the same thing, and if she puts up a kick, you give her a smack in the mouth, and she'll probably lay for you too. Sometimes that doesn't seem right to me, but that's what all the boys say. You know sometimes a bunch of us run across a broad who's out to have a good time and we all take a crack at her. Getting in a line-up like that isn't much fun, but it's better than nothing. If you haven't got the dough to take girls out, why you don't have much chance otherwise. The younger guys don't have the guts to make a deal with a broad so they let the guys with a fast line do the talking and then they just get in line. You can get in a hell of a jam with the law if they ever catch you, but the girls almost never holler. Some of 'em like it and others figure it won't do any good to holler, and if they did they'd embarrass themselves and their family anyway.

The squad car just pulled around the corner and I'll bet they stop here and give us the chase. I wonder if Harry called them because he figured we robbed some cookies or maybe that girl that went bouncing by called them because one of the boys made a fast remark. Yep, yep, they're gonna stop all right. Oh, it's all right though. Chippie is a hell of a nice cop. He probably was a knock-around guy just like us when he was a kid. He just told us to move, and kinda grinned and said something about they got a complaint at the station house about us. We're all taking a walk. But there's no place to walk to. In about 15 minutes we'll be back by the candy store again.

9:30 P.M.

Say, that sounds like music. Oh, yeah, this is Friday night. Jerry's gin mill has dancing every week end. He's got a speaker hung outdoors to attract the customers. I think I'll take a walk down there. There's Milly, Rosena, and Fay standing over there. There are three Jigs in this band who really know how to play jump music. The trumpet player is especially good. We know the guys in the orchestra personally because they always come out here on the sidewalk during intermissions and a lot of times we stand and talk to them. They're nice guys. They're really hep. I sure like to listen to that fine jive talk. A couple of times when we've had a bottle, we gave a couple of them a drink. They like us a lot. Fay just started dancing with Milly, so Joey and I split 'em up. The rest of the boys out here on the sidewalk can't dance so good but they formed a circle and they're giving us a little encouragement by clapping their hands. You get tired when you really jump so fast, but then we change off. One of the other guys takes over and by the time we get through the girls are really worn out. The people that come along on the sidewalk always like to watch us dance and before we get through we get quite a crowd. Jerry doesn't care about the crowd just so the neighbors don't complain too much about the sidewalks being blocked up. If the cop makes everybody move on once in a while nobody complains to Jerry.

10:30 P.M.

The law broke up our jump session and we're back by the candy store again. The boys are kinda wound up so we've been horsing around a lot. Kid Ralphie's brother got up on the newspaper box and started being the king of the hill. He didn't stay up there but about two seconds. About half of us have been up there and down again. Harry's been crying about us making so much noise, but he's crying most of the time anyway, so we don't pay too much attention to him. I'm going to take a walk with some of the boys.

11:30 P.M.

We've been back by the candy store for about 15 minutes. We just started a bull session about driving cars. When some of these kids start to drive cars, they don't know nothing about it and they drive all over the streets, and get in all kinds of jams. Sometimes we rob cars just to take a ride. One of the boys robbed a car and kept it for about two months.

I'm going over for coffee now. The guys ought to be back from the movies pretty soon. Yep, they're already in, having coffee. At night we come into this place. It's a big cafeteria with a bar on one side. I don't think the guys who own the place like to have us come here too much, because once in a while we get in a little fight, but they try to be nice to us. They know damn well if they weren't we could make it plenty tough for them.

We've been in here now for about three-quarters of an hour. The paper came out a little while ago and we've been talking about baseball and who's going to win the pennant, and then we got to talking about Rocky Graziano and a couple of other fighters. Georgie, who's kind of a quiet sort of guy, was reading the front part of the paper, and he said that he figures we're gonna have to fight Russia. We had a hot argument about that, because a couple of boys who've been in the service said if we have to fight Russia it's gonna be a hell of a mess, and if we do they're gonna find a nice little place in the mountains till the whole thing blows over.

12 Midnight

The boys that have been out dancing just came back with their girls. While two of them were over getting the coffee, a guy sitting at the bar figured he'd try to make a deal with one of the girls, so he whistled at her and motioned to her to come over. Larry just walked over to see what he wanted, and the guy said he figured that there was a couple extra girls there and he wanted one of them to have a drink with him. The guy sounded like a rebel (he's a guy from down south) and he made a couple of snotty remarks, so Larry sized him up and dropped him. His buddy started to take a swing at Larry and by then Rudy and a half a dozen of the boys were over there and they gave both of them a good going over. They kicked hell outa one guy and they hit the other guy with a bar stool. The bartender hollered like hell, but we told him to shut up and mind his own business, and if he gets smart with us we'll drop him too. The boys that were in the fight just took a walk because the law will probably be around in a few minutes. Nobody would call up the law from here; they're afraid we might give them the business, too.

Sure enough, the law just walked in. They came right over

to the table where we're sitting. I don't know why it is these bulls always have to put on such a big deal act. The guy comes over with the billy club in his hand and says, "I see you guys are getting in trouble again." We tell him we don't know nothing about it, we haven't been in no trouble, we just been sitting here drinking coffee. He tells us to finish up and get the hell out and not to be hanging around in here. The manager just came over and told them that we weren't in the fight—it was somebody else.

I A.M.

Well, that's how it goes. Every day it's the same old business. I think I'll cut out and go to bed now because the boys who work on the docks think if I go along with them tomorrow they can get me in on their job. I sure hope so because I could use a little extra dough.

You know, I've been thinking since we been telling you about what us guys do. You probably wonder how we like this kind of life. Well, it's like this. It's not so bad. We kinda like it because we can do whatever we want to. We don't have to take any crap off of anyone. At least it's not like in the army or the navy. Around here you take a chance getting your beatings from the law, but except for that you don't get pushed around without having anything to say about what happens to you, like in the army or the navy. You know, a lot of the guys from here get discharged from the service by putting on some kind of an act. One guy acted like he was a homo, another guy acted real nervous, and so on. Pretty soon the army gets disgusted and lets them go. If we had a place where we could play cards and hang out without the cops always figuring we were wrong, it would be good.

A lot of the boys would like to have jobs, but some of them figure they ought to get the money they got when the war was on, and there ain't no such thing any more as a 60-buck-a-week job for just labor. Most of the guys haven't got enough schooling and don't know enough about a trade to get a good job, and they kinda hate to take a cheap one where they have to work so hard. Besides, finding a job is kinda hard. You have to know someone who can get you in. Sometimes I get to thinking about working and I really wish I could find a job that I would like. It's no fun to work like hell all the time. Then, too, you figure that maybe some day you want to get married and you'd like to have a job where you could make a little more money after you've been at it for a while. There's no chance like that in most of the jobs we get. Like on the docks, when business gets bad nearly everybody gets laid off. So half the time you don't know whether you really got a job or not.

Well, I'm gonna cut out now. So long.

From this account, several points become clear. The underlying pattern is one of frustration and the disorientation that results when a youth has no goals and is apparently free to do as he pleases. These negative elements are compensated for by attitudes of aggression and sensitivity to status—the need to achieve a reputation, even though a bad one; the need to defend himself; the need to distinguish himself and his group from "the others." Anti-minority activities may be only a small part of his overt behavior, but the attitude is usually present as part of his over-all personality, which includes resistance to control, assertion of superiority, emphasis on others' inferiority, sensitivity to others' differences, sensitivity to real or imagined insults, readiness to resort to physical aggression.

Milder manifestation of these characteristics which are so clear in the acts of street gangs are also present in other adolescent groups. Usually aggression and the seeking of status are directed at adults but in a more socialized way, such as verbally or passively resisting control or setting aside certain areas in which the group can feel superior. For example, in a community center organized only partly through the efforts of a youth council, a bitter battle rages over naming the center, as though adults had no part in it. Youth in this case say, "Let's name it the Westview Youth Center. It was our idea and our effort which started it. Even if adults participate in its programs, it is our center and adults are more or less guests."

Adolescent groups also set themselves apart in a manner of dress distinctive from both that of children and that of adults. Special language, such as "jive talk" or more complicated language modifications, also appear. The gang, then, is not something unique but a highlighted and somewhat exaggerated example of this general state of adolescent adjustment. Where in one case costume, language, and verbal battles become satisfactory forms for expressing a desire for independence, the gang goes further —to physical aggression.

The account of a gang's "typical" day set forth above offered the following examples of this desire for superiority, this insistence on status: ganging up on individual members to keep them in their place; establishing the inferior status of the "bum" by using pain or payment of money; taking advantage of the store owner; resistance to accepting money from younger members and exaggeration of the amount of money acquired and the ease of earning it; relations with girls; dancing in a specialized way and subsequent exhibitionism; telling tall tales and verbalizing lack of fear. Fighting, of course, is the most obvious method of establishing superiority.

In such a setting any identifiable minority may become a focus of resentment simply because it is identifiable as different. Such groups may have been established as inferior through the bigoted remarks of adults and their treatment by society; they simply become the more obvious targets, people to be "kept in their place." Slighting remarks made to members of minority groups often prompt the answering "insults" that call for fighting. Conflict then reinforces the anti attitude. Bigoted expressions take on the value of contributing to the need for feeling superior.

Such a desire to feel superior, to assert status, frequently springs from feelings of insecurity.

Leadership Skills[2]

The adult group worker who assumes the task of working with gangs has one basic aim: to redirect youthful energies toward behavior that is constructive or at least non-destructive and socially acceptable. He must take stones that seem to have been rejected and left over and must help to integrate them into the structure of a democratic society, even if he cannot convert them into material suitable for the cornerstone of the building. His task is to a certain extent facilitated by the fact that basically everyone wants to be accepted—a great many so-called "delinquents" simply have to be given the proper guidance and offered the opportunity to participate, to belong. Following the modern theory of learning, the adult leader concentrates on redirecting behavior, trusting that desirable changes in attitudes will inevitably follow. Thus his skills and his methods are simply those that a good teacher would exploit. The difference is that his task is much harder; frequently the boys are older, they are more set in their ways, they already have a history of failure, and they are suspicious of outsiders.

The leader must have a strong liking for young people and must have the ability to get next to them. His success in large measure depends on his personality and on training for such work. Only through a strong personal relationship to the group is the leader able to cope with its hostility and aggression and steer it toward socially constructive goals.

It is important that the gang see the adult leader as a person who accepts them as they really are. They should see him as a friend and a counselor—one who possesses a deep respect for

[2] See the reports, available through the Department of Justice, of a panel discussion on Youth Participation of the National Conference on the Prevention and Control of Juvenile Delinquency, held at Washington in November, 1946.

the intimate relationships he establishes and for the confidential information that may be revealed to him.

The leader's first task is to get *himself* accepted. At first the boys view the worker with suspicion because they are afraid of "stool pigeons." They will question him thoroughly and carefully and will demand an explanation for his presence in the neighborhood.

How a gang feels toward an adult worker in the first few months was portrayed in a dramatization at a session of the Wellesley School of Community Affairs in which the problems of autonomous youth groups were discussed. The scene takes place in front of a candy store. Two members of the gang are discussing a visit which the worker and Artie had made to the local police station. The visit was for the purpose of enlisting the support and interest of the police in helping the boys to organize a club and secure a meeting place. The worker has been in the area for two months.

BILL: I heard that you and Ted went to talk to the cops today.

ARTIE: That's right.

BILL: What was it all about?

ARTIE: I don't know. I didn't hear all of it. They asked me to leave the room for a while and then they talked. After that I came back and they talked about helping us to get a club house. The cop talked pretty nice and promised to help us.

BILL: What do you think about it? Do you think that we can trust Ted?

ARTIE: I'd sure like to know what they talked about when I was out of the room. I don't know whether I trust him or not. He has only been with us for two months and he has acted O.K. But you can never tell. He might be a dick; he's built like one, you know. Anyway, we'll string along with him but keep our eyes open at the same time.

It is difficult to establish confidence between adults and boys in street gangs. Two months, as shown in the above portrayal, is a short period in which to achieve that goal. As indicated, suspicion gradually melts away under constant observation during which the worker always "seems to be O.K." The style of leadership adopted by the worker has a great deal to do with the speed of assimilation and achievement of acceptance.

It is important that the boys see in the leader a participant-consultant who is young and has enough new skills to offer so that he is able to assimilate into the group. He brings with him a program so dynamic, so glamorous, so naturally established as to be at least as attractive as the spontaneous activities of the group. They see a man who is willing to give and take on a mutual basis. The group itself sets up the standards, maps the program, and makes the rules. Its members feel that the leader works *with* them, not *on* them.

When the group engages in some clearly anti-social activity the leader does not participate in it himself. He makes it clear to the boys that he disapproves of it, and he gives his reasons. He also uses his personal prestige with them in an effort to persuade them to modify their behavior. He does not attempt to forbid activities except under the most extreme circumstances, nor does he make the boys feel that they must do good deeds continually in order to keep his friendship. They see in him a person who sets an example for a new activity pattern.

Lastly, they see in the leader a person who has an understanding of their attitudes, community patterns, and codes and who has the emotional capacity to accept them by working on an informed rather than a moralistic basis.

The following account of a year with a gang illustrates the difficult tasks of leadership.

A Street-Corner Club

My work in the Eastern district began some years ago. The neighborhood was one of the blighted low-income areas marked by high rates of juvenile delinquency. It was my responsibility to help operate a large-scale recreation program for the youth of the community.

In our work we tried to involve the adults in the planning and conducting of activities. We also worked with the youth and their indigenous leaders in natural gangs. A large number of these autonomous boys' clubs participated in our sports tournaments. In the summer we organized camping programs which reached hundreds of the boys.

In August, 1940, a group of the older boys prevailed on me to organize a one-day canoe trip through a chain of lakes and streams in the vicinity of the camp. In the fall a camping club was proposed with a canoe trip as the highlight of its yearly program. The boys asked me to serve as group leader. We agreed that there should be as little red tape as possible, no minutes or bylaws, and no officers. When we needed money we would raise it together rather then have anyone drop out because he did not pay his dues.

By the process of heated discussion we selected a name, the Xavier Club. In the beginning the more interested members had to buttonhole the others in corner candy stores and poolrooms to get them to the meetings. We purchased club sweaters, and this helped to identify the club. Our first activity was a small social dance, and here we began our policy of trying to give our friends and patrons their money's worth instead of concentrating on making a big profit.

Many clubs have broken up because boys who brought in a lot of money and boys who did little or nothing received the same benefits. To avoid this, we devised a system by which a definite proportion of each member's earnings was held in the club treasury in his name to be used when needed for club activities.

Our first canoe trip was a great success in spite of the fact that we ran into a lot of mosquitoes. Ten members participated. The Xavier Club continued to grow and some activities became annual events. The following highlights of the sixth year give some notion of the progress, problems, and pleasures of the club:

June. There is much excitement at meetings, working out menus and completing arrangements for the sixth annual canoe trip.

July. Fifteen club members went on the canoe trip.

August. With my family, I went to the north woods for my vacation. Six club members organized a party to come up camping and fishing for ten days.

September. Arrangements have been made for us to use the lounge at the public park for meetings. The club is now publishing two thousand copies of our monthly community newspaper, and it looks as though the paper will soon be self-supporting.

November. We held our sixth annual football game. It has become a tradition that these games are slam-bang affairs with plenty of roughness.

December. We held the sixth annual Christmas party. Some of the boys had a fight by spraying pop and beer at one another. Afterwards everybody agreed it was the best party we ever had.

January. I tried to read a financial statement for the year, but all they wanted to know was whether the club owed any money.

February. Paul and Sonny, two of the main leaders, have been on the outs. I suggested that the club meet once a week to play cards and selected a neutral location. On the second card night both Paul and Sonny were present and in the course of the evening their difficulties were resolved.

March. We have been practicing for a minstrel show to raise money to pay the deficit on our newspaper.

Club members often call on me for help when they run into difficulties. For instance, Tom was close friends with a young girl who had run away from home because of a very strict stepfather. Now both he and the girl were objects of an intensive police search. I could not reveal their whereabouts until some arrangement for them was worked out. Fortunately, an understanding probation officer arranged for the girl to live with a relative and for Tom to have regular opportunities to visit her.

April. Plans for our big minstrel show blew up when we tried to get the auditorium at the neighborhood settlement house. We were told that we could not put the show on if it was in black-face. I suggested that we do it in hill-billy style, but some of the members objected that it is not a minstrel show unless it is in black-face. I told them that Negroes generally did not like black-face minstrel shows. The argument reached an impasse, and the wisest thing seems to be to forget about the show for this year.

May. We are working hard on plans for our annual dance, through which we hope to raise the money for our traditional canoe trip. Members of the club have been meeting with representatives of other clubs to plan the dance.

June. Our sixth annual dance was a big success, and the Xaviers realized a profit of over $500. The co-operation with the other clubs was satisfactory, although there was some criticism of a group of similar background because they seemed to shirk some of the minor responsibilities. The members were enthusiastic about the performance of the Jewish boys and expressed their willingness to co-operate again with this club next year.

A Constructive Program

The group feeling shown in the above account facilitates development of good relationships with other groups of persons who are of different backgrounds. Dynamic programs are needed, provided they are carried out with leadership that fits into the setting and can operate practically in any area of life from fights between leaders, or girl friend troubles, to livening up a Christmas party.

A program which seeks to involve the autonomous gang in constructive inter-group relations must have the following qualities:

1. In the inter-group co-operation there must be practical advantages which make the program attractive to each group.
2. The program must be set up in such a way as to preserve the basic autonomy of each group.
3. The program must be one that enhances the prestige of each co-operating group.
4. In accordance with the ages and experiences of the groups involved, the program must be challenging and stimulating.
5. The informal and spontaneous spirit of the natural gang must be incorporated into the inter-group enterprise.

Experimental programs have been carried on in Chicago by the Commission on Community Interrelations of the American Jewish Congress. The results of this work have indicated that there are many points within the framework of our present society at which inter-group co-operation will result in better understanding between groups. Since the development of mutual understanding is an essential first step in the process of building a better society, these experiments, even though they are only small-scale working models, seem to offer hope for the future.

One such opportunity for intercultural co-operation is the neighborhood dance. The neighborhood dance has traditionally been one of the chief means by which autonomous social and athletic clubs and gangs have financed their activities. By hiring a hall and an orchestra and by selling tickets and advertisements in a souvenir program many clubs manage to raise money to pay rent on their clubhouse, buy club jackets or team uniforms, and have enough left over for occasional refreshments at club meetings. The annual dance is a matter of considerable pride to each club and enhances its status as a group in the community.

The Commission on Community Interrelations in Chicago invited four such groups, representing different community, nationality, and religious backgrounds, to consider a plan for a cooperative dance. The plan was carefully worked out and had the following advantages:

1. By sharing the expenses for the dance hall and the orchestra, the expenses of each club were reduced to one-fourth of what they would have been if each club had independently conducted a dance with the same facilities. This increased the margin of profit for each club.

2. By sharing the expenses, the clubs could afford to conduct their dance in one of the world's finest ballrooms with a well-known band. This greatly enhanced the prestige of each club in its own community.

3. Each club retained complete control over its own ticket sales and souvenir program advertisements. After paying its share of the expenses, each club profited in accordance with its own efforts in promoting the dance. This preserved the autonomy of each club.

4. The experience of working in a larger group and conducting the dance in fine facilities, as well as the thrill which comes from successful large-scale co-operation, was stimulating to the participants.

5. The planning was carried on by the clubs themselves and in an informal manner which effectively incorporated the dynamic gang spirit of the groups into the larger organization.

The success of the co-operative dance was such as to indicate the great possibilities of such inter-group programs. The dance was followed by a canoe trip involving members of the same groups which had co-operated in the dance and also representatives of other groups. In addition to bringing together representatives of different community, nationality, and religious backgrounds, the canoe trip was inter-racial.

With imagination and good leadership, programs such as this can be expanded in local situations to include mutually advantageous co-operation between groups in the field of sports, in securing employment and educational opportunities, and in solving personal, family, and community problems.

The encouragement of intercultural co-operation in matters of mutual interest offers an effective means of developing better understanding between groups and of removing the barriers which customarily keep groups apart or pit them against one another. Such programs must be initiated in and carried on through the natural social groupings in our society. With the proper encouragement and opportunities, natural gangs which have derived status and a sense of power through destructive activities can find even greater strength and a new kind of status through constructive and socially acceptable channels.

CHAPTER VII

THE HIGH SCHOOL TEACHER[1]

Although important changes have been taking place in the elementary schools in the last generation, the high schools have generally been more resistant to basic innovations. This chapter examines some of the sources for a secondary school curriculum, the attitudes and practices prevalent today, and the approaches that may offer the greatest hope for the future in fostering democratic human relations.

A Panel Discussion

The teachers in service who made up Middletown's Curriculum Workshop were considering a panel report. The topic was: "What Curricular Experiences Are Essential in a High School Program?" Ann Smith rated it one of the best sessions she had attended during the summer weeks. She kept wishing that more of her colleagues from West High were registered in the workshop. At the moment, the panel members were discussing experiences in intercultural education as among the essentials in today's school program. Ann listened intently; the field of human relations was the area on which she was concentrating in the workshop.

One teacher was urging, "If the members of this workshop intend to stress the most needed centers of experience in the program of today's high school, they must include intercultural edu-

[1] This chapter was written by WILLIAM VAN TIL, Director of Learning Materials, Bureau for Intercultural Education.

cation. In my school, cliques dominate some clubs; kids of lower-class background and of foreign parentage do not even try to join these clubs any more. Jewish youngsters cannot gain full acceptance; the invisible walls rise at school social affairs, for instance. We have had our share of locker-room and corridor 'incidents' between Negroes and whites. Nasty names get tossed about lightly, whether in the balcony chatter at basketball games or in would-be humor over the cokes.

"But if you ask the faculty or administration about tensions, you get that big bland smile and the classic response, 'We have no problems here.' I would certainly rank intercultural education high among essential experiences because of the outstanding importance of problems of human relations in the lives of many students I meet."

"While I should never claim we have no problems in our school," added another panel participant, "the conflicts you mention are not obvious with us. The youngsters who come to our high school are largely white, native-born, and Protestant. Yet I, too, would urge intercultural education as an essential in the modern American high school, regardless of what has to be shoved aside to make room for it. But I have another reason—the brutal facts of life in the society these kids are inheriting. These youngsters are going to live in a society in which prejudice, discrimination, and bigotry are wicked realities. It is a world still all too familiar with racism, anti-semitism, lonely refugees. You do not have to look any farther than Georgia to recognize that the war against fascism is not over even in our own country.

"As a matter of fact, you do not have to look any farther than our own community. Our community has slum housing for Negroes and restrictive covenants to 'keep them in their place.' It has 'Christians only' advertising, and snobbish clubs, and queries about nationality and religion on employment blanks, and news-paper editorials against the admission of refugees to a land where Liberty is getting weary of holding up her torch."

A third panel member chipped in: "But there is an even

sounder reason for dealing with racial, religious, nationality, and socio-economic problems in the classroom. It is a reason that relates fundamentally to what we are trying to do through education—help youngsters understand and live the democratic way of life. What an opportunity these problems of relationships give a teacher to contrast ways of life! What an opportunity to put democracy into practice rather than rest content with words! It is these emotion-ridden areas like human relationships that test the extent to which democracy has roots in the life of the student."

"Want to open discussion now?" asked the workshop leader.

The panel members nodded. Ann then asked, "You three seem to be in agreement that intercultural education is one of the 'musts' for the high school. I'd certainly go along with you. But do we all agree on why it is needed? It seems to me that you might each advocate quite different ways of looking at intercultural education if you see quite different reasons for stressing human relationships."

"Such as?"

"Well, if you stress the problems that students now face, you might take up only those problems of student relationships which have become obvious with individual students or in group situations in your school. If you stress the broad social problems as the only reason for learning about human relationships, students in your classes might study fair employment practices or housing or races of man. But will you then be sure that such broad social problems are important to the student? If you relate everything to values and to achieving a philosophy, you have a third angle which I know is important but of which the content, I will admit, is none too clear to me."

But it was another workshop member who touched off the day's more pyrotechnic verbal fireworks: ". . . and I'm not too sure whether intercultural education is as important an area of experiences as, let us say, physics or some other subject that discipline your thinking. . . ." Ideas came fast and sometimes furiously, until finally the discussion had to be stopped for lunch. That afternoon, in a talk scheduled by the planning committee, the workshop leader, a curriculum worker from the university that was co-sponsoring the workshop with the Middletown City system, offered some extended last words on the matter. Ann listened hard and applied the ideas to her efforts to foster democratic human relations in the school in which she taught.

The Sources of Experiences

The workshop staff member said: "Most of you agree that intercultural education and certain other centers of experience are essential to a contemporary high school program. Yet, as you also point out, they gain entrance with the greatest difficulty. Then—

"How can we tell what are important centers of experience for the high school curriculum?

"What are the high schools now teaching that makes the introduction of those essential experiences so difficult?

"To determine the important curricular experiences for today's high school student, some educators turn to the social realities of contemporary civilization as the primary source. Others find the source of curricular experiences in the needs of adolescents. Still others, who regard the development of a philosophy of life as basic, advocate the selection of those curricular experiences which throw light on conflicting value choices. In other words, one school of thought finds the primary source of curricular experiences in social realities, another finds it in the needs of adolescents, and a third chooses whatever learning experiences best contrast ways of life and values.

"Each blind man who tried to describe the elephant, it will be recalled, claimed to know the only true shape of the beast. I hope my friends on the panel will not refuse to speak to me tomorrow when I say that we saw something of that this morning when the panel dealt with intercultural education. All believe that intercultural relationships are important. Yet each found a different reason for their importance. Actually each of these reasons is important, and each explanation of the source of desirable curricular experiences is inadequate and incomplete if taken in isolation.

"A curriculum based only on needs, or only on social realities, or only on formulating a philosophy just will not do. We cannot have learning experiences which leave out student needs and problems, for these are essential if any learning is to take place. Nor can we afford experiences which ignore the culture in which we live, the social realities of our time; a grip on an understanding of these, too, is essential if we are even to *exist* in this complex society made up of what the sociologists like to call persons-in-culture. Nor can we neglect the constant development and practice of a philosophy of life, which is crucial if young people are to have a sense of direction rather than to drift aimlessly.

"Educators today can venture an answer to our first question: 'How can we tell what are important centers of experience for the high school curriculum?' Centers of experience for high school students can grow only from the three curricular sources, all of which interact—the needs of adolescents, the social realities of the culture, and the democratic philosophy which gives us our sense of direction. A close reading of the curricular specialists of the past two decades will indicate that, unlike the blind men, each school of thought is willing to admit that other sources than the one selected as of the greatest importance play a significant role.

"To decide, then, what centers of experience the program of the modern high school should include—intercultural, or international, or consumer, or health, or vocational, or psychological, or any other particular kind of education—we must ask ourselves whether such experiences are based on needs, throw light on social realities, and help the student steadily to develop a philosophy.

"In our quest for the most essential learning experiences for high school students, let us look at the social realities of our contemporary culture. Let us ask what kind of world we are living in. If we would determine whether intercultural experiences, for instance, are essential, we should ask ourselves whether the problem of establishing decent human relationships and of minimizing hatred, hostility, and prejudice is not one of the basic tasks in today's pattern of social realities. We should ask whether the experiences we encourage will help youngsters to understand the intercultural conflicts, trends, and problems of our culture.

"But, while we seek answers to these questions, we should remember that to determine desirable experiences for the education of high school students we must do more than examine social realities. Some social realities may as yet be beyond the ken of high school pupils. If we are going to make any impact on the attitudes of youth and avoid meaningless expenditure of breath, we must be familiar with the actual problems, concerns, and needs of the adolescents who are the heirs to this culture. One might rightly make a plea to educators to help teen-agers to solve their pressing life problems because dealing wisely and effectively with their problems is essential to achieving intelligent adjustment, responsible citizenship, or whatever similar goals are most prized by the individual educator. But, even if the case for meeting adolescent needs is argued on no higher basis than the possibility of communicating any idea or attitude or way of believing whatsoever, is it not obvious that the educator must deal with the real problems of youngsters whom he, ostensibly, is educating? Again, if we believe certain experiences to be important, we should ask ourselves whether these experiences grow from the real and vital problems of the youngsters whom we are trying to educate. For instance, if the intercultural education we foster is not related to the students' drives, tensions, and concerns, we'd better shut up shop. For people learn only what they live and they cannot truly learn what does not matter to them.

"And are the student's experiences used to develop his viewpoint on life and to give him opportunities to practice our chosen democratic way of living? We do not want students simply to learn facts about bigotry and prejudice or any other social realities and then stay neutral toward them. We reject a limp cynicism; our adolescents have to develop and apply a positive philosophy, since a philosophy is our only source of direction.

"We cannot dodge the issue of developing a philosophy by vaguely stating our purpose to be 'meeting needs' or 'growth in relationships.' Growth must be toward a certain desirable *quality* of relationship. As the Nazis have well taught us, growth may be directed toward fascist as well as toward democratic or still other goals. Similarly, we have only to think of the need of the old soak for a drink or the need of a bully to punch the innocent by-stander in the nose to realize how far we are from aiming to meet any and all needs. We both select and direct needs in the light of our values, be they authoritative or democratic. Meeting needs and learning about social realities without developing an ac-companying sense of direction can only produce chaotic thinking. Intercultural education that does not come to grips with an understanding of the democratic way of life is Hamlet played without the melancholy Dane himself.

"Yet, what is the fearful paradox? Too often at present, ex-periences which will meet needs, illuminate social realities, and develop values can only smuggle their way into current high school curriculums. Urgent and undeniable as the grass which forces itself between pavement cracks on a busy city street, they merely take root in extracurricular activities, optional or free choice courses, or in clubs, or work their way into the occasional interstices between ivy-covered traditional subject matter. They sometimes infiltrate into the established and respectable subjects only to produce odd, hybrid blossoms—as, for instance, when a class hears about intercultural relationships through a study of ancient Rome, or when a student encounters personal or health or consumer problems through some tortured distortion in gram-mar or intermediate algebra or chemistry classes. Is this the best we can do to make high school education vital and to center it on life problems?

"In America we keep saying that we hold to the democratic way of life and that we are for education for *all* American youth. Yet, save for a few honorable exceptions, in community after community a high school designed for the elite still carries on an education appropriate for the eighteenth-century British aristocrat, if for anyone. Grammar and Greek history; classics, cosines, and conjugations; frog dissection (which is a relative newcomer!) and French; Shakespeare and chivalry; elegant lettering and English literature; binomial theorems, the rise of Phoenicia, for ever and ever, amen. From the teacher point of view, it is mine not to reason why, mine but to teach a subject matter which some obscure destiny once dictated. From the student point of view, it is mine not to reason why, mine but to absorb mechanically, give back phonographically, and wait for the bell. For both teacher and student, life begins at 3:30.

"Have inroads on this conception of education been made in the American high school? Of course they have; we can all cite evidence. And more power to those who are trying to bring actual life and the American high school into their proper relationship! But my portrait of the paradox, unfortunately, is all too close to the actual situation in too many American high schools.

"The confusion in the American high school comes about because the new is struggling to be born and the old refuses to lie down to die and be buried."

To at least one listener, Ann Smith, teacher of social studies in the West High School, the talk summed up the problems she was facing in developing intercultural experiences in her school. She felt sure that she could document the importance of intercultural education for West High. Prejudice, discrimination, and bigotry were woven into the social fabric of the community in which she lived and worked. As a real problem of the student body, it showed itself in a dozen obvious ways: in the social-economic discrimination which marked elections to Hi-Y membership; in drug-store table cliques; in the rudeness of some minority group members; in the obsequious, studied politeness with which still others reacted to discriminations; in the lifted eyebrow and meaningful exchange of smiles during the reading of literature that contained stereotypes of Jews; in the embarrassment with which a second-generation youngster waited for the substitute teacher's inevitable mispronunciation of his name; in the expressed gratification of some students at not going to East High where so many Negroes went; in the loose use of slurring epithets; in scurrilous jingles popular for the moment. If America really meant its education to help the young to understand and practice the democratic way of life, such social and personal problems—the ones that really count—are the raw material for the making and application of a philosophy.

To Ann it was evident that the extension of democratic human relationships was an integral phase of democratic education. The need was inescapable. The major question seemed to be which approaches were most fruitful. But all this was not so self-evident to many others on the West High staff.

"It's None of Our Business"

To a large group it seemed a self-evident truth that human relations, democratic or undemocratic, were none of their business. What *was* their business? Miss Jones, who was nothing if not outspoken, may have phrased the matter in an extreme way when she asserted, "The people of this community are paying me to put some mathematics into their children's thick heads." Yet putting knowledge into children's heads was apparently the accepted business that she and many others methodically and systematically undertook. Thus administered, some knowledge of mathematics (or of grammatical construction, or physical law, or Spanish, or military campaign, or mechanical drawing) lingered somewhere in the student's organism, presumably in his thick head, until examination time. Later, blessed forgetfulness set in.

Stirred by the meeting just described, which had occurred early in the workshop course, Ann found for herself a short-term problem on which to work immediately. She began to look for the results in human relationships with the "none of our business" approach, as she termed it. What happened when the teacher supposedly abdicated so far as human relationships were concerned? Was even *neutrality* achieved when such a teacher concentrated on conveying traditional content through formal methods? Or did the traditional type of education, still powerful in the American high school, unwittingly run counter to democratic human relationships? Ann contrasted what the traditionalists most prize with what democratic human relationships apparently necessitate.

Democratic human relationships involve respect for the individual. But, in the classes of those who feel that relationships—democratic or undemocratic, human or inhuman—are "none of their business," mastery of a fixed quantity of subject matter and maintenance of teacher-enforced discipline frequently take precedence over what happens to human personality.

Democratic human relationships involve co-operation and the development of a group process. But, where subject matter reigns supreme, co-operation yields to competition for grades and scholarships, to appeals to personal ambition, to striving for scholastic victory over others.

Democratic human relationships involve sharing of purposes—the common concerns of teachers and students. But the traditional classroom is a miniature authoritarian state.

Democratic human relations involve the use of intelligence. But, even here, behind the façade of respect for intellectuality, highly formal education prizes memorization, conformity, passive acceptance.

And prejudice? Although Ann was no scholar in this phenomenon, she knew that psychologists were demonstrating the relationship between frustration and aggression—which made her wonder about the results of a traditional school education which condemns some youngsters, by their very nature and make-up, to a steady and losing fight against low grades, failure, or competition with those with higher I.Q.'s. She had watched the excessive explosions of energy which occurred when the class hour bells reprieved such youngsters who had been "cabin'd, cribb'd, confined" to sitting still for periods. Maybe restrictive school arrangements helped to explain the "meanness" that sometimes seemed to crop out spontaneously in corridors, in locker rooms, on school steps, and in street cars when the clamped lid of school had been pried off. From what little she knew of human behavior, Ann was dubious about the solution proposed by those who valued restrictions—to make the restrictions ever tighter, ever more comprehensive.

When war was coming over the horizon, Edna St. Vincent Millay wrote, "There are no islands any more." And in human relationships, reflected Ann, there are no neutrals any more—if there ever were. Those who claim human relationships to be none of their business are, wittingly or not, shaping lives. Consciously or not, teachers contribute toward building self-security, acceptance, and friendliness to others, or they contribute toward the creation of self-doubt, frustration, and suspicion. True, they only contribute, but Ann recalled the proverb about the constant dripping that wears away the stone. In education we are all in the business of building human relations—inevitably so, she concluded. Only the quality of the relations thus built remains in doubt.

The Brighter Side

That there is a brighter side to the high school picture Ann well knew. Although the American senior high school is still lagging perhaps decades behind the better elementary schools in developing functional education, and although general education approaches are as yet only in their infancy in the senior high school curriculum, still the new *is* struggling to be born. Ann therefore tried next to analyze what it was that the group of West High teachers who recognized the establishment of democratic human relations as a goal actually *did* to move toward this purpose. She took up the school's outstanding teachers one by one.

According to the office records, Mary Flood was a mathematics teacher—as was Miss Jones, the advocate of the instillation of knowledge into thick heads. But, unlike Miss Jones, Mary Flood never forgot that primarily she was teaching youngsters. True, she had found no ways of directly relating the prescribed materials of mathematics content to human relationships. But she had a willing ear for adolescent trials and tribulations, and she had a warm heart. Hence many a conference after school and during study periods began with angles and arcs and ended with a personal confidence and the discussion of a non-mathematical problem. "And so, when Doris has her party next week, Miss Flood, some people I know will be left out again. Why do certain people think themselves better than others?"

Miss Flood did the best she could with the two hundred and five youngsters who came to her classes daily. She could not know all of them intimately, but for more than a few Miss Flood—who never would have recognized her rule-of-thumb, friendly guidance as in the realm of relationships—was an indispensable safety valve.

Jane Tilson taught Spanish. She was a rebel against total immersion in learning to speak and read the language. She took as much class time as was politic for building appreciation of Spanish and Latin-American culture. She felt that perhaps 95 per cent of the students in her classes would neither travel in Latin-American countries nor read Spanish literature in the years ahead. From all her experience, and from follow-ups she had made of graduates, she could not persuade herself that knowledge of the life of a people was less significant for these average American youngsters than a partial and stumbling introduction to a foreign tongue. Yet perforce she kept an eye to windward. She was being paid for teaching Spanish, wasn't she?

Mantillas, gay combs, slippers, castanets, peasant embroidery, and Argentinian newspapers contributed to the vivid exhibits her classes gathered. Earnestly she told them of the dramatic wreck-age from the pre-Spanish past and of the contrast in ways of living that marked the South American land she had seen one ever memorable summer vacation. In every way she could devise she tried to acquaint Middletown youth with Hispanic culture. Since she knew the low regard in which the Spanish-speaking minority were held in her community, she even ventured once with a class to the local settlement house in the Latin-settled neighborhood. The dinner and the evening at the settlement house were a magnificent experience.

Yet the wary eye to windward must be maintained. Somehow penalties in education were so much more tangible than rewards. The rewards for work she considered well done included the ap-preciative comments of some students and parents. The penalties included the steady struggle with formal college requirements, with colleagues who maintained inflexible academic standards, with examinations dedicated to the measurement of skills, and with parents uncritically loyal to the academic *status quo* and fearful of any deviation from the respectability of the socially accepted. Jane Tilson therefore went about as far as she could go in stressing human relationships in her Spanish class and kept watching over her right shoulder for flank attacks.

Then there was John Mandoli, the English teacher. When in the high school classics and in free reading there were problems of how man dealt with man which could be made communicable to the younger generation, one could count on John to find them. It was even rumored that he could teach *The Merchant of Venice* in such a way as to build mutual understanding among Jews and Christians; some, however, found this hard to believe.

But it was generally agreed that the most skillful work in human relations in the West High School went on during extra-curricular activities—that "wing" added to the educational struc-ture to house the realistic problems and interests of youth deemed too vigorous and vulgar to come into the "main house." In this realm one came into contact with "that bunch" and with instructor Herb Delmar, to whom even the principal was now accustomed to referring community inquiries on whether the school dealt with intercultural affairs. "That bunch," in spite of this designation so persistently used by most of the faculty, was not really homogeneous. It was made up of a miscellany of the kids who did not belong—the hard-boiled, rootless, low-income youngsters. Though the faculty lumped them together, there were at least two dominant groups, "the Irish" and "the foreigners." Who "the Irish" were needs no explanation; "the foreigners" were Polish, Slovakian, and Italian youngsters, joined in an uneasy coalition.

The members of "that bunch" were not staying in school until they were old enough to work; they were staying in school simply until they were legally old enough to leave. They showed no conspicuous interest in their own futures. And, to hear them tell it, dramatics, debating, glee club, and school parties were for "punks." They resembled Shakespeare only in that they had little Latin and less Greek . . . to say nothing of history, biology, English, civics, and similar West High requirements. In classes it was a blessed day for teachers when members of "that bunch" actually endured the monotony rather than concocted devices to relieve it. It was steadily evident that they had few middle-class virtues.

Only the industrial art shop stirred them to occasional spurts of activity, and it was there that instructor Herb Delmar got acquainted with them. They were typical of generations of their kind whom he had seen pass through high school untouched by education, unaffected by the motto graven over West High's doors, "Knowledge and Brotherhood." There were bitter faculty complaints about "that bunch" after a lamp illuminating the school steps was broken during one of the frequent internecine after-school wars between, as usual, "the Irish" and "the foreigners." It was then that Herb Delmar decided to see what he could do. After all, the members of the bunch had arrived at a stage of cordiality in their relationship with him where they no longer tried to steal his tools. Maybe he had a chance.

"That bunch" was suspicious of adults and of proposed organizations. According to reports of past performances, organizations suggested to them had turned out to be milder versions of school and fundamentally no more pleasurable or meaningful. Herb therefore said nothing about organizing, but started with an experience and trusted in the logic of events for the later development of an organization, if any. He interested four key leaders, two "Irish" and two "foreigners," in a week-end hiking trip into the hills. Then when they returned, vainglorious and argumentative over the mileage they had covered and the speed with which they had hiked, he suggested a longer trip for the coming spring vacation. More fellows, both "Irish" and "foreigners," wanted to be counted in. In each crowd there were mutterings about the inclusion of "those others," but, when the competitive aspects were stressed—let's see who's *really* rugged —and when bicycles were chosen as the vehicles, the proposed trip took on the aspects of a sporting contest, almost as exciting as throwing rocks at train windows or playing football.

Most of "that bunch" had bicycles; the few who did not own any found ways of persuading friends to lend theirs. But camping equipment was another matter. With nudgings from Herb, however, they decided to stop at youth hostels, farm homes with simple facilities for hikers and bikers who stop overnight.

By day the two sub-groups of what the faculty still mistakenly lumped as "that bunch" took different routes and raced each other. By night they sat about the hostel fire swapping prodigious exaggerations of their feats. They slept in a common bunk room and were too worn out for much horseplay; they drew lots for such hostel chores as meal preparation, dishwashing, and washroom clean-up. Whether they would or not, they inevitably grew better acquainted. Rivalry remained, but enmity diminished.

They came home with something in common; they talked of

the trip night and day. They set a time after school for those who wanted to meet and plan ahead for a summer trip. Capitalizing on their feeling of personal proprietorship of the hostels, Herb encouraged them to build simple games in the shop—box hockey, for instance. They used the games during lunch hour and planned to leave them, on the next trip through the hostel loop, at the hostel most lacking in recreation materials. Herb got them to reading topographic maps (and that, reflected Ann, was more geography than she had been able to teach them in social studies the year before). Over two week ends they marked a new hikers' trail from hostel to hostel through a state park. The ranger who went with them on a first survey of the trail seemed more impressed by readiness to swing an axe than by the boasts of a few, a minority now, about the toughness of the crowd they hung out with. With more important things to do, the bunch showed less of a tendency to think along nationality lines and began to think and act together.

Late in the spring "the Wanderers," as they now called themselves, sent delegates to the local hostel committee in the region; the delegates reported back on hostel needs. Plans got under way for work holidays, days of doing such needed work at hostels as converting a shed into a boys' bunk room, building an outdoor fireplace, and putting up guide signs along roads. It was even rumored that some of the bunch were writing a guide book to the hostel loop, with maps locating roads, hostels, and stores and with advice to the hosteler on what to see and do in the neighborhood. Apparently something was happening to the interests and attitudes of these rootless kids. What was happening stemmed in part from the way the project was handled and in part from their "adoption" by Herb.

Despite community approval and the shift in administrative attitude from indifference to recognition, Herb Delmar knew that he was still largely on his own and that support of his work with the boys would consist of words rather than deeds. For instance, he told his colleagues that he had learned that sheer contact, such as rubbing shoulders in class or shop, is not enough to build bridges between groups. The key to what success had been achieved here was in working and sharing together for purposes which all thought important. He talked about acceptance, starting where youngsters were, informal relationships, the importance of prizing individuals, the need for youth to have a sense of belonging. Many of his colleagues told him that they agreed completely and that he was doing fine work, but in their classes they went right on ignoring the importance of common purposes and human acceptance and continued to wage a losing battle against the hostility or indifference of many students, including "that bunch."

There were others than Mary Flood, Jane Tilson, John Mandoli, and Herb Delmar who worked toward democratic human relationships in West High. There was Adeline Levy, who had coached plays written against prejudice, such as *Look Beyond the Label;* there was Nina Zachary, who had included in vocational discussions a talk on the job-getting problems of minority group youngsters; there was Ann Smith herself, who had tried to make the democratic idea come alive for her American history students. In general, though, conscious activity in human relations included only scattered endeavors—except for Herb Delmar's all-out effort to change the attitudes and behavior of the dispossessed of West High.

How the Score Stood

After her review of how the teachers dealt with democratic human relations in her school, Ann tallied up the score. It seemed to stand about as follows: To most of the teachers in West High, intercultural education was none of their business—they were neutrals. Yet what they did choose to regard as their business was handled by too many of them in such a way as to militate against democratic human relations. Others on the faculty regarded intercultural education as important, and attempted to squeeze attention to relationships among people into a curriculum fundamentally oriented toward a mastery of logically organized subject matter. They also used extracurricular time for introducing intercultural experiences; after-school activities, they found, afforded opportunities for working shoulder to shoulder on common enterprises and offered possibilities of using intercultural themes for plays, forums, clubs, and councils.

How successful was the effort to pervade the various branches of established subject matter with concern for human relationships? Could intercultural education—or for that matter consumer education, international education, health education, or any contemporary imperative—permeate instruction in geometry, or Spanish, or English literature, or world history, or typing?

To Ann it seemed that pervasive emphasis on new imperatives within established subject matter was most successful when two conditions were present. The pervasive emphasis was most successful when sensitive and guidance-minded teachers of any subject helped youngsters develop democratic attitudes in class and out. It was also most successful when the established subject matter was adaptable to illuminating intercultural relations. For instance, certain phases of social studies, of English, of biology, of physical education, and of the arts could be so handled as to foster intercultural understanding; but other phases of the same subjects and areas, however charitably regarded, seemed entirely unsuited for it.

Conversely, pervasive emphasis on intercultural relations within traditional subjects was most likely to fail when teachers of any subject neglected guidance and disregarded attitude formation. The pervasive emphasis was most likely to fail when the subject matter was so remote from racial, religious, nationality, and social-economic affairs that the content of a course had to be twisted to the point of ludicrousness to relate it to intercultural education. For instance, teachers of bookkeeping, mathematics, and such sciences as physics and chemistry in any such attempt faced well-nigh impossible tasks of reinterpretation and adaptation. To insist on teaching centers of experience through subjects or major phases of subjects designed with different ends in view was like pouring new wine into old bottles.

Sensitizing all high school teachers to the critical importance of guidance in human relationships and encouraging occasional intercultural emphasis in the most adaptable established subjects or areas—was this the only possible approach in the American high school? Was this approach more promising than developing general education which cracked the pattern of logically organized subjects and dealt with functional centers of experience for a substantial part of the school day?

In the world of the American high school—where democratic experimental education was struggling to be born, where traditional formal education refused to accept decent burial—one faced hard choices. Certainly, thought Ann, no opportunity for education in human relationships within the traditional subject-centered curriculum should be neglected. To take advantage of each opportunity serves not only to further functional areas of experience but also to build democratic attitudes in the current high school generation for whom the time is now.

But she hoped that high school educators were not going to allow the use of a pervasive emphasis on crucial centers of experience to substitute for facing the two basic curricular questions: What should the American high school attempt to do? What experiences should be the focus of high school education?

To rest content with occasional pervasive emphases on essential experiences, rather than to press on toward a general education based on life problems and supplemented by vocational and avocational electives, was to reside in a halfway house in the land of almost-but-not-quite. In a halfway house, Ann reflected, compromise is the order of the day—rather like moving in with relatives, a procedure which all too often affords full satisfaction to neither party.

There were some in the workshop, Ann knew, who thought it immaterial whether the high school dealt squarely, or sporadically, or not at all with problems of human relationships. They argued that society and its agencies were the potent forces in the making of attitudes. They claimed that the attitudes and understandings of the adolescent were shaped by his family, by the clubs he joined, by the people he ran around with, and by the total molding power of the prevailing culture—but not by the school.

Ann rejected the pessimism of these futilitarians. Their viewpoint seemed a rationalization for inaction. She had no intention of joining the defeated of her profession who, like King Richard II, chose to "sit upon the ground and tell sad stories of the death of kings." She counterclaimed that the school was part of society and a delegated agency for the building of attitudes. It could pretend to abdicate and yet, through its spurious neutrality, actually foster anti-democratic human relations. It could also approach intercultural relations obliquely, spasmodically, and with relatively minor effectiveness. It could regard human relations as extra and assign intercultural experiences to the extracurricular program. Or the school could regard intercultural education as a major task and bring to bear its potential power to shape lives toward democratic human relations.

The Search for a Master Plan

For the rest of the workshop weeks, then, Ann concentrated on getting herself ready for a school year in which she would work urgently for the advancement of decent intercultural attitudes. First of all, she sought the best Master Plan, for she had heard much of "plans" in intercultural education. It is true that she was a bit discouraged to learn that what was sometimes referred to extravagantly as the Chicago Plan was no more than a single mimeographed Negro history unit developed by an excellent teacher and completely ignored by the overwhelming majority of her colleagues. But there were other "plans"—even more comprehensive and more effective—such as the Springfield Plan. Perhaps all that was needed was to learn about the best plan and then install it in her school?

But what magic blueprint could change the total orientation

of the majority of West High's staff, for whom intercultural education was someone else's business? What was the recipe for intercultural education in a curriculum geared to other objectives? How, in using another city's plan, would one allow for differences in the social pattern and in the needs of students from community to community, from school to school, from person to person? How did "taking over" another's plan dispose of the authoritarianism so deeply rooted in American education, where line-and-staff philosophy is so prevalent? What magic wand of a school superintendent or other mystical educational force would exorcise these obstacles?

She concluded that education is not plumbing. Schools simply cannot "put in" or "install" another school system's plan. Educators must adapt, not adopt.

Planning was possible, even necessary, but not "a plan" in the form of final answers, attractively packaged. The essence of educational planning, Ann learned, is that it proceeds through the united effort of teachers and administrators thinking together about the unique problems imbedded in their own unique situation. Planning will then eventuate in the development of appropriate experiences. Good education is indigenous. For example, excellent as the experiences of Springfield, Massachusetts, must be in meeting the needs of that community, a Springfield Plan cannot be transplanted elsewhere *in toto*. In reading of that plan, Ann found that responsible leaders in the Springfield schools have consistently opposed the idea that Springfield had a plan which was a set pattern, importable anywhere and guaranteed to produce a utopia within a week. They knew full well what it had taken to develop experiences appropriate to the Springfield situation.

As she read on, Ann found many materials, approaches, and promising practices available to those truly concerned for the long-term educational task of changing a nation's attitudes. There were many assumptions and beliefs as to which approaches were most workable but little of the proof positive which advertisers usually profess to have. In fact, there were skeptics who maintained that there can be no proof positive in intercultural education, which is to say, no science of human relationships, since when dealing with that creature of infinite variety—man—the closely controlled experimentation of the science laboratory is impossible. Be that as it may, Ann found that many teachers were adapting to their own use numerous practices judged by them and by the teaching profession generally as promising. But nowhere did she discover a Master Plan, sprung full-grown from the brow of some educational Jove. She concluded that babies and good educational programs are not born and matured so easily as that.

There were, then, no easy answers. There was only the long way that could not be shortened, despite the pleadings of those who yearned for "quickies" as substitutes for the use of intelligence. The long way involved learning from the experience of others and experimentally developing curricular experiences built up from the needs of particular students, throwing light on the social realities of our culture, and affording opportunities for the formation and application of a consistent philosophy. It involved co-operative work, shared purposes, and friendly relationships with colleagues as well as with students—in short, a democratic group process.

Learning with Others

As Ann equipped herself better to help build democratic attitudes and behavior in the adolescents with whom she worked, she purposely rejected the role of a lone wolf, for she knew how meaningful learning with others could be. With two of her colleagues and with interested teachers from other schools she formed a group that specialized in intercultural education. They met regularly during the Middletown curriculum workshop.

Many are the sensible courses the group might have adopted. There is no mandatory road to learning on the intercultural frontier; many roads lead to the Rome of better teaching. This group chose to initiate a long-term study of intercultural needs, social realities, and values; their meetings were primarily devoted to learning what teachers actually did to foster democratic human relations with their students.

A major competitor to this choice was the proposal to focus solely on understanding the intercultural needs, problems, and tensions of adolescents through surveys and case studies of adolescents in Middletown. This was proposed because the group members judged themselves less informed on the nature of their own students than on society and world views. Had it been adopted, this approach might have involved the careful observation and study of particular individuals and of friendship groups in the workshop's demonstration class. It might have included learning sociometric techniques, such as the measurement of social distance and the devising of interest inventories to help determine student concerns; such techniques Ann judged to be helpful ways of supplementing the indispensable combination of the naked eye and common sense. To her list of planned reading she added *Reorganizing Secondary Education,*[2] a report on years of study by a commission of the Progressive Education Association; *Teacher-Pupil Planning,*[3] *We, the Children,*[4] and *The American High School.*[5]

After time spent fruitfully in orienting themselves with respect to such sources and to new approaches to the problems of adolescents, the group decided to reserve intensive study of the needs of youth in our culture for the school year, when the teachers might relate their reading, techniques, and study of individuals and groups to the individuals and groups who made up

[2] *Reorganizing Secondary Education,* by V. T. Thayer, Caroline B. Zachry, and Ruth Kotinsky, for the Commission on the Secondary School Curriculum, Progressive Education Association (New York: D. Appleton-Century Co., 1939).

[3] *Teacher-Pupil Planning,* by H. H. Giles (New York: Harper & Brothers, 1941).

[4] "We, the Children," in *Educational Leadership,* March, 1945.

[5] *The American High School,* Hollis Caswell, chairman; eighth yearbook of the John Dewey Society (New York: Harper & Brothers, 1946).

their particular classes. Similarly, the participants in the study laid plans for gaining a broader understanding of both social realities and values, initiated reading and other experiences, but decided on a program of continuous learning in the months ahead rather than on one of intensive emphasis in their few precious weeks together. They planned to meet occasionally throughout the school year to share reports on progress and perplexities.

Ann found that, like many social studies teachers, she had a fairly substantial grounding in social realities. Yet workshop trips to various cultural groups and talks with teachers of youth from varied stocks opened up vistas whose existence she had only suspected. She knew her community fairly well but learned still more of the patterns of segregation through a mimeographed report prepared by the local Urban League. Although antagonisms between the children of new and old Americans persisted in her neighborhood, the ever growing antagonism was between established whites and incoming Negroes. Maybe that was a community front on which in the year ahead she should work with parents.

Mentally she ticked off the authors on cultural relations whom she had read in the past few years: Carey McWilliams, Louis Adamic, Lillian Smith, Ruth Benedict. Of the extensive available literature, she chose to begin now and continue into the school year with what seemed most relevant to the emerging problems of the northern Middletown in which she lived: *Black Metropolis*,[6] a study of Negro life in Chicago; *Primer for White Folks*,[7] an anthology; *Sense and Nonsense about Race*,[8] a pamphlet against racial mythology; and *An American Dilemma*,[9] the monumental

[6] *Black Metropolis*, by St. Clair Drake and Horace R. Cayton (New York: Harcourt, Brace & Co., 1945).

[7] *Primer for White Folks*, Bucklin Moon, editor (New York: Doubleday, Doran and Co., 1945).

[8] *Sense and Nonsense about Race*, by Ethel J. Alpenfels (New York: American Missionary Association, 1946).

[9] *An American Dilemma*, by Gunnar Myrdal (New York: Harper & Brothers, 1944).

study of the Negro and the American conscience. Such reading would strengthen her ability to help white students and parents to understand not "the Negro problem" but the white man's problem of hostility toward a minority group. It was a plan of reading which would lead into action, and that Ann deemed important. She began to ponder ways of sharing what she learned with parents; she listed possible consultants for PTA sessions.

As to reconstructing values, Ann refused to assume that she had arrived at a final philosophy and had no more to learn. With years of teaching experience behind her, she found new meaning as she began to reread Dewey, Kilpatrick, and Bode on the democratic way of life which is our American commitment. Since she was one of the many for whom writing clarifies ideas, she wrote down during the summer, on a single page, what her basic educational purposes now were. She tried out her statement of purposes on workshop friends, and she thought long and earnestly of what such a philosophy meant in her daily classroom living. Thus she and others continued the endless process of building better backgrounds for experimental and functional teaching.

The Study of Practices to Develop "Know-How"

In meetings of the intercultural study group, it was "know-how" that they were after. The practices which they had themselves developed, or of which they had learned, were the subject of many vigorous and rewarding sessions. The group came early to an acceptance of a multiple approach and to a realization that —given varied teacher personalities, student needs, and community situations—one man's meat might be another man's poison.

Based on her experiences and the curricular conclusions she had tentatively reached, Ann believed that the greatest hope for vital intercultural education lay in general education approaches which dealt realistically with community situations and with individuals. She admitted that she was not impressed with the potentiality of pervasive emphasis (the absent-minded approach, as she sometimes termed it), for she was not convinced of its far-reaching effect on student attitudes. It was not that she ruled pervasive emphasis out; she refused, however, to rest content with it or to regard the subjects which the high school of today has inherited as the perpetual and only channel for the experiences important to all students. She did not believe in cutting the person to fit the suit or in letting the tools that happened to be at hand determine the architecture of the house.

History and Human Relations

Certainly, she admitted, the pervasive approach in her major subject, American history, sometimes seemed well used. Central High School in Tulsa, Oklahoma, used history to help youngsters to think critically about the melting pot and the adequacy of such concepts as "tolerance." The Long Beach, California, history units repeatedly raised questions about minority groups in America, how and why they became American, what contributions to America they make, what problems they face. At Friends Central School in Philadelphia the importance of studying people was stressed in a course that opened with the question: "What is an American?" At the Central High School in Columbus, Ohio, history teaching condemned intolerance and stressed the recognition of services made to the nation by members of minority groups. In East High School in Akron a special study was made of the application of the principles of democracy to the attitudes of the majority toward minority groups.[10] The cases of which she read strengthened her resolve to try to produce a greater impact on student attitudes through the history courses she probably would continue to teach.[11]

For instance, she determined to take better advantage of opportunities afforded by the American history course for the under-

[10] *Democratic Human Relations*, Hilda Taba and William Van Til, editors (Washington: National Council for the Social Studies, 1945), Chapter IV.

[11] *The Study and Teaching of American History*, Richard E. Thursfield, editor (Washington: National Council for the Social Studies, 1946), Chapter V.

standing of the democratic way of life. American documents
from the Mayflower Compact to the Atlantic Charter, as well as
American experiences from the persecution of Roger Williams
to the war against the racist state, were replete with democratic
meanings. The real problem of the history teacher was to stay
close enough to student concerns to make such matters vital to the
learner. With able teaching a group might profit interculturally
at such points in our history as the following: the treatment of
the American Indian; the struggle for religious freedom in the
colonies; the conflict between the haves and the have-nots in
Revolutionary and post-Revolutionary days; the varied nationalities who settled the new nation; the "peculiar institution" of
slavery; the growth of sectionalism; the tragic Civil War; the
scars of reconstruction; segregation enforced by custom and by
Ku Kluxism; the tide of immigrants, their problems of adjustment,
and their contributions; the hate groups in American life and
their scapegoats; the discrimination against Orientals; the influence of urban living on hostilities; conflicts among class groups;
restriction of immigration; American attitudes toward war enemies; and the handling of Japanese-Americans in the Second
World War.

Some General Education Experiences

Yet Ann confessed to feeling excitement at the potentialities of
intercultural experiences unrestricted by the limitations of subject
matter—even those of such a subject as history, which is one of
the natural channels for the pervasive approach. One recognizes
such general education experiences not by the label of a course,
for labels—biology, social studies, or even the noncommittal term
"core course"—may be misleading. One recognizes these experiences by other signs: a readiness to begin with the actual persistent problems of youngsters; an earthy realism involving community participation and facing of the social situation; and a repeated application of democratic principles as the test of practice.

Among such experiences of which Ann's group learned were

those of a senior class of the Longfellow High School in Yonkers. That group decided to look into the composition of their own class and their own community. They dug for facts about their families and their town; they interviewed, read, and ferreted out data. They turned up stories of the lives of their parents and grandparents; they learned that, in their own class, 47 per cent of the children were sons and daughters of immigrants and 33 per cent more were grandchildren of immigrants. They looked critically at the facts which they unearthed and determined how they could best communicate them. They decided to produce a student-written commencement program, *America Is Only You and Me*. Before the assembled parents, finally, the program began with a conventional graduation address on Americanism and our Pilgrim ancestors, but this address was interrupted by students who pointed out the new-stock American background of the class and presented informal dramatic sketches of their parents' perplexities as they adjusted to a New World environment.[12] To Ann it seemed inevitable that such an experience, carried on over a period of months, would have a lasting influence on the adolescents who participated and would be long remembered by all involved.

Could she use such an approach? She thought of Miss Levy, the English teacher charged with responsibility for dramatics. Adeline Levy had often wished aloud in the faculty room that youngsters might some day write a play of their own, rather than always choose from the Samuel French catalogue, which offered dramatic delicacies with such titles as *Minnie's Mad Monday*.

Perhaps if Ann's history students came upon an issue that genuinely stirred them—hate groups in America or labor-management struggles, for instance—they might concentrate for a month on the documentary approach of fact finding, discussion, and evaluation. Through joining the extracurricular dramatics group of Miss Levy they might develop, and eventually present,

[12] *They See for Themselves*, by Spencer Brown (New York: Harper & Brothers, 1945).

a play based on community research. In *They See for Themselves*, a book on the documentary approach used in schools in New York City and Westchester County, New York, there were many leads on how to proceed. This book, thought Ann, would help to give Adeline Levy assurance.

With one successful experience behind her, maybe Adeline would be able to develop a democratic group like the radio class of the Glenville High School in Cleveland. Glenville's radio group, in a neighborhood formerly populated largely by Jewish people and now housing increasing numbers of Negro residents, has specialized in interpreting problems of the neighborhood to the school. Student-written plays on native American fascism and on the intercultural facts of life have been presented by the group. To Ann it seemed that these presentations must have been important to the participants, since members of the radio class joined with an area council of adults formed to deal with intercultural problems. And the best test, perhaps the only real test, of the strength of an attitude is whether it results in behavior consistent with that attitude. . . . So went Ann's reflections as she applied the documentary approach to her own school situation.

Since the workshop intercultural group shared what they had learned, Ann heard of still other ways in which teachers established a two-way passage between the school and the community.

Exchange of visits among schools, for instance, was an approach increasingly used. The quality of the visits ranged widely. At one extreme there was the possibly damaging kind of trip in which whites went to schools attended by Negroes to stare at those strange creatures, colored people—or vice versa. At the opposite extreme were the significant social travel experiences of New York City's Lincoln School students who lived for a time in the homes of West Virginia miners and of families in the Georgia hills and the Shenandoah Valley. But, in order to be significant, the trips did not have to be so extended and expensive as the Lincoln School trips, Ann found. Most American communities have immediately at hand cultural islands which can serve as laboratories for intercultural education.

Perhaps, Ann thought, she might join with Jane Tilson, the Spanish teacher, on another visit to the Spanish-American community house. She and Jane had best tie the experience in closely to the contents of their respective classes, so that the enterprise would not be a mere tourist lark. Maybe when Ann's history classes were studying the new immigration, the students might spend less time on memorizing a battery of facts about the entrant groups and on learning about the contributions of their great men. Thus the students would be able to spend more time on getting a realistic acquaintance with the everyday lives of the oldsters and the youngsters in one selected immigrant group. Jane would certainly tie in wholeheartedly on a Spanish-American project; perhaps her class and Ann's could meet in joint sessions while they were planning and preparing for the trip. Maybe, too, in planning the trip, the students and Jane and Ann could find ways of developing common experiences with their hosts—singing, dancing, eating together, and the like—as Edward G. Olsen has suggested in his pamphlet on social travel experiences[13] and as Rachel Davis DuBois has demonstrated through her life work.[14] And might not a trip of this sort sow seed that would grow into an experience of working together on a common enterprise—such, for instance, as the redecorating and refurnishing of a playroom in the community house?

Too bad that such an experience could not enter the curriculum as the school was now organized, but instead would have to be relegated to Saturday morning or late afternoon! As a matter of fact, thought Ann, one of the school's greatest failures was in not carrying out the democratic principle of working together with

[13] *Social Travel*, by Edward G. Olsen (New York: Hinds, Hayden & Eldredge, 1947).

[14] *Get Together Americans*, by Rachel Davis DuBois (New York: Harper & Brothers, 1943); and *Build Together Americans*, by Rachel Davis DuBois (New York: Hinds, Hayden & Eldredge, 1945).

others for shared purposes. Maybe she would have to depend on the extracurricular activities and out-of-school programs of work camps, youth hosteling, and community-oriented agencies if her youngsters were to have experiences with cultural groups other than those now included in the school population. She was troubled that the school waived such experiences, which she felt properly belonged in the curriculum.

However, she could do her best to see that adolescents of varied backgrounds worked together in shared activities—not only in sports, dramatics, and debating but also on planning committees, classroom panel discussions, work groups, interviews, and visits. She could work with adult-sponsored youth groups and extracurricular activities. And if the schedule and requirements permitted curricular opportunities for community participation of the kind described in *Learning the Ways of Democracy*,[15] and foreshadowed in that collection of intercultural practices, *School and Community Meet*,[16] she could be ready to proceed.

Essential Experiences

That the same need for time and freedom to teach the meaningful to individuals existed for other centers of experience than intercultural education, Ann knew well. Some of these all-important yet all but neglected centers are: personal development and self-understanding; home, school, and friends; health; recreation and leisure-time use; consumer education; vocations and work experience; education beyond high school; proposed roads for the American economy; workers, management, and government; communication and public opinion; ways of living in other nations; war in the modern world; efforts toward enduring peace; human, natural, and technological resources; world

[15] *Learning the Ways of Democracy*, prepared by the Educational Policies Commission, National Education Association (Washington: National Education Association and American Association of School Administrators, 1940).

[16] *School and Community Meet*, Samuel Everett, editor (New York: Hinds, Hayden & Eldredge, 1947).

views and ideologies. All involved adolescent concerns; all dealt with basic social realities; all could be used to develop understanding and practice of democratic living. Bringing out the wider relations and implications in each would, incidentally, supplement the more direct approach to intercultural education as one essential center of experience. If such centers of experience were actually important, then time would have to be set aside for them and opportunities provided for the teachers to know their students as individual persons. Teaching in such general education centers would have to become at least as respectable as is the present teaching of subjects required for college entrance to the 70 per cent and more of high school students who never enter college!

Ann judged that a partial solution to the riddle of how to develop such centers of experience—including the extension of democratic human relationships through intercultural education —might be in curricular reorganization. If the high school program could be revised to include a substantial block of time for general education and, supplementing this, a program of electives based on vocational choices and avocational needs, there would be a mandate to proceed with educational opportunities in the centers of experience most important in specific class situations. With fewer students working together in a longer block of time, teachers could meet individual needs and develop group activities. Putting across specific subject matter would no longer be the chief aim of teaching; helping adolescents to grow through solving life problems in a democratic society would become the goal. Subject matter and skills would be utilized and developed, but they would serve as means, not as ends. History, for instance, would become a tool to use in understanding personal-social problems instead of being taught as an end in itself. This would mean much more teaching and, more important, much more *learning* of functional history through both general education and elective courses.

Leads for the Future

Perhaps general education was not so remote from the immediate future as it sounded, Ann reasoned. She and John Mandoli, the English teacher, frequently were scheduled to teach twelfth-grade students at the same hour. Perhaps they could join their classes together for, say, a period of two months. Thus as she read of projects dealing with human relationships Ann stored up leads for future use.

The project or problem-centered approach was not confined to the experimental university schools, as she had thought; nor was intercultural education taught only in a few Northern states. One comprehensive study, "Americans All," involved a biological and psychological consideration of races and a psychological approach to prejudice and discrimination in Amarillo, Texas.[17] In Milwaukee, Wisconsin, the study of discrimination against Negroes in employment was skillfully carried out.[18] In Detroit a study of restrictive covenants and housing relations was part of a unit which helped to dramatize the American dilemma of democratic ideals and discriminatory practices.[19] In the Lincoln School in New York City a study of the people of the city introduced a variety of topics. There were studies of the youngsters' own backgrounds and the acquisition of anthropological insights; there was research into Negro life in New York City through committees on journalism, health, and so forth; there was a work experience as Lincoln School youngsters cleared a play space in a polyglot neighborhood.[20]

Various groups handle the same general topic in different ways, depending on the composition and needs of the particular class

[17] *Democratic Human Relations*, Hilda Taba and William Van Til, editors (Washington: National Council for the Social Studies, 1945).

[18] "Negro Employment: A Curriculum Unit," by Helen B. Goetsch, in *Social Education*, December, 1944.

[19] *Promising Practices in Intergroup Education*, prepared for the Administrative Committee on Intercultural Education (Detroit: Board of Education, 1946).

[20] Unpublished material in the possession of Alice Stewart, formerly of the Horace Mann–Lincoln Schools.

making the study. Take Japanese-American relationships. Ninth-grade children in a Japanese-American relocation center school studied prejudice not only to round out their personal knowledge of prejudice against themselves, but also to learn more of the rocky road to acceptance for other groups in America. They learned that prejudice, like peace, is indivisible and that the discriminations directed against them were similarly experienced by others. They looked carefully at their own prejudices. Consequently, when they had the Bill of Rights printed for their center, they also prepared their own Bill of Responsibilities.[21] Meanwhile, in a West Coast high school, eleventh graders were studying "what shall we do about our Japanese Americans?" These white youngsters discussed the meaning of democracy, gathered information, and, fired by their findings, began a program of all-school education. This program involved school newspaper editorials, speakers from the community, films, and teams of students to talk to community groups.[22]

In West High, thought Ann, there are any number of intercultural matters close to student lives—the cliques in school life and their influence on elections, the change in the cultural composition of the community with the increase in Negro neighbors, the relations between youngsters and foreign-born parents or grandparents, to cite only a few.

Suppose we started with the last of these, she reflected, and through interviews and data gathering built some understanding and sympathetic appreciation of our immigrant backgrounds. We could discover why our parents and grandparents came to America, what they found here, how they adjusted to this brave new world, what values they cherished, how their children differed from themselves. And we should not forget fiction and biography as tools. We could think together about whether a youth should

[21] *Democratic Human Relations*, Hilda Taba and William Van Til, editors (Washington: National Council for the Social Studies, 1945), Chapter V.

[22] *The English Journal*, prepared for the National Council of Teachers of English (Chicago: University of Chicago Press, June, 1946), p. 340.

accept the mores of his parents or the ways of his contemporaries, or whether he should find principles for himself on which to depend. The youngsters of our school, largely white and children of the newer immigration, might, after self-study, be more ready to meet their new neighbors, the Negroes. Small groups might study housing. To make the study real, we should have to become personally acquainted with actual situations. That is still another thing for me to talk to the Urban League director about, mused Ann. If ignorance bars some of my group from acquaintance with others, I may have to get help from our science staff to make known the results of blood experiments and share meaningful anthropological knowledge. And I must never let the group experience, important as it is, replace friendly relationships with individuals and the steady building of self-acceptance and self-understanding. Group experiences must be a supplement, not a substitute.

What we learn must eventually be applied to school life, for the injunction "physician, heal thyself" is still good. The policy of blackballing in one of our clubs has long been a bone of contention. Maybe. . . .

And so went Ann's thinking before she began her final workshop self-assignment, setting down a battery of possible initiatory, central, and culminating activities in a resource unit which she might draw upon in working with her students in the school.

A Teacher's Role with the Faculty

If she had been a utopian, Ann would have dreamed of engaging all the faculty in fundamental rethinking of the curriculum. As a realist, she knew that administration held the key. In the actual not-so-perfect world, Ann hoped to share ideas with the faculty and administration through a school intercultural committee which might well be appointed if she and her fellows in the workshop continued to stress the need for the Fourth R. She hoped that membership on the committee would be open to anyone who wished to join, and thus prevent the development of the fatal feeling on the part of neutrals and the few hostile staff members that they were being consciously excluded.

Maybe at first any such committee would be composed of a small group of like-minded staff members, the teachers about whose work Ann had thought when she looked for the brighter side of the picture of human relationships in her high school. Perhaps plans for joint teaching of general education units could grow from a conviction of common purposes. Fortunate, too, that among these faculty members there were no zealots who offensively flaunted their own virtues and sagacity and addressed others as though bringing the gospel to the heathen. Ann had met one or two teachers of this type in the workshop and judged them intercultural education's worst ambassadors.

If work and fun were joined, the committee might grow. Perhaps, Ann reflected, they would hold their evening meetings at one another's homes, at foreign restaurants, and in community centers, rather than at school. The main business of the evening might be the swapping of experiences in building relationships, or it might be getting acquainted with the ways of their community's various culture groups through visiting or entertaining members of these groups, or through sharing what they had learned from the reading they could find time to do. If John Mandoli, for instance, joined the committee, his intention to become an administrator would lead him to explore further the techniques of democratic school administration. And, if John did get the vice-principalship which Ann suspected he was yearning for, then what a good chance there would be for a program focused on the essential experiences!

Ann Smith, an American high school teacher in Middletown, was going back to her work this fall with a new glint in her eye.

CHAPTER VIII

THE SCHOOL AS A WHOLE[1]

A school system, like the families described in Chapter II, is seldom either all good or all bad with regard to its handling of intercultural relations. The present chapter realistically examines how one more or less typical system might appear to an enlightened observer. In a final section it delineates criteria for determining the extent to which a school is fostering democratic intercultural living.

A Visiting "Expert"

On a November evening in 1946, John Peregrine, a teacher from a neighboring community, arrived in Amtown, a midwestern city of 100,000 population, where he was to study intercultural education in the Amtown schools.

John was one of those teachers who want actively to help children live together democratically. In recent years he had taken a deep interest in intercultural education and had worked hard to develop a program for his own classes and his own school. At the same time he had felt the need of enlarging his understanding of the problem by studying the work of other schools in his vicinity. Finally the board of education, urged by John's superintendent, had granted him a long-deserved leave with pay so that he could assemble material that would help his colleagues develop an enriched program in intercultural education.

[1] This chapter was written by C. O. ARNDT, Professor of Education, New York University.

John and his superintendent had carefully thought through the purposes of the Amtown study. The plans they laid out included interviews with and a study of (1) the citizens, (2) the board of education, (3) the superintendent and teachers, and (4) the students and parents.

Contact with the realities of several communities had already taught John to vary his approach according to the situation. He had to consider the local patterns of segregation and the type of minority group problems to be found in the community— whether racial, religious, ethnic, or socio-economic. He also had to consider the administrative organization of the school and the relations that existed between teachers, administrators, and students. He had usually found that teachers were surprisingly fearful of him at first, apparently mistaking him for a snooper or "an expert."

What Some People in Amtown Were Thinking

John had found no better way to investigate intercultural attitudes or to learn what the public thought the schools were doing than through informal conversation. He therefore engaged the hotel desk clerk in talk on the subject.

The hotel clerk had graduated from the local high school fifteen years before. Said he: "We have no problem with Negroes here. They know we won't let them register in the hotel, so they don't even try. Any white person is admitted so long as he pays in advance. Our elevator man is a Negro and a good worker. I don't think we will have any problems with Negroes so long as we don't try to change our present customs."

"Are the local schools working on the problem of group relations?" John asked him.

"I don't know," the desk clerk said. "Never heard of such a thing. I don't think it is any of the school's business."

Early in his stay in Amtown, John Peregrine interviewed the local president of the NAACP. "One of our main concerns is to see that Negroes get the protection due them under the law. We find that the number of grievances is decreasing somewhat as the result of our efforts. On the positive side, we are trying to inform Negroes about desirable attitudes and, in turn, to develop good relationships with whites, including members of other minority groups. This work needs to be enlarged and strengthened."

John was not quite satisfied with the comments of the president, since they gave evidence of work only with Negroes. "Why don't you try to get Negroes and whites together so that by discussing and thinking together they may grow toward mutual understanding?" The president's reply gave evidence of serious thought. "We have tried that more than once, but without success so far," he said. "You see, we are a minority group and therefore not in a position to take the initiative. The invitation for co-operative action must come from the majority group that controls our community life. Our group will go more than halfway once the opportunity is offered for us all to meet and work together. Thus far we have found the legal approach the only one through which we can operate successfully."

A CIO labor organizer was another of John's informants. To his query, "Are members of minority groups eligible for membership in your union?" the response was strongly positive: "Our union does not draw the color line. We are of all religions, and many of our men are second-generation and some foreign-born. We look upon all workers as entitled to equal rights. That is simply good democracy, the American brand."

"But that is also contrary to the customs of this community," said John, thinking of the hotel clerk and the experiences of the president of the NAACP. "How are you able to bring it about?"

"Through education," said the labor leader. "In the CIO we tell our men that a strong union can be built only by bringing all workers under one roof. Every American citizen must have the right to a job and be protected at that job. If you keep some workers out because of race or nationality or religion, they will work against the union. They will break strikes, work as scabs. They have to live some way. By signing them up we prevent a break in labor ranks and at the same time strengthen our organization. Sure, that is a selfish reason, but I think it is good democracy, too."

"How did you come to your own democratic attitudes?" asked John.

"I guess through a teacher in the local high school. He still gives us advice. He is not a member of our union, mind you, but he helps anyway. I wish we had more teachers like him."

John went next to Amtown's best-known clergyman, a young Methodist who had lived in the city only three years. Some citizens thought he was no clergyman at all. They claimed he did not preach the Gospel in his church on Sundays but was always talking about politics and social problems. His job was not confined to the pulpit. Trying to help the underprivileged, he worked harder on week days than on Sundays. And it was this extracurricular work which won for him public acclaim among Amtown's more socially sensitive citizens.

"I understand that you are working toward the development of an adult education program," John began; "I hear you are trying to bring people from the various groups of the community together. Do you get support from the local schools in this work?"

"Yes, we do," the clergyman replied. "The adult education program in this community is receiving direct support from staff members of the local public and parochial schools. You know, we have both Catholic and Lutheran parochial schools in our community. I couldn't say exactly who started this project. The local superintendent had long been interested in the idea. So had some of his teachers. When they found that I was interested and also some other local citizens, the idea began to take form. The superintendent and the board of education quickly made classrooms and library facilities available. The public library helped.

"More and more people in this community are realizing that education continues beyond school. We learn as long as we live. But there are some things which we will not readily learn unless we plan certain learning experiences carefully.

"You are interested in human relations work, you say. My idea at first was to organize adult classes on human relations or intercultural education. As a matter of fact, I did this and for a while we held evening classes in the basement of my church. People from different churches attended. We did not go so far as to include Negroes. People did not seem to be ready for that. We got people with different religions and different jobs together, though. You will be glad to know that two policemen became interested in our class and attended quite regularly. We began to see their problems in a new light, and I think they gained from friendly discussions with us. After all, policemen play an important role in the development of group relations in the community. They can become human relations engineers rather than merely law enforcement officers if the community trains them well."

"Why, then, did you discontinue your classes?" asked John.

"Because, by talking with the superintendent, teachers, and others, I began to see the possibilities of adult education as broader than simply one class on one great problem. I still feel that intercultural education is a central problem in this community and in America generally. But we should offer training in other fields as well. Just working together on common problems is itself important intercultural education.

"We now have a steering committee made up of the school superintendent, a teacher, a clergyman, a lawyer, a labor leader, and a mother of school-age children. We are planning courses for next summer and fall at the Central High School in homemaking, gardening, current events, new books, and last, but not least, intercultural education. All classes are open to all citizens of the community. People seem more willing to have all races together in the school than in the church. We expect to get still more non-Protestants, too, when the sessions are held on public ground, such as the public school. If we do not get all citizens to take a course in intercultural education, we still are moving forward in this area by getting adults from all groups together in classes so that they can talk and work together."

"How about some recreation in your adult education program? I mean such things as volley ball or indoor baseball. You have a fine gymnasium at the high school."

"There has been some talk about that," said the clergyman, "but no decision thus far. It seems that the gymnasium is used almost every night. Right now it is basketball practice and games."

"But how many people take part in basketball? Are the numbers large enough to warrant the present use of the gym?"

"I do not think so," said the clergyman. "I will try to delve into this matter further. Offhand, I think we might have better luck in getting the art and music rooms. You may be right in implying that the program is too academic."

As John talked to others in the community he found that each person displayed similar friendly or hostile intercultural attitudes. Finally, he felt he had a good sampling, and upon return to his hotel room one evening he wrote the following summary into his record book:

The influence of the school as a whole on group relations in this community is making itself felt very slowly. Some citizens know nothing of its efforts and consider work in this area to be none of the school's business. But there is definite evidence of progress as shown by the plans for an adult education program.

It appears significant to note that the school as such need not always be the initiating agency for desirable social changes in a given community. At times it can work more effectively through other channels, such as churches or labor unions. As citizens, teachers may also be church members or members of unions, and, if they can use their influence toward furthering constructive work through these agencies, they are merely broadening the scope of attack on inter-group problems. At the appropriate moment, they can enlist the active support of the school.

It should be noted further that the school as a whole includes parents and other citizens. As their active co-operation is enlisted in intercultural education, the school becomes in a fuller sense "a community school."

The Board of Education

John had a short discussion with the superintendent of schools the following afternoon. The superintendent was definitely interested in John's study, invited him to attend a scheduled monthly business meeting of the board of education the following evening, and asked him to plan for a half hour of discussion with the board.

The day of the meeting John spent profitably. He visited classes in a grade school during the morning and in a high school during the afternoon.

At the board meeting the superintendent, in introducing John, commented briefly and favorably on the purpose of his visit.

In closing his remarks, John said, "As you gentlemen know, the recent war made this nation aware, as never before, of the value of its human resources. Threatened by invasion, we quickly organized our natural, industrial, and human resources to defeat the enemy. A Fair Employment Practices Committee was set up to assure fair and equitable treatment of all laborers in the war effort. This planning and action on a national scale brought results that astounded the world. We achieved a miracle in production; we developed a military force second to none in the world. All this was achieved in a very short period of time.

"The purpose of my study of inter-group relations or intercultural education is to learn what Amtown and other cities throughout this country are doing toward preserving and enlarging the national solidarity which we moved toward so significantly during the war years. Specifically, I am interested to know how the schools of this community are working toward the development of understanding among its various religious, racial, nationality, and economic groups. My major question to you, therefore, as the elected representatives of the citizenry of this community, is: What is your policy toward your minority groups?"

What John was after was not too clear in the mind of the president of the board. Since, however, all eyes turned to him, he attempted to rise to the occasion.

"Do you mean whether we admit Negroes to our schools? Of course we do. Our schools are for all of our young people. It has always been the law to have all schools of this community open to all youth. We had some complaints about this during the war when many new people moved in from the outside, but we still follow our old policy."

Board member Smith said, "The policy is O.K. for our own people, but I am not so sure what we should do if we get more outsiders in here or if those who came during the war stay on. They are not like our children."

A third and a fourth member stated that they favored the established policy as given by the president. That seemed to settle the question for the present.

John thought he ought to determine whether the board was merely following precedent or whether it was really concerned with the equal rights of all people.

"I hope you won't mind my next question, gentlemen. Would you hire a Jew as a member of your faculty?"

The president now turned to the superintendent. "Do we have any Jewish teachers in our schools?"

"Not to my knowledge," said the superintendent, a bit uneasily.

"But that is not because our policy prevents it, is it? We just have never done it. I suppose we have not had any good Jewish applicants. Is that right?"

"The fact is that since I have been here I have never paid attention to the race or religion of an applicant. I wanted to know only whether he or she was a good teacher." John watched the superintendent as he made his point, and the latter did not seem too comfortable on this issue.

"I think," said Smith, "that we should follow our established policy about teachers. We have an unwritten policy and everybody knows it. Let us hire the kind we have been hiring. We know our community wants that."

After some apparent hesitation the superintendent decided to speak out. "It seems to me," he said, "that the time has come for the board to make a clear-cut public statement of policy on education for better human relations. The school personnel and the community will then know the official position of the board, which I trust will be opposed to all discrimination. This will prevent misunderstandings and confusion on the part of those of us who work with the schools. I suggest that we discuss this matter further at an early meeting rather than right now."

John did not wish to wear out his welcome. He thanked the board members for their attention.

"You know," said the president, "I'd like to read your report sometime. We would all profit from learning what you found not only in Amtown but also in the other places you are studying."

"I shall be glad to supply you with a copy."

The president's interest encouraged expression of an idea which was taking form in the mind of the superintendent. "I'm interested in the 'so what' of your study," said he. "That is, what concretely we can do to strengthen our school policy. Yesterday, Mr. Peregrine, you told me that a foundation was supporting your study. Let me make a suggestion to you if it meets with the approval of the board. I wish to propose that the foundation match the board in providing funds for conducting a workshop or conference for members of the school board, say sometime next summer. Let us find out what school boards are doing over the country in this important field of intercultural education. Maybe the workshop should run for only a week end as a start."

"Sounds like a good idea to me. Any objections?" asked the president.

Every board member concurred.

"Pick out a cool place on a lake that has fishing," jovially added one of the members.

That night John's notebook entry was as follows:

Apparently the board is quite sensitive to community pressures. And the superintendent is sensitive to what the board approves. As problems are posed for solution the board seems immediately to refer to precedents. My question about the Jewish teacher is a case in point.

The superintendent must be encouraged in his obvious desire to overcome this policy of expediency and develop in its place a reference to democratic principles. This cannot be achieved overnight. But it must become standard practice if the school is to become a vital training center for citizenship in American democracy.

The suggestion of a conference or workshop for school board members is deserving of special note. Even as teachers learn from one another through such experiences, so also may board members. The Kellogg Foundation has already sponsored some work in this area. Write to the X Foundation about this matter.

The Superintendent

John had acquired some understanding of the superintendent as a result of the meeting with the board. He wished, however, to know the superintendent better and to learn particularly how he worked with his staff. To this end he made an appointment to visit the superintendent in his office and later to attend a staff meeting.

"What did you think of the board meeting the other evening?" was the superintendent's first question.

"I enjoyed it and appreciated, among other things, the suggestion about a conference for board members. I will follow up on that idea. Maybe such a conference will be a key to your problem of working with your board toward implementing democracy in the school program."

"I am sure you noted," said the superintendent, "that there are obstacles to the progress of school policies. One board member, Smith, is a particular problem, and he has strong backing from certain pressure groups in the community."

"Apparently his objections were not sustained last evening. Can he be overridden?"

"I don't believe in that method, because I do not think it is fundamentally sound or enduring. It appears sounder to trust to the educative process, particularly when important problems need to be solved and one has the support of at least some other board members. You see, Mr. Peregrine, I have to work with these people year in, year out. It is not possible to hand-pick a board of education. They must learn on the job and I can't do their learning for them."

"That will take a long time," John said, "particularly in the field of intercultural relations, where patterns are so firmly set. How are you assured of progress?"

"I'm not assured. In this world, the gods give no guarantees. My assumption is that we are trying to train youth for life in American democracy. The very foundations of our way of life are based on the principle that all people are created equal. Few Americans will quarrel with this assumption, though many will work against its practical implementation. In my work with the board, I am working toward the development of a frame of reference based upon this principle. As problems arise we try to examine them carefully and then check the analysis against this and other democratic principles."

"I am not so sure that the board is conversant with these principles in view of our discussion of the Jewish teacher," said John.

"That is quite true, and I appreciate your frankness. The fact is that the board showed readier agreement in your presence than they usually do on a question of this kind. They knew the object of your visit and wished to make a good impression. Smith, for example, was on his good behavior and accepted the leadership of the president for the evening. A forthright statement of intercultural policy on personnel or instruction is not yet written and accepted, nor will it be before much more work is done.

"Now you can help me. As a result of your study of other school systems do you have any suggestions to make toward democratizing our board procedure and policy?"

"Well," said John, "that is not exactly my function, but your direct question apparently disposes of this technicality. There are no easy answers and I am doubtful whether there is any plan that can be installed in all communities like standard plumbing. But there are at least two ideas I have picked up.

"In the Westville High School the superintendent and board last year, when the subject of released time for religious instruction was under consideration, invited to their meetings community leaders who represented different religious groups and varied viewpoints. By consulting with these leaders before the establishment of board policy, many difficulties were avoided. In fact, the results were so beneficial that this board subsequently consulted labor leaders and professional men in the community when employment policy and wages were being worked out. Therefore it does seem that getting community participation in policy making is a good idea.

"Then there is a community school in Alabama in which the school administration is carried out largely through teachers' and students' committees. It has become standard procedure there to invite the respective chairmen of these teacher and student committees to attend board meetings when problems in their area are being considered. I remember reading an account of such a board meeting at which the student council was under fire. Three high school students attended this meeting. They developed an even greater sense of responsibility after talking directly with the board of education. In turn, the board members gained valuable insight into the actual operation of the school. They came away knowing what the youngsters were thinking."

"Thanks for those illustrations," said the superintendent.

"You will find many more in Theodore Brameld's *Minority*

Problems in the Public Schools.[2] It is a survey of administrative policies and practices in seven school systems and well worth your reading. Brameld is a realist, and he calls a spade a spade."

"That is the kind of help I need," said the superintendent.

"The Methodist clergyman here told me about the adult education program for next summer," said John. "Shouldn't the initiative for this enterprise have come from the school?"

"That is a fair question when asked by a survey maker from another community," the superintendent said amiably. "My view here is that a superintendent should have wide interests, including an interest in adult education. It is not necessary, however, that he be the originator of all things educational. Let's not be utopian. I grant that he should work on problems of this kind; but, if a citizen or citizens have seen the light and are ready to move, why not work through them? Doesn't this project promise to enlist many local citizens in the educative process and also afford them a positive outlet for their energies? Remember, we are building educationally for the entire community."

"Fair enough," said John. "By the way, I suspect that the clergyman still believes that inter-group understanding is best built through a fixed course of study in intercultural education. What is your thinking on this point?"

"You don't know the whole story of this. Some of us school people thought that the break-up of his church class in intercultural relations might not have been too unfortunate. At any rate, we hoped he would learn a lesson from it. Our point was that through our offering a wide range of courses and experiences based on adult needs, the same results the preacher had in mind would be achieved. We stressed the principle of equal educational opportunities for *all* citizens. Classes are to be open to *all*. Our belief is that, for adults, intercultural understanding will come as a byproduct of studying together and exchanging ideas as between citizens."

[2] *Minority Problems in the Public Schools*, by Theodore Brameld (New York: Harper & Brothers, 1946).

"As a teacher," said John, "I honestly wonder whether inter-group understanding does come about just because people of varying backgrounds meet in classrooms. If this were true, then this community and indeed this nation would inevitably change during the next several decades, for do not people of various races, creeds, and nationalities go to school together in most parts of this country? The evidence seems to be that to effect the desired change in attitude you will have to plan your courses and other experiences in such a way that the people involved will actually learn to work and play together. They will have to think together about their common problems and actively work together to solve social problems. And some of these problems are intercultural."

"I agree with you," interrupted the superintendent, stimulated by this comment. "We must go further than merely incidental meeting of problems. We must come to grips with the socio-economic inequalities which exist in our community and in the nation at large. I have deep convictions on these matters but I can't see how I can attack them openly until community support has been built up sufficiently. In this community, these adult education classes will provide a way of building support.

"We have our problems, even though we tend to deny it. Just think of it, our local churches discourage Negroes from attendance though they profess to worship a God who is no respecter of persons. We have 'Christians only' advertisements in our newspapers. Our hotels and restaurants are closed to colored people. Real estate men look with suspicion on southern European buyers of property. Such inequalities must be removed if our community and nation are to become strong, if we are to become a united people. And until in this whole community we develop democratic human relationships based on the equal socio-economic rights of all people, regardless of their race, creed, or nationality, the work of the school in this direction will not achieve its purpose."

"But the school can help achieve those relationships," said John, "through adult education centered on working and playing together and attacking community problems, through an education for children centered on democratic living, and through teachers who regard themselves also as responsible citizens."

"I think you have a good point and I like your definition of the front I have to work on," said the superintendent thoughtfully.

A Faculty Meeting

At 3:30 P.M. John went with the superintendent to the faculty meeting. He had asked not to be introduced, since he wished merely to be an observer.

The meeting was devoted to routine business. One of the last items on the agenda was a report on relationships with parents. The superintendent, who presided, called for a report from the Committee on Co-operation with the PTA at the Amtown High School.

"We have had several meetings with representatives of the PTA," said the chairman of the committee, "and I wish you would look over a mimeographed copy of our report which is being distributed. You will note that we list the programs for each meeting this year, together with the names of those who will be responsible for each meeting. This is in line with our procedures in other years. We have also listed some things which the school needs by way of equipment. We did this at the request of parents who wished to do something really helpful for the school. Are there any comments on the report?"

There were a few desultory comments of approval. Then an English teacher spoke up, somewhat hesitantly. "Since we are on the subject of the PTA, I would like to make some suggestions about other ways by which we can involve our parents in the work of the school, aside from those which we have always used in the past. As you know, I am doing experimental work this year in classes called 'General Education.' I have two classes, each of which extends over two periods. Much of the work grows out of student-teacher planning and is quite different from the English literature classes which I have taught in other years.

"Now here is my point. I wish to have the parents of the students in my classes know what we are doing and have them know it by direct observation. I'd like them to visit my classes and then arrange for meetings, first at school and then in the homes of the different parents, in order to discuss the work we are doing. They may be able to give me some suggestions. And then I have another reason—I want to learn to know the homes of my students, who not only are individuals but are also of various races, religions, and social classes. I have discussed this suggestion with the superintendent, and he has told me to bring it up for discussion in a staff meeting at some appropriate time. I think this is the appropriate time."

"My reason for making this suggestion," said the superintendent, "was that I wanted to hear your comments on the proposal. I think it is worthy of serious thought."

"I wonder whether you have thought of what your proposal really means," commented a mathematics teacher. "If all of us urge all our students' parents to visit all the classes which their children attend, we are going to have an awful lot of parents in this school. How shall we find seats for them all? Is this visitation really necessary?"

"Why do we have report cards, anyway?" asked another teacher. "If parents really want to know about their children's work, they not only have the reports but can also ask their own children or the principal or teacher whatever they want to know."

"There is another point which I wish to make," said another teacher. "I am concerned about holding parents' meetings in parents' homes. It seems to me that the school is the place for the PTA meetings. It always has been. And, more important, you are going to get into trouble with minority group parents. Our well-to-do parents will not mix with them, and vice versa. I do not think you have thought through what you plan to do."

Many hands were in the air asking for the floor. The English teacher, noting the direction of the comments, took time out to say a few things herself in response to questions already raised. "To me," she said, "the important question is not how busy we are or what we are doing now to inform parents about our school. It is, rather, this: Are we using the parents in a manner that is really most helpful educationally?

"Might I add a word regarding the mixing of parents and the anticipated ill effects? I think that many parents will want to know the parents of their children's friends. That is quite natural. And I think it's healthy. Many kinds of people make up this community. They live here, and they are going to continue to live here. People need to get acquainted if there is going to be any working together in this city."

One teacher, desirous of reaching a compromise, rose to say: "It seems to me that it would be shortsighted to prevent this proposed work with parents. We do not all have to do it. After all, we always have had some parent visitation in our school. I favor the proposal for the General Education classes."

The realization on the part of a number of teachers that they need not follow this plan took the edge off their desire to protest, and a lull took place in the discussion.

The superintendent then summarized the discussion as follows: "It seems to me that we are not all agreed about parent visitation on a larger scale. However, no one has suggested that we should not try out parent visitation and participation in the General Education classes. I should like to suggest that the Committee on Cooperation with the PTA discuss this question with the parents to ascertain their attitude and then bring a report back to the staff. Any further discussion?" There was none, and the meeting was adjourned.

In summarizing his impressions of the superintendent and the teachers, John wrote as follows:

The superintendent would like to develop in the school as a whole a frame of reference which is in harmony with basic democratic principles. At times he appears to forget this purpose, but I believe it is deep-seated. His comments on the need for board members and others now in charge of public education to be re-educated with reference to intercultural relations were reassuring.

The superintendent's comments about the need to work toward a change in the socio-economic conditions which now obtain in the local community and the nation as a whole were significant. The fact that the adult education program is designed as a step in this direction lends credence to the superintendent's good intention. But one is forced to ask whether the superintendent has got very far in sharing his democratic ideas with the board and the teachers.

One of the first requisites would seem to be enlisting the active co-operation of a larger number of the school parents in community enterprises he hopes to foster. The families whose children attend the schools have problems and needs. Why not launch community changes by beginning with these? If the problem is garbage disposal, begin there! If the current major problem is an epidemic, begin there! In social science classes, for example, problems studied could be made live and significant by relating them to their manifestations in the local community. Socio-economic problems of the local community should be studied at first hand with a view to finding solutions for them. This would enable parents and students of all groups to work together on common problems. There may be better ways of breaking down intercultural antagonisms—but, if there are, I don't know of any.

As for the teachers, they are of varied abilities. As educators, some are good, some bad—and many seem, in more ways than one, indifferent! Avenues for the exchange of ideas are open to them, and apparently they can carry through constructive projects. If the teachers can catch a vision of what education could be, a school-community program is possible. But there has apparently been no progress beyond the formal PTA thus far, though individual teachers are beginning to move.

The Students

Following the faculty meeting, John spent a number of days in the schools of Amtown, visiting classes and watching students at play on the school grounds and in the gymnasium. In short, he observed the life of the school as a whole and particularly looked for the quality of human relationships exhibited and for the practices which helped and hindered. Only a selected number of his experiences can be related here.

There was, first of all, the social studies class which was zealously studying "the cultural contributions of minority groups to American life." In this work they were aided by their tireless teacher, who had a veritable museum of international curios in her classroom, as well as many pamphlets and books descriptive of Irish, German, Italian, and other groups in American life. Apparently this was not the first time she had taught these topics, and each year, as parents became involved in the studies undertaken by their children, some articles were given to the school and thus swelled the resources of future classes.

Asked whether they enjoyed this study, the students were generally favorable and even enthusiastic in their responses. The reasons given were that they did so many different kinds of things, including the preparation of scrapbooks, the gathering of curios from foreign countries, the writing of playlets, and the putting on of pageants. Several students mentioned the ready help given and interest shown in this course by their parents, some of whom even came to the class and gave talks. They claimed that they had learned a lot of facts about other cultural groups and had found everything very "interesting."

In the course of conversation, John found opportunities to say to some students, "I find that there are a number of Negro and Mexican-American students in your school. What kind of work do their parents do?"

"I don't know for sure," said one boy, "but I think the Negroes do mostly janitor work. Our school janitor is a Negro."

"All Mexicans are truck farmers, I think," added another.

"Do you happen to know where they live and what their houses are like?" asked John.

"They live on the other side of the tracks in old houses or shacks."

"Why do many Negroes do janitor work, and why do Mexican-Americans live in shacks?" pursued John.

"I guess they have always done janitor work. Mexicans don't have enough money to live in better houses. I like Negro spirituals and orchestra music."

"What about the Irish- and German-Americans?" asked John. "What kind of work do they do? Where do they live?"

"I don't think they have any special kind of work, and they live in clean places," replied one of the students. "They're just like we are. Mike here is Irish and proud of it."

"In your course have you studied questions like those I have just asked?" queried John.

"Not so far," was the reply.

Further inquiry revealed that questions about contemporary socio-economic conditions in relation to minority groups were not, according to present plans at least, to be dealt with in this social studies class. John seriously questioned how important the study of cultural contributions as presently taught could be in changing public attitude toward minority group members. It seemed to him that, until the socio-economic forces which control the lives of our citizens are changed and barriers to free association are broken down, the ability to describe the cultural contributions of the Italian- or Spanish-born to our national life might serve only as evidence of ability to memorize facts. Students must become aware of the need for such changes.

During the noon hours, John went to the cafeteria for lunch. He found that faculty members ate in a dining room separate from the large room which accommodated the student body. A teacher acted as general supervisor of the student lunchroom. Apparently students could sit wherever they desired. There was no segregation. It was apparent, however, that the Negroes tended to cluster together at separate tables, as did the students of Mexican extraction.

Once John chose to sit at a table which was occupied largely by Negroes.

"Do you boys always sit at this table?" asked John.

Most of the boys nodded in the affirmative.

"Why don't you move about from time to time so that you get to know other boys?" he continued.

"We do, once in a while, but we like to be with our pals during the noon hour," was the consensus of response.

"Do the teachers ever eat in this room?" asked John.

"No, they've got their own room," was the reply.

"Mr. Johnson, our coach, eats in this room during the next lunch period," said one of the boys; "I know because Jack told me. He's a swell guy. He sits with us sometimes. He sits with everybody."

"Would you like to have other teachers eat with you?" continued John.

Most of the boys thought they would feel better if they were alone.

As John reflected on the segregation practiced by both teachers and students, he saw that an opportunity for interaction had been lost. Why not work out a plan by which a given number of teachers in rotation would eat with the students in their dining room for a period of say one month? This would serve both to divide teacher responsibility and also afford the students an opportunity to meet all the teachers over the period of the school year. The emphasis at mealtime naturally should be on friendly talk, not on discipline.

Similarly, why not work toward breaking up the racial and national and the less noticeable but very real social-economic cliques at the luncheon tables? Perhaps the school might initiate occasional luncheon groupings based on common interest—members of a team, club, or council. For on the playground and in the gymnasium John had observed that in organized sports, such as basketball, baseball, and football, the boys best qualified to represent the school were put on the team. There was no discrimination. He learned, however, that a swimming pool had not been built in the high school because of the opposition toward having Negroes share the pool with whites. In the informal, spontaneous games there appeared to be a clustering of minority group students, and no apparent effort was made to change this situation. John made a mental note of the fact. It was characteristic of the all too frequent school situation in which intercultural education would be included in the course of study but left out of the day-by-day activities of school life.

The work of the student council appeared to be extremely helpful in developing good relations among students of all groups. Made up as it was of elected representatives from the freshman, sophomore, junior, and senior classes, under the guidance of a faculty adviser, it was given definite responsibilities and authority to act in such matters as bicycle and car parking and traffic on the school campus, the supervision of halls and lockers, and the guiding of visitors to their destinations. Though these functions appeared limited and mechanical, they were clearly defined and apparently no adult interfered.

John asked members of the student council whether they had any other duties and responsibilities and was informed that the limited area of operation had been given them by the superintendent at their request the year before. They wanted to have a clear understanding of exactly what their duties were. They also wanted to be sure that they could really act without interference. In former years their duties had been more numerous, but the staff had sometimes overruled their decisions. This they had resented; hence the request for a limitation of their function.

The Parents

On the night before his departure from Amtown, John attended the parent meeting called by the English teacher. He hoped for the best, since he knew that the achievement of democratic human relations called for parent participation.

After the General Education classwork had been described and discussed, several mothers hesitatingly indicated their desire to visit classes. Some others feared their boys or girls would not like it. It just was not customary to visit classes in Amtown. But almost all indicated their own personal readiness to visit the school.

Toward the close of the meeting one parent said, "I'd like to see us have some more meetings like this one so that we can ask more questions about your classes and the school generally. This meeting has cleared up for me many questions about what you are trying to do. For instance, I could not understand till now why the class made a study of fair employment practices in Amtown."

"I'd be glad to meet with you any time," said the English teacher. "But how about meetings in some of your homes instead of in the schoolhouse? We ought to get better acquainted with each other. I have visited many of your homes and plan to make the rounds completely before the year is over, if you will let me."

"That idea of meetings in our homes sounds good, but I'm not so sure," said one mother. "Some of us have big houses and some small homes. Maybe those whose homes are small would be ashamed to invite people."

"I think it would be better if we met in the school. Then nobody would have a problem in inviting people to their homes," was the comment of a Negro mother.

"Let's try it for once," said one of the few fathers in attendance. "My house is not new, but it is big and you are all welcome."

They set a date and the meeting adjourned. Now, thought the English teacher, if the next meeting focuses as successfully as this one on the central problem of their children's education, these parents may have a chance to know each other—a chance that reaches across class lines, nationality backgrounds, religious differences, racial barriers. Maybe we'll do more than meet in the months ahead. Maybe we'll find common problems to work at that will serve the welfare of all the children or all the people.

John's notes on the students and parents of Amtown read as follows:

Curriculum: Patterns of human relationships are confused. There is no formal legal segregation at the school, but sometimes there is integration and sometimes self-imposed segregation. Apparently the pattern of segregation is deeply established in the customs and habits of the community, and education must therefore move beyond the four walls of the school to break it down. The students pattern their behavior on the community mores. Persistent application of the democratic idea to student problems may be a real help in aiding students to apply beliefs consistently.

In the social studies class there was much good and interesting work on the contributions of minority groups to American life, but not a word thus far about why some minorities live in shacks, hold menial jobs, and face quotas or discrimination. Youth needs to learn more than the names of minority group leaders and artists and their contributions to American democracy; education must also be directed toward doing something to change the inequalities and discriminations which persist in our socio-economic world. Unless the pattern of the community also moves toward social change, the efforts of the school will be largely academic. That is why I think the General Education work, centered on real problems like job discrimination, is important—especially now that parents are being related to the program.

The student council is doing good work. Why? Because it has worked out ways, based on principles, by which to deal with students. And these principles are applied to all the students alike, whether they be Mexican, or old-stock American, or Catholic, or Jewish. All are treated as people. This experience of living by principles which are accepted by all, and of being punished if those principles are violated, is of the essence of democracy. We need to find more ways to enable more youth to have this vital experience.

Parents: Something has been started by the English teacher. Not only do the parents want to visit the school; they also want a chance to ask questions about the curriculum. They want to meet together to talk about something that ties them all together, namely, their children. Parents want to know the parents of their children's friends. This beginning is a "natural" for inter-group education.

My guess is that there will be quite a bit of parent visitation in the General Education classes this year. From there it can spread to the whole school—if the English teacher knows how to work with her colleagues, building friendships with them, gaining respect for her daily performance, and achieving status with the administration without appearing pampered. And there are other ways.

Some parents wanted to visit in one another's homes. Some parents were afraid of this. They noticed the Negro mothers in the audience. But with careful handling and determination to include *all* parents there is a good chance that this plan will go through. I'll bet on the English teacher and those parents.

Much later, back in his home community, with Amtown behind him as one of several communities he had visited and studied, John Peregrine wrote in an article for an intercultural magazine:

HALLMARKS OF A WHOLE-SCHOOL APPROACH TO INTERCULTURAL EDUCATION

What is the best way by which to develop a program of intercultural education for my class and for the school as a whole? Give us an outline, duly tested in practice, and we will follow it. Questions and comments such as these are not unusual among teachers in this country.

Now the plain fact is that there is no one way by which to do this job unless we would become totalitarian schoolmasters. Hitler's success in minority group persecution was marked and rapid, but his program was a negation of our way of life. Ostracism and persecution were his prime media of implementation. On the other hand, the job of building respect as between people through the educative process is delicate, involved. As we teachers strive to develop respect for the dignity of human personality we cannot, unless we would be grossly inconsistent, force a plan which has developed successfully in one community upon teachers who are working with different people in different situations in another community. Teachers in a democratic society must ever build and rebuild programs of intercultural education which grow out of local needs.

There are, however, certain questions you must ask of your school and community to determine whether they are enabling youth to learn the ways of democratic intercultural living. They are given here as aids in determining the measure of progress which has been achieved by a given school as a whole:

1. *Has a philosophy of education consonant with democratic human values been developed and put into practice in your school system?*

The failure of this nation to live such democratic principles of human relationships as those expressed in the Four Freedoms has caused many critics abroad to scoff at the high-sounding ideals in which we profess to believe. And their criticism is obviously warranted when practice lags too far behind principle. The fact remains, however, that the enunciation of principles is also evidence of a desire to improve the conditions which now exist. These principles serve as evidence of a sense of direction on the part of those who enunciated them and therefore constitute an essential step forward in a systematic effort to effect change.

If a philosophy of education consonant with democratic human values has been developed in your school and is really operative, how was this brought about? Again and again we find that a democratic philosophy is operative to the extent that the various elements in the school—parents, teachers, and administration—have participated in the development of the policy. The surest way to kill democratic human relations is to have any one group rule by fiat—as administration so frequently does.

2. *What evidence exists in the life of your community that intercultural education is being seriously undertaken by the school as a whole?*

To measure growth toward healthy, democratic inter-group relationships in the life of a given community, it is well to determine first of all the measure in which freedom to live and work is enjoyed by all. The numbers and kinds of agency which have been set up to bring about intercultural understanding and co-operation, of course, are important indices of effort. It should be noted, however, that they may also reflect a low ebb in human relations. Thus a study of the community must be designed both to determine the status of the inter-group relations which exist, and then, if these relations are in need of improvement, to assess the success of constructive measures which have been undertaken to improve relations.

3. *What is the policy of your board of education regarding intercultural education?*

For various reasons, including that of alleged strategy, a board of education may have developed no clear-cut policy in reference to intercultural education. Presumably, however, every board of education does have a policy, even though it may be vague in its outline.

The constituency or membership of the board of education is important with respect to policy development in intercultural education. Does the membership of your board represent all local citizens? Is community interest in intercultural education strong enough and based broadly enough to warrant advisement with the board of education?

A board with members having varied backgrounds will be likely to avoid provincialism and to create a forum for the hearing of many interests in the community life. This is a healthy state of affairs. It should here be noted, however, that a sound program of intercultural education will not necessarily grow out of the fact that a Czech-American or a union member or a Negro has been placed on the school board. Mere reorganization is not a sufficient answer. The change desired must come from a true dedication to the implementation of democratic principles on the part of the board membership as well as on that of the staff of the school as a whole.

4. *What is the attitude of the local school administrative officers toward intercultural education and toward democratic administration?*

Since the principal or superintendent is the highest professional and administrative authority in the school, his attitude toward intercultural education as an aspect of democratic education is of first importance. What does the record show regarding the work of your principal or superintendent (a) in the local schools and (b) in schools in which he has served previously?

The administrative procedures developed by the superintendent for operating the school system serve as a significant index to his philosophy of education as well as to his attitude toward intercultural education. Does he (a) run the school himself by giving orders or (b) reach administrative decisions in consultation with the board of education and with the teachers and parents? How does he work with the adult public of the community? The first task of intercultural education is sometimes to find ways of moving administrators toward democratic practice.

5. *Are minority students given "minority group" status in your school?*

A careful analysis of the learning process, with special reference to intercultural education, must center attention on the prime importance of the role of the learner. According to such an analysis, the student learns what he accepts as a basis for action, that is, what he lives. In other words, the significance which his experiences have for him determines both what he learns and the degree to which he learns it.

It appears, therefore, that approaches to education in which students—regardless of race, creed, or color—are afforded a maximal opportunity to interact in work and play and to plan co-operatively their educational experiences under the guidance of experienced teachers must be developed. Only through experiences in which living and learning are one will they be enabled to grow toward understanding and acceptance of one another.

Moreover, to assure success according to this conception of the learning process, all students must have vital experiences not only in the classroom but in the total life of the school as well. The measure to which such a complete participation has been successfully developed is an important index of the maturity and stature which intercultural education has achieved in your local school or school system. In what measure, then, do students from varying backgrounds have opportunities really to study, play, and work together as people? Is the climate of the school favorable or unfavorable toward such interaction?

6. *Is the intercultural work of the school rooted in the ongoing life of the community?*

In too large a measure the work in intercultural education—whether as a regular course or as an extracurricular activity—is academic and structural only. Questions as to why the members of some minority groups are largely laborers or why they are poorly housed are not often and seriously raised. Even more rare is the effort on the part of the school to work energetically toward the change of discriminatory practices in the community.

The extent to which the inter-group work of the school is based on a two-way passage between the school and the community largely determines its dynamic quality. Is your school working on real problems in human relations as they exist in your community, or are its efforts largely academic?

7. *What role do parents play in the development of the intercultural work of your school?*

A fuller understanding of the way in which students learn

reveals the importance of life outside the school in the learning process. The forces which influence and give direction to the student outside of school hours are large, diverse, and of great significance to the teacher.

Ready helpers for every teacher are the student's father and mother. They know the student's background, since they have been vitally interested parties in the development of that background. Parental information about students is available to the teacher, guidance worker, and administrator of the school once the essential relationships for communication are established with the parents.

With reference to school policy generally, including intercultural education, the parents constitute a vital link with the local community. If the school program can be developed with their active co-operation, their support for that program in the community will be forthcoming. And parental support is of telling significance, since the parents are taxpayers in the local community. If they can share in common enterprises as the school and community grow interrelated, a great leverage for social action is achieved.

Is your school using parents significantly in the development of its intercultural program? In what ways? How can their usefulness be enlarged?

No, there is no one or best way by which to begin or develop work on intercultural education in a given school or community. Detailed operation must be developed in view of the nature of the local situation. But recognition of the importance of democratic principles is fundamental to intelligent experimentation and operation.

The carrying out of democratic principles and attendant consistent practice at any of the levels here described will tend strongly to lead to further democratization at other levels. For the principles involved in a healthy program of democratic human relationships are powerful and persuasive. In writing of the prospects of intercultural education Brameld in his recent book, *Minority Problems in the Public Schools*,[3] says:

> In this connection we are reminded once more of Myrdal's important theory of the vicious circle of discrimination and segregation. Once such a circle is begun, it rises and expands into a spiral; the situation becomes increasingly vicious, and then it is difficult to reverse the trend. Once a reverse direction does begin, however, there is likewise an acceleration—this time away from segregation and discrimination and toward integration and equalization.

So it is in the school as a whole. There is no substitute for the democratic philosophy resolutely translated into practice. There is no authoritarian road to the quality of human relations we seek.

[3] *Minority Problems in the Public Schools*, by Theodore Brameld (New York: Harper & Brothers, 1946).

IN CONCLUSION[1]

The book is now before us. Such is life as the young person lives it. Ceaselessly, he is shaped by social forces. His life experiences are myriad, each in its way educative, each carrying its own meanings. Day by day, as the young person meets with the people who comprise his personal world, are his intercultural attitudes in the making. People, themselves shaped by the culture, become the agents of society in molding the young. Especially deep-rooted in the young person's personality structure are his experiences with family, groups, and school.

First of these three is the family, first to the child in point of time and first, at least usually, in the strong influence it exerts on the child's personality and his life outlook. By its chosen and cherished ways the family builds either feelings of security and acceptance or feelings of dissatisfaction and resentment. Sometimes a family most concerned for decent human relations may in its child rearing follow the very approaches most conducive to the creation of hostility and suspicion toward others!

Next off to school goes the child, possibly to meet inside its doors blindness to all but subject matter standards, or possibly— and how much better so!—to meet acceptance, belongingness, welcome as a person. Across the school's threshold thus may lie coldness, rejection, indifference, enforced conformity; or across it may lie acceptance of the importance of good relations, knowl-

---

[1] This chapter was written jointly by the two editors.

edge that a child is what he has lived, recognition that mere uniformity of treatment creates conflict and denies freedom.

The child grows older; horizons widen. Out of the cocoon of family and school he comes into close relationships with chosen ones of his fellows. His "crowd" now matters greatly to him, perhaps most of all. In it his quest is still for participation, acceptance, belongingness, a relationship in which he will have status.

The more favored youth will likely join adult-sponsored groups. Of these groups the ones that value the vital interests of the young person and operate with proper democratic processes may skillfully lead him through self-directing experiences toward satisfying maturity. These educative experiences can occur spontaneously or they can be fostered carefully by skilled leadership. But the adult-sponsored groups may not be wise, and the young person may be repelled by an authoritarian, sterile club dominated by adult personalities and patterns.

Or the young person, instead of joining an adult-sponsored group, may find his security, acceptance, and status in autonomous groups beyond the reach of adults. Such voluntary groups may, to be sure, be characterized by a democratic atmosphere and by wholesome intercultural attitudes. But, as in the case of some gangs, the outlook of members may be so resistant to control, so assertive of superiority, and so sensitive to status as to develop positive anti-social behavior. To such gangs those minority group members who seem in any way visibly "different" make ideal scapegoats, and on them are the self-superiority and status of the gangs often assertively demonstrated.

Meanwhile, the young person as he grows continuously older is still being educated in attitudes by the school, the institution in society formally dedicated to education. Alas, frequently only formally so dedicated! For there are American schools in which arrangements and practices hostile to good human relationships exist. There are schools where authoritarianism elbows out any effective democratic living, where community settings are ignored and no two-way passages built between the school and community, where intercultural attitudes are regarded as none of the school's business, where help in thinking through intercultural problems is denied the young person because of traditional pressures to which such a school gives priority. As between such anti-democratic practices or the more democratic, the choice must be made by the local citizenry, the board of education, the school administrators, the teachers, and the parents. These must decide which they will support. And no decision at all is, in effect, a decision against democracy; neutrality is a point of view—in effect, a vote of confidence in a status quo which includes discrimination and group hostility.

But, increasingly, school people are taking seriously the democratic mandate. They are recognizing that a democratic atmosphere must pervade school relationships if desirable intercultural attitudes are to be fostered. Such relationships, they are finding, must be as characteristic of board—superintendent relationships as of teacher—student relationships, or any other relationship among persons in the educational structure.

School people are thus now learning the importance of examining the total school environment to eliminate discrimination and to foster the healthiest possible attitudinal climate in which to educate against prejudice, educate for the American dream. They are learning, too, that school and community meet and that bad attitudes and discriminatory practices in either gets into the other; so that both must work consciously together if effective education is to result. School people are further learning the importance of knowing children as persons, studying them in their family and cultural settings, and working with them as individuals. In all of this they are learning to tap the potential power of parents and turn this power to educational ends.

They are still further learning that content based upon actual values and social realities and vital needs is better education than courses inappropriate to child nature and current life. They are learning that intercultural education, certainly an integral part of a modern school's curriculum, best proceeds in a school program based upon the findings of experimental education.

Finally, our school people are learning the importance of a democratic philosophy at work, implemented by appropriate board of education policies, by the efforts of aroused administrators, by parents and teachers eager for children's welfare, by a program with roots in the ongoing life of the community, by practices made to fit individual and class and community rather than rigid plans made in advance and without particular reference either to individual or life. In short, school people are learning to create schools which can play their part in developing youth accepted and secure, sensitive to others, responsible in all they do.